# THE
# TEMPEST

# THE
# TEMPEST

*William Shakespeare*

EDITED BY
JF Bernard and Paul Yachnin

BROADVIEW PRESS

BROADVIEW PRESS – www.broadviewpress.com
Peterborough, Ontario, Canada

Founded in 1985, Broadview Press remains a wholly independent publishing house. Broadview's focus is on academic publishing; our titles are accessible to university and college students as well as scholars and general readers. With 800 titles in print, Broadview has become a leading international publisher in the humanities, with world-wide distribution. Broadview is committed to environmentally responsible publishing and fair business practices.

Library and Archives Canada Cataloguing in Publication

Title: The tempest / William Shakespeare ; edited by JF Bernard and Paul Yachnin.
Names: Shakespeare, William, 1564-1616, author. | Bernard, J. F. (Jean-François), editor. | Yachnin, Paul Edward, 1953- editor.
Description: Includes bibliographical references.
Identifiers: Canadiana (print) 20200394215 | Canadiana (ebook) 20200394290 | ISBN 9781554814954 (softcover) | ISBN 9781770487932 (PDF) | ISBN 9781460407448 (EPUB)
Subjects: LCSH: Shakespeare, William, 1564-1616—Criticism and interpretation. | LCGFT: Drama.
Classification: LCC PR2833.A2 B47 2021 | DDC 822.3/3—dc23

*Broadview Press handles its own distribution in North America:*
PO Box 1243, Peterborough, Ontario K9J 7H5, Canada
555 Riverwalk Parkway, Tonawanda, NY 14150, USA
Tel: (705) 743-8990; Fax: (705) 743-8353
email: customerservice@broadviewpress.com

For all territories outside of North America, distribution is handled by Eurospan Group.

# Canada

Broadview Press acknowledges the financial support of the Government of Canada for our publishing activities.

Copy-edited by Denis Johnston
Book design by Michel Vrana
Typeset in MVB Verdigris Pro

PRINTED IN CANADA

# CONTENTS

# ACKNOWLEDGEMENTS

We would like to thank everyone involved with the Internet Shakespeare Editions for making this project possible, beginning with Michael Best. We also wish to particularly thank Janelle Jenstad and James Mardock for their help, guidance, and patience along the way. We would also like to express our gratitude to Broadview's coordinating editor, Marjorie Mather, for her precious assistance with this endeavour. We also extend our heartfelt thanks to Denis Johnston, whose eagle eye enhanced the overall quality of the edition.

We have likewise benefited from crucial contributions by (then) graduate students Karen Oberer and Amy Scott. Brent Whitted collaborated on the edition at the start of the work, and he and Karen Oberer did the original transcriptions of the texts included in the Appendices. Without these talented young scholars, this edition would have not seen the light of day.

The Tempest has always generated productive discussion about Shakespeare, his theater, the arts more broadly, and a wide number of substantial questions about how we live in the world. Accordingly, this edition grew from enlivening and challenging discussions with colleagues over the years. With this in mind, we thank Anthony Dawson, Patricia Badir, David Schalkwyk, Harry Berger Jr., Michael Neill, Tiffany Hoffman, Michael Bristol, Charlotte Artese, and the late Sandy Pearlman.

The two brief essays on Shakespeare's life and theater are reprinted from the late David Bevington's Broadview edition of Hamlet. Quotations from Shakespeare's plays other than The Tempest are from David Bevington's Complete Works, updated 4th edition (Longman, 1997).

Finally, our heartfelt thanks to our families for their support and for allowing us to spend so much time on Shakespeare's Island in the process of creating this edition.

## FIRST PERFORMANCE AND PUBLICATION

What do we know about the first performances and first publication of *The Tempest*? A note in the Revels Account for 1611 tells us that, "By the King's players: Hallowmas night [i.e., 1 November] was presented at Whitehall before the King's Majesty a play called *The Tempest*" (Chambers 2: 342). A second record, from the Chamber Account, includes the play among those performed at court in 1613 during the wedding celebrations of King James's daughter to a German prince, Frederick V, Elector of the Palatinate:

> Item, paid to John Heminge upon the Council's warrant dated
> at Whitehall 20th day May 1613 for presenting before the Princess
> Highness the Lady Elizabeth and the Prince Pallatine Elector fourteen
> several plays, viz. one play called *Philaster* ... one called *The Knot of Fools*
> ... *The Maid's Tragedy, The Merry Devil of Edmonton, The Tempest, A King
> and No King* ... (Chambers 2: 343)

Because of these references to court performances and also because there is a court-like masque in the play, some readers have concluded that *The Tempest* was written expressly for the court. This idea about the play is consistent with a still-lingering notion that Shakespeare aligned his art with the interests and views of the king. Since the idea is historically unfounded and deeply misleading about Shakespeare's art, it is good to get it out of our way at the outset.

There are three strong objections to the view that *The Tempest* was written for the court. One is simply that records that survive tend to be official ones such as the Chamber Account quoted above. The absence of evidence of early commercial performances of the play therefore is not at all significant. Two, it was Shakespeare's normal practice to write plays that could be performed both at court and on tour in English towns outside London, as well as at the two playhouses that the King's Players owned in London—the large open-air amphitheater, the Globe; and the more exclusive indoor venue, the Blackfriars. Three, we know that *The Tempest* was performed at a public, commercial theater because Shakespeare's contemporary Ben Jonson (1572–1637) makes fun of at least one such performance in his 1614 comedy *Bartholomew Fair*, which was also performed at a commercial playhouse. At the start of Jonson's play, a character called the Scrivener takes the stage and speaks to the audience on behalf of the author (remember that *The Tempest* features a "servant monster," "a living drollery," and a good deal of dancing):

> If there be never a servant-monster i' the Fair, who can help it, he [i.e., Ben Jonson] says, nor a nest of antics? He is loath to make nature afraid in his plays, like those that beget *Tales*, *Tempests*, and such like drolleries, to mix his head with other men's heels, let the concupiscence of jigs and dances reign as strong as it will amongst you. (Induction, ll. 130–35)

That *The Tempest*, like all of Shakespeare's plays, was written for one or more public playhouses in London, for rural audiences in the provinces, and also for the royal theater at Whitehall can help us understand the complex political meaning of the play, which, as we will see, is able to knit into a coherent vision a spirited argument for the value of labor and the community of laborers at one end and a defense of something like absolute loyalty to monarchical government at the other.

   *The Tempest* was written by someone who himself was a working actor, a shareholder in the most successful playing company in England, and a part-owner of two splendid playhouses. He was a consummate man of the theater. But Shakespeare also wrote his plays as literature, as texts to be read as well as staged. His plays were printed in quarto editions throughout his lifetime; and in 1623, seven years after he died, *The Tempest* was published as the first play in a handsome folio edition of his works, *Mr. William Shakespeare's Comedies, Histories, and Tragedies, Published according to the True Original Copies*. John Heminges (1566–1630) and Henry Condell (1576–1627), Shakespeare's fellows in the King's Players and the sponsors of the volume, might have arranged to have *The Tempest* appear as the first play in the volume because they thought of it, as many have since, as Shakespeare's summing up of a career in the theater or as his farewell to his art; or they or the publisher might have thought that the play, being previously unpublished, would be more likely to persuade browsers to buy the book. In the epistle "To the Great Variety of Readers" that appears over their names, Heminges and Condell remember their friend tenderly ("he was a happy imitator of nature [and] a most gentle expresser of it"), and they offer the book to potential purchasers as a fitting remembrance of him; so perhaps they did mean their readers to regard the lead-off play and especially the character of Prospero as a memento of the playwright and a reflection on the "rough magic" of theater. But, of course, we do not know how they expected the purchasers of the volume to regard the plays, only that they expected that the book would appeal, as they said, "to a great variety of readers" who would find his plays, which had been, they claimed, "maimed and deformed" in previous editions, now "cured and perfect of their limbs as he conceived them," and who would "read him therefore, and again, and again."

The Folio edition of *The Tempest*, which provides the copy-text for the present edition, does seem "cured and perfect of [its] limbs"; it is a carefully produced text, mostly error-free. While most of the stage directions are what we are used to seeing in Shakespeare's early texts— phrases such as "Enter Prospero and Miranda" or "Exit Caliban"—a significant number of them read as if prepared for a literary text rather than for a theatrical script. The first stage direction in the play says, "A tempestuous noise of thunder and lightning heard," which is more detailed than usual for a playhouse-derived text, and a number of them describe the action as if they were bits of narrative instead of instructions for actors: "Enter certain reapers, properly habited," one says, "they join with the nymphs in a graceful dance, towards the end whereof PROSPERO starts suddenly and speaks, after which, to a strange, hollow, and confused noise, they heavily vanish" (4.1.139, TLN 1805–08).

The Folio text of *The Tempest* itself is unusual in the volume, not only because it comes first, and not only because of the appearance of literary-seeming stage directions, but also because it was very carefully proofread as it went through the printing process: according to Hinman, the printing of the first page of the play (the first page of the body of the book, of course) was stopped four times to make corrections (1: 251). The text was set up from a transcription that appears to have been made by the professional scrivener Ralph Crane from a copy of the play in Shakespeare's own hand. Scholars have suggested that Crane did more than merely copy the text; in fact, he appears to have changed it in a number of ways, and he—not Shakespeare—might have been the author of the elaborate stage directions. Performances and printed plays are the work of many hands. In all, we could say that both the first performances and the first publication of *The Tempest* were collaborative and highly accomplished productions of which Shakespeare was the author but not the sole producer.

OCCASION AND DATE

What do we know about why Shakespeare wrote the play, and why did he write it when he did? One part of the answer has to do with current events. In the summer of 1609, an English ship, the *Sea Venture*, bound for the colony at Jamestown, Virginia, was separated from its companion vessels in a terrible storm and wrecked on the uninhabited Bermudas. For over a year, people in England had no word from the ship that had been carrying Virginia's governor-designate Thomas Gates and Admiral George Sommers as well as some 150 others, including women and children. News of the miraculous survival of the colonists did not reach England until autumn 1610. Along with the wonderful news came a narrative report in the form of a letter, *A True Reportory of the Wracke*, by William Strachey, a man who had suffered the shipwreck and survived the ten months on the island. The Strachey Letter circulated in manuscript (it was not printed until 1625).

We think that Shakespeare must have got hold of a copy since so much of the Strachey Letter turns up in the play. Certainly it seems to have fired Shakespeare's imagination. The title of Strachey's first section is "A most dreadful Tempest ... their wracke on Bermuda; and the description of those islands" (see Appendix F, p. 196). Shakespeare read about how the ship was beset: "the clouds gathering thick upon us, and the winds singing, and whistling most unusually ... a dreadful storm and hideous began to blow from out the northeast, which swelling, and roaring ... at length did beat all light from heaven" (p. 197). Shakespeare picked up the idea of the ominous sound of the wind here: in the play, Trinculo says, "another storm brewing! I hear it sing in the wind" (2.2.19, TLN 1058–59). And later, Alonso expands the metaphor:

> Methought the billows spoke and told me of it;
> The winds did sing it to me, and the thunder,
> That deep and dreadful organ pipe, pronounced
> The name of Prosper—it did bass my trespass. (3.3.96–99,
> TLN 1633–36)

Did Shakespeare also begin at this point to think about the uncanny music of the island, which is one of the dominant features of the play's setting? "Where should this music be?" Ferdinand wonders, "I' th'air or th'earth? / It sounds no more, and sure it waits upon / Some god o' th'island" (1.2.91–93, TLN 530–32).

Shakespeare read about ball lightning in the Letter. Strachey describes it as "an apparition of a little round light, like a faint star, trembling, and streaming along with a sparkling blaze, half the height upon the main mast, and shooting sometimes from shroud to shroud" (Appendix F, pp. 201–02). Ariel imitates it when he wants to terrify the mariners. On the *Sea Venture*, the sailors and their passengers worked together for three and a half days as the ship took on water. Strachey says that it was "not without his [i.e., its] wonder (whether it were the fear of death in so great a storm or that it pleased God to be gracious unto us) there was not a passenger, gentleman, or other, after he began to stir and labor but was able to relieve his fellow and make good his course" (Appendix F, p. 201). In the event, the tempest did not abate, and they were saved as if by a miracle when, on the fourth day, they spotted an island and were able to run the ship aground near land. Once the survivors were together on the island, their governor, Sir Thomas Gates, had—like Prospero—to manage a recalcitrant element among the men and even put down several mutinies. One of the mutineers argued fascinatingly that "it was no breach of honesty, conscience, nor religion to decline from the obedience of the Governor, or refuse to go any further led by his authority (except it so pleased themselves) since the authority ceased when the wreck was committed, and with it they were all then freed from the government of any man" (Strachey 1744).

And as in the play, the island that saved the lives of Strachey and his fellows was both a haven and a place of strangeness, even terror: "the dangerous and dreaded ... Islands of the Bermuda ... because they be so terrible to all that ever touched on them; and such tempests, thunders, and other fearful objects are seen and heard about them that they be called commonly the Devil's Islands ... Yet it pleased our merciful God to make even this hideous and hated place both the place of our safety and means of our deliverance" (Appendix F, p. 204).

Shakespeare's attentive reading of the Strachey Letter demonstrates his keen interest in the English and European voyages of discovery, even though, as has often been pointed out, the play takes place on an island in the Mediterranean somewhere between Italy and north-ern Africa—very far indeed from the New World. We can say that the occasion of *The Tempest* was an English shipwreck in the New World that marooned a group of English men and women on a wonderful but frightening island and transformed a tragedy of loss and separation into a comedy of deliverance and reunion. "The events of 1609 in Bermuda," comments Frank Kermode in the first Arden edition of the play, "must have seemed to contain the whole situation in little.... The Bermuda pamphlets seem to have precipitated, in this play, most of the major themes of Shakespeare's last years" (xxv). On the basis of when Shakespeare could have first read the letter that so sparked his imagination and when the play would have been first performed in one or the other of the London playhouses (in advance of the 1 November performance at court), we can determine that Shakespeare wrote the play sometime between late fall 1610 and fall 1611.

### SETTING THE STAGE

At the start, all hell breaks loose. The beginning of the play is spectacular and action-packed. There are flashes of lightning, rolling thunder, and urgent shouts of distress. People are running about, either in sheer panic or in rapid, orchestrated labor. After the opening stage direction, "A tempestuous noise of thunder and lightning heard," the actors are heard shouting over the noise of the storm:

> SHIPMASTER. Boatswain!
> BOATSWAIN. Here, master. What cheer?
> SHIPMASTER. Good. Speak to the mariners. Fall to it yarely or we run
>     ourselves aground. Bestir! Bestir! (1.1.1–4, TLN 4–9)

In the face of dire danger, the mariners work together with admirable skill and courage. "Yarely" (nimbly and diligently) and "cheerly" (1.1.10) (heartily) characterize their cooperative action. The courtiers, who are their passengers, show far less patience or fortitude. Shakespeare differs from Strachey's description of how both the sailors and passengers worked to save the ship. The change makes a political point about the possible failings even of high-ranking people just as it does about the possible abilities and virtues of commoners.

The usually good-humored counselor Gonzalo turns his own fear of dying into a wish to see the Boatswain hanged: "his complexion is perfect gallows," he says. "Stand fast, good Fate, to his hanging. Make the rope of his destiny our cable, for our own doth little advantage" (1.1.27–28, TLN 37–40). Prospero's villainous brother Antonio, also terrified of the storm, puts the same wish more directly and rudely: "Hang, cur. Hang, you whoreson, insolent noisemaker!" (1.1.38, TLN 62). The Boatswain is abrupt enough in his turn, shouting at his social superiors to shut up and to get out of the way: "What cares these roarers for the name of King? To cabin! Silence: trouble us not!" (1.1.15–16, TLN 24–26).

This scene of deafening noise, exploding fireworks, whirling action and angry exchange is, however, also one that features moments of poignant fellow feeling. The mariners work together yarely and cheerly. Once there seems no hope of saving the ship, they leave the stage to pray. At the moment the ship seems to be breaking up, we hear them taking leave of their absent families and of each other—"We split, we split! Farewell, my wife and children! / Farewell, brother! We split, we split, we split!" (1.1.57–58, TLN 72–73). Even the villains Sebastian and Antonio, finally face-to-face with death, have the sense to think about someone beside themselves:

ANTONIO. Let's all sink wi'th' King.
SEBASTIAN. Let's take leave of him. (1.1.59–60, TLN 74–75)

Shakespeare writes not only as an accomplished artist of human psychology but also as a clear-eyed philosophical thinker. From beginning to end, *The Tempest* explores the coupling of harshness and tenderness in human life. The play shows us how to live in the world as it is, especially by taking on these very different ways of seeing and feeling.

The harshness can come from nature, as it does, or seems to do, in the storm. And it can also come from humankind, as when Antonio, frightened for his own life, curses the Boatswain and wishes him hanged. Prospero has a well-developed harsh side, which he keeps turned toward Caliban (who fears him more or less as the tortured fears the torturer), and a harshness that he can on occasion turn against Ariel or even his own daughter. His most acerbic remark is aimed at Antonio—"most wicked sir—whom to call brother / Would even infect

my mouth—I do forgive / Thy rankest fault" (5.1.131–33, TLN 2094–96).
Antonio himself is capable of real cruelty, as we learn once Prospero
begins to tell his story to his daughter Miranda in the second scene.

Twelve years before the action of the play, Antonio handed his brother
Prospero and Prospero's three-year-old daughter Miranda over to a
"treacherous army," a small commando force directed by the Neapolitan
counselor Gonzalo. Father and child were cast adrift at sea in an unseaworthy boat—"A rotten carcass of a butt; not rigged, / ... The very rats
/ Instinctively have quit it" (1.2.128, 146–48; TLN 229, 251–53). But
tellingly, the injury done to him as well as his own physical suffering
engendered in Prospero an enduring tenderness toward his daughter
Miranda, who, he tells her, was an angel that kept him going through
his hardship:

> ... a cherubin
> Thou wast that did preserve me. Thou didst smile,
> Infusèd with a fortitude from heaven
> (When I have decked the sea with drops full salt
> Under my burden groaned), which raised in me
> An undergoing stomach to bear up
> Against what should ensue. (1.2.152–58, TLN 259–65)

Or consider this moment near the end of the play. Prospero has rein-
troduced himself to those who nearly killed him and his daughter.
He transforms his anger into a painful lesson for Alonso, the King
of Naples and the man whose imperialist ambitions meshed with the
treachery of Antonio. Alonso has been made to believe that his son
has drowned, and he has suffered inconsolable grief, until, in the final
scene, Prospero reveals the very much alive Ferdinand playing chess
with Miranda. So preoccupied are the two young lovers that it takes
them several moments to notice that they are not alone. Once they do
become aware of Prospero, decked out in his duke's finery, and all the
other members of the court party, Miranda says,

> ... O wonder!
> How many goodly creatures are there here!
> How beauteous mankind is! O brave new world
> That has such people in't! (5.1.183–86, TLN 2157–60)

Prospero responds in a bitterly ironic remark, "'Tis new to thee" (5.1.186, TLN 2161). How can we compass both Miranda's joy in the face of the beauty of humankind and Prospero's harsh response to the wickedness of people? How can we hold two so diametrically opposed ideas about "mankind" in our minds? Shakespeare seems to want us to feel Miranda's wonder and also to grasp the soundness of Prospero's judgment of the men who stand together on the stage.

We might say that learning to think and feel both harshly and tenderly about others is the point of Prospero's story, a story that culminates in his decision to forgive those who have wronged him. The forgiveness is not merely an intellectual choice made in the teeth of his anger but rather a reorientation of his whole personhood in the direction of forgiveness. Ariel tells him that his enemies are entirely at his mercy and, in a weirdly subjunctive voice, comments that he would feel sorry for them if he were human. Prospero does not abandon his anger, but, as if in answer to Ariel, he nevertheless forgives his enemies. Indeed, his ability to forgive depends as much on his "sharply" passionate nature as on his "nobler reason" (5.1.23, 26; TLN 1973, 1976). His passion, we might say, awakens his reason. Because he is "kindlier moved," Prospero is able to call on his "nobler reason" in order to assuage his "fury" (5.1.26, TLN 1976).

## THE WORLD IN THE PLAY

The world that Shakespeare creates in *The Tempest* has many features that make it recognizably like the world we live in. There are bad, self-seeking people; brothers fall out with brothers; people who have power are reluctant to give it up; people fall in love; fathers (such as Prospero) love their children, wish for their happiness, and yet are sometimes irritated by them; children (such as Miranda) love their fathers but can find them overbearing and can want to break free; people commit great crimes against others; and people forgive others who have wronged them. But there are also elements in the *Tempest* world that are very unlike the world we live in. There is a monster on the island (or a human being that is unjustly called a monster); there is a fairy-spirit named Ariel who can produce storms, prepare a sumptuous dinner from thin air, organize a wedding masque "with a twink" (4.1.43, TLN 1698); there is music in the very air; and there is a powerful magician who can command the elements and even, he tells us, bring the dead back to life.

Beyond these strikingly magical features, there is something about the world of the play that is deeply out of keeping with the world that most of us know. In the world of *The Tempest*, events are meaningful in ways they are usually not in the real world. In the real world there are real accidents; in the play, accidents, even shipwrecks, are part of a meaningful pattern. It is not at all that the play has a simple moral: Shakespeare would have had no patience with the Duchess in *Alice's Adventures in Wonderland*, who says to Alice, "Tut, tut, child! ... Everything's got a moral, if only you can find it" (Carroll 96).

How does Shakespeare create an intelligible world, but not one that is reducible to a simple moralist message? The answer has to do with how Shakespeare creates the formal features of the world of the play— its genre, design, themes, and characters.

First is the question of genre. What kind of play is *The Tempest*? Heminges and Condell placed it as the first play in the Comedy section of the 1623 Folio. That makes good sense since the play, like romantic comedies such as *Twelfth Night* and *As You Like It*, is in part a story of the love and courtship of Ferdinand and Miranda. Prospero even takes on the conventional role of the curmudgeon who stands in the way of the happiness of the young lovers. But since much more happens in the play than courtship, many readers have not been satisfied by Heminges and Condell's designation and have preferred, usually, one of two genres that are related but not identical to comedy—one being romance and the other tragicomedy. Romance is an expansive narrative genre that features adventures, long journeys, accidental happenings, the marvelous and magical, and key story elements having to do with separation and reunion, loss and recovery. Northrop Frye remarked wryly that in Greek romance, "the normal means of transportation is by shipwreck" (4). In Shakespeare's time, two of the most important longer narrative works, Philip Sidney's *Arcadia* (1581) and Edmund Spenser's *The Faerie Queene* (1590–96), are well characterized as romances. Tragicomedy is a genre, imported from Italy, that was fashionable in the early seventeenth century and that Shakespeare's younger colleague John Fletcher (1579–1625) defined as a form that has too little violence for tragedy and too much for comedy: "A tragicomedy is not so called in respect of mirth and killing, but in respect it wants deaths, which is enough to make it no tragedy, yet brings some near it, which is enough to make it no comedy" (Fletcher 3: 497).

Does this mean that we cannot identify the play's genre? The answer will depend on what we mean by "genre." Stephen Orgel has remarked that "[m]odern conceptions of genre are not those of the Renaissance, and our categories tend towards different ends: ours are exclusive and definitive, theirs tended to be inclusive and analytic. To find a new category for a play was not, for the Renaissance critic, to abandon the old ones" (4). In light of this insight, we can say that Shakespeare's idea of genre was not of something rigidly prescriptive but rather like a set of guidelines for experimentation with dramatic form.

*The Tempest* is only the latest instance of Shakespeare's usual practice, which is always to push the boundaries of genre in ways that renovate literary form from the inside. Like all his plays, this one is hybrid in terms of genre. The play is able to orchestrate comic, romantic, and tragicomic conventions. Stanley Wells is right to point out how the play's mixing of genres produces "an attitude firmly though sympathetically judicious": "*The Tempest* is a romance containing a built-in critique of romance; not a rejection of it, but an appreciation both of its glories and of its limitations" (77, 76). The play's genre, then, is hybrid and self-critical. Its mix of comedy, romance, and tragicomedy is capable of giving us the pleasures that belong to stories of loss and recovery, and of giving us also the pleasurable challenges provided by a critical view of such stories.

The design of the play is twofold. It has a narrative dimension that is sequential and diachronic (unfolding over time) and a structure of parallel incidents and characters that is synchronic (not unfolding over time, but there all at once). The diachronic and synchronic sides of the play's design are interrelated. The narrative weaves together three strands: (1) a courtship plot, (2) a revenge plot modulating into a story of restoration and forgiveness (Prospero and the members of the court party), and (3) a parallel revenge plot, in which Caliban conspires with Stephano and Trinculo to take back the island. The foundation of the three plots is the extended exposition in 1.2, where Prospero tells Miranda (and us) the story of the original conspiracy that led to their exile on the island, and where Prospero, Miranda, and Caliban recall for us, in their angry exchange, how their harmonious living arrangements were violated by Caliban's attempted rape of Miranda.

The play's narratives are filled with parallel and contrasting elements. There are three conspiracies bent on the violent overthrow of rulers—two in the play and one prior to its beginning. All three engender pathological relations of domination among the conspirators: Antonio sought the throne of Milan but became a subject of the King of Naples. Now he seeks to seduce Sebastian into killing his brother, the very same King of Naples, so that he, Antonio, can gain the upper hand at last. Caliban wants to overthrow Prospero and get back the island that was his by inheritance from his mother Sycorax. To do that, ironically enough, he becomes the slave of two Italian servants.

The parallel conspiracies are one instance of the metaphorical webwork in the play, where one cannot pluck one string anywhere in the play without awaking an answering resonance somewhere else. Consider how Caliban celebrates his abandonment of his wood carrying, among other tasks, at the end of 2.2:

> No more dams I'll make for fish,
> Nor fetch in firing at requiring,
> Nor scrape trenchering, nor wash dish:
> 'Ban 'Ban Ca-Caliban
> Has a new master. Get a new man!
> Freedom, high-day, high-day, freedom, freedom, high-day, freedom!
> (2.2.57–63, TLN 1226–32)

—and how his exit is followed by the entrance of Ferdinand, who struggles onstage "bearing a log." These contrasting characters—one casting off service and embracing "freedom," which is really his new slavery, and another embracing service as a higher form of freedom—show how the play's network of mirroring moments can invite us to think critically about all the characters. Prospero shares many features with Caliban's mother—both are powerful magicians who were banished from their homelands but not killed when they might well have been, both arrived on the island with offspring, and both made Ariel their servant. Does that mean that Prospero is no better than the "foul witch Sycorax"? Caliban is paired with Ariel as opposing figures of the natural world—one all air and the other earth, one strangely without emotion and the other burdened with an excess of passion—although they both seem to feel a certain vexed devotion to Prospero while both also long for freedom.

We could go on cataloguing the many correspondences among incidents and characters in the play. As Reuben Brower has commented, "the harmony of the play lies in its metaphorical design, in the closeness and completeness with which its rich and varied elements are linked together through almost inexhaustible analogies" (95). Like the design itself, the purpose of the play's inexhaustible analogies is twofold: the beauty and intricacy of the relationships arouse pleasure and provoke wonder; and the ways in which parallels are drawn between incidents (the usurpations of power, the multiple conspiracies, the escapes from drowning), or between characters that seem to be opposites (for example, Caliban and Miranda, Prospero and Sycorax) invite us to respond alertly to what the characters or even what the play itself seem to be saying about the world.

THEMES

### Animality and Humanity

*The Tempest* is the culmination of Shakespeare's long-standing interest in the relationship between the human and the animal. Most often, he defines the human as qualitatively better than the animal. When Hamlet wants to express his distress at his mother's hasty re-marriage, he says that "a beast, that wants discourse of reason, / Would have mourn'd longer" (*Hamlet*, 1.2.150–51, TLN 335–36). Elsewhere Shakespeare puts in question Hamlet's conventional distinction between animality and humanity. King Lear says that "man is no more but ... a poor bare, forked animal" (3.4.106, TLN 1887)—we are no better and perhaps a bit worse than animals. And still elsewhere, Shakespeare raises the relative standing of animals by suggesting that the bestial can embody virtue above the human. In *The Winter's Tale*, King Polixenes says of his boyhood with his friend Leontes, "We were as twinn'd lambs that did frisk i' the sun ... / what we changed / Was innocence for innocence" (1.2.67–69, TLN 130–32).

For Shakespeare, furthermore, not all humans are the same. A unitary idea of personhood is automatic and obvious to us: all persons regardless of race, sex, class, ethnicity, or sexuality are entitled to the recognition of their human dignity and the social, legal, and political rights that flow naturally from such recognition. But the boundary between human and animal was more porous for Shakespeare and his contemporaries than it is for us. It was not obvious to them that women or non-Christians or people of lesser rank were human in the way male members of the upper ranks were human. That means that in Shakespeare, some characters might be far closer to the nature of beasts and some others might be more fully human; and it also means that all his characters have elements of both humanity and animality.

The Tempest and Caliban represent the most radical phase in Shakespeare's thinking about humans and animals. Caliban is a "thing of darkness," a creature apparently made up of appetites and instincts. One of his first lines is "I must eat my dinner" (1.2.333, TLN 469). He might seem the very emblem of the animal as opposed to the human. When Prospero accuses him of attempting to rape Miranda, he responds with glee and the suggestion that, had he succeeded, he would have sired a litter of offspring:

> Oh ho! Oh ho! Would't had been done!
> Thou didst prevent me. I had peopled else
> This isle with Calibans. (1.2.352–54, TLN 489–91)

The word "peopled" troubles a simple view of Caliban as a mere animal. He is also capable, as we have heard, of articulate and dignified speech, which is very unlike an animal; he seems to have a deep appreciation for the beauty of Nature and the wonder of music; and (though Prospero seems not to see it) he is capable of rational thinking and good judgment, which is evident when he realizes just how wrong he has been about Stephano and Trinculo:

> What a thrice-double ass
> Was I to take this drunkard for a god
> And worship this dull fool! (5.1.299–301, TLN 2292–94)

The coupling of human and animal qualities in a single character is usually a recipe for making a monster, such as the ass-headed Bottom in A Midsummer Night's Dream or the ghastly insect-human hybrid in the 1986 David Cronenberg film The Fly. Caliban is repeatedly called a monster: "a very shallow monster.... very weak monster ... most poor, credulous monster" (2.2.124–26, TLN 1188–89, 1191) and "Servant monster" (3.2.4, TLN 1355). But while there must be something remarkable about Caliban's appearance, he is not, on the evidence of the text, intended to resemble a monstrous hybrid. That is the conclusion of Trinculo's delightfully roundabout examination of him, which demonstrates that Caliban has human arms in spite of Trinculo's working assumption that he is a fish with fins:

> What have we here—a man or a fish? Dead or alive? A fish. He smells like a fish ... A strange fish. Were I in England now, as once I was, and had but this fish painted, not a holiday-fool there but would give a piece of silver. There would this monster make a man. ... Legged like a man, and his fins like arms. Warm o'my troth—I do now let loose my opinion, hold it no longer: this is no fish but an islander that hath lately suffered by a thunderbolt. (2.2.23–29, TLN 1063–75)

Caliban is neither a monster nor a fish. His human but in some respects bizarre physicality, strange speech, ability to reason, love of natural and musical beauty, and failure to understand or to defend himself against the charge of attempted rape—and the attack itself—suggest not that he is a monster but rather that he is, just like us, a creature that is both human and animal. It can even be argued that he is not guilty of attempted rape because his share of animality renders him pre-moral rather than immoral. Shakespeare is not being merely mischievous when he draws parallels between the "servant monster" and the magician-ruler, especially their hankering for revenge and their love of beauty. The connections between the two men are a necessary feature of Shakespeare's understanding of humanity and animality as adjacent and interpenetrating categories. Caliban is the "thing of darkness" (5.1.280, TLN 2270) that Prospero acknowledges as his because Caliban is his servant and, more importantly, because he knows that they share a capacity for violent rage. Prospero's fury is expressed in the storm and the other frightening shows he puts on, in his harsh speech even to those he loves such as Ariel and Miranda, and in his vindictive treatment of Caliban. The figure of the dark beast Caliban is necessary for Prospero to be able to safeguard his own humanity, since acknowledging the servant monster allows Prospero to recognize the dark rage in himself and yet keep it separate from his supposedly pure human nature. Since Prospero seems determined to maintain a clear division between humanity and animality, he would not wish to acknowledge the kinship of his aesthetic delight and Caliban's love of nature and music; however, as we have seen, the play makes the connection clear enough by way of their allied dream-like visions of beauty and harmony. Prospero's devotion to an unyielding boundary between the human and the animal prevents him from seeing the good qualities in his servant and also the complexity of Caliban's character as the perfect figure of Shakespeare's understanding of the hybridity of humanity itself.

## Colonization

While the island of *The Tempest* is in the Mediterranean, the play nevertheless invites us to think about the European conquest and colonization of the Americas. Caliban apparently had no language before Prospero and Miranda taught him theirs, but he remembers non-European words like "scamels" (2.2.150, TLN 1216) or the name of his mother's god, "Setebos" (1.2.376, TLN 516), which Shakespeare picked up from one of the New World travel narratives (Frey 29). Caliban claims ownership of the island on the strength of inheritance from his mother, but his right to a homeland is stripped from him by Prospero. He also suffers rough punishment at the hands of Prospero, especially when he is hunted by dogs, which is a barbarism reminiscent of the reports of Spanish mistreatment of the native peoples.

Caliban's apparent slavishness to Stephano puts into play Aristotelian ideas about "natural slavery," the notion that some humans were simply unfit for self-rule and so needed the firm hand of "natural" masters who would do them—so the argument went—a kindness by governing their lives and making use of their labor (see Appendix A). In a formal debate against Bartolomé de las Casas (1484–1566), a man who was a tireless defender of the Indigenous peoples of the Americas, the Spanish theologian Juan Ginés de Sepúlveda (1494–1573) supported his country's conquest of the Amerindians by drawing on Aristotle's idea of the "natural slave." "Those who surpass the rest in prudence and intelligence," Sepúlveda says, "although not in physical strength, are by nature the masters. On the other hand, those who are dim-witted and mentally lazy, although they may be physically strong enough to fulfill all the necessary tasks, are by nature slaves. It is just and useful that it be this way" (Appendix C, p. 170). Caliban sometimes fits this description, so his character can serve to support the idea that the European domination of the Indigenous peoples was natural and just. On the other hand, Caliban keeps up a courageous verbal campaign against Prospero, he uses slavishness to manipulate Stephano into joining a war against Prospero, and he seems to have a capacity for intellectual and moral growth as well as a love of beauty and an aptitude for poetry, all of which make him perhaps more like Prospero himself than like an Aristotelian natural slave.

### Service and Freedom

Shakespeare's society was characterized by a system of rank, by ingrained habits of deference to one's social superiors, and by relations of service in every quarter of social life. In his brilliant study of master-servant relations in Shakespeare, David Schalkwyk comments that service was "the *predominant* form of social organization and personal experience in early modern England" (3; emphasis in original). Shakespeare himself was a member of the King's Servants; no doubt he proudly wore the King's livery (distinctive clothing worn by household retainers) on several state occasions. People from the highest to the lowest were in service to some master or other—from domestics such as the butler Stephano to counselors such as Gonzalo. Ferdinand, who is a prince and therefore not in domestic or political service, plays at being a servant to his beloved mistress after the fashion of poetic lovers going back at least to the twelfth century. Shakespeare gives the motif a twist by making Ferdinand's love-service into real work. And beyond the social, political, and amatory realms, every single person in Shakespeare's society, including nobles such as Prince Ferdinand, his father the King of Naples, and all the others, served God, their divine master.

Given the ubiquity of relations of service, it is no surprise to find the play is concerned with different kinds of service and with the possibility of being liberated from servitude (the apparent goal of both Ariel and Caliban) or of finding freedom *through* service, which is what Ferdinand achieves by his loving labor for Miranda. It is important to note how

Ariel achieves his freedom by following a conventional pattern: in the London trade guilds, young men signed a contract to serve as apprentices, usually for seven years, before being advanced to the "freedom" of the guild, which allowed them to practice their trade on their own account. Ariel follows that pattern except that he agrees to contractual service under extreme duress and the "freedom" he earns amounts to an escape into a radically non-human state of nature. He sings as he helps Prospero dress again as the Duke of Milan:

> Where the bee sucks, there suck I;
> In a cowslip's bell I lie—
> There I couch when owls do cry.
> On the bat's back I do fly
> After summer merrily.
> Merrily, merrily shall I live now
> Under the blossom that hangs on the bough. (5.1.88–94, TLN 2045–51)

The play borrows from Montaigne (1533–92) in order to describe Ariel's natural freedom in social and political terms. Montaigne's essay "Of the Cannibals" (see Appendix E) provides the core of Gonzalo's utopian imagining of a commonwealth without service, sovereignty, or the violence that takes root in political communities, especially on account of their unequal distribution of wealth, status, and power:

> I'th' commonwealth I would by contraries
> Execute all things, for no kind of traffic
> Would I admit: no name of magistrate;
> Letters should not be known; riches, poverty,
> And use of service, none; contract, succession,
> ...
> No sovereignty—
> ...
> All things in common nature should produce
> Without sweat or endeavor. Treason, felony,
> Sword, pike, knife, gun, or need of any engine
> Would I not have; but nature should bring forth
> Of its own kind all foison, all abundance,
> To feed my innocent people.

...
I would, with such perfection, govern, sir,
T'excel the Golden Age. (2.1.139–48, 150–55, 158–59, TLN 824–28, 833,
837–42, 845–46)

The problem, as Gonzalo understands well since he serves the King
of Naples, is that men and women live not in a state of nature or a
"Golden Age" but rather in relations structured by habits of domination
and deference. It is with great surprise, therefore, that he declares near
the end of the play that each of the characters has achieved the freedom
that comes from being one's own person—the self-fulfilling capacity
to choose one's own course of action and identity:

... O rejoice
Beyond a common joy, and set it down
With gold on lasting pillars! In one voyage
Did Claribel her husband find at Tunis;
And Ferdinand, her brother, found a wife
Where he himself was lost; Prospero, his dukedom
In a poor isle; and all of us, ourselves,
When no man was his own. (5.1.208–15, TLN 2188–95)

We can begin to discern in what Gonzalo says how service and freedom are linked, and even how human freedom, which is necessarily
fostered by relations with others, might be more valuable than Ariel's
radical liberty within nature. For Ariel, "freedom" is essentially a liberation from anything that might constrain one's acting and thinking.
Against this, human freedom is the freedom to undertake something
meaningful. "Freedom to," as opposed to "freedom from," is active
and productive and requires the presence of others as witnesses, stake-
holders, and partners.

The play suggests that human freedom is founded on a renunciation of private interests in favor of a commitment to be useful to others. The emotional tone of Prospero's recovery of his dukedom and
the work of government is more somber than his daughter's youthful
discovery of love, but both are movements toward a freedom founded
in service to others rather than by a flight from community into

self-cultivation—"transported / And rapt in secret studies" (1.2.76–77, TLN 171–72), as Prospero describes his earlier abdication of political responsibility.

Even Ariel finds a measure of freedom through service, despite being tortured by the human model of service. Sycorax and then Prospero drag him into a life of labor quite against his nature. Sycorax uses physical coercion, at the end binding him "[i]nto a cloven pine" (1.2.278, TLN 404); and Prospero threatens worse punishment in order to ensure his compliance. Yet even in the face of violence, Ariel's feelings for his master develop to the point where he asks, "Do you love me, master, no?" (4.1.48, TLN 1703). Ariel's freely given love for Prospero and his wish to be loved in return grow because he takes delight not only in his own art but also in the delight his service arouses in his master (note how their love is founded on the model of working relations between playwright and boy-actor and also how the passage ends with Ariel's parodic imitation of Ferdinand, a theatrical gesture designed to please Prospero and the audience too):

> PROSPERO. Hast thou, spirit,
>     Performed to point the tempest that I bade thee?
> ARIEL. To every article.
>     I boarded the King's ship—now on the beak,
>     Now in the waist, the deck, in every cabin,
>     I flamed amazement. Sometime I'd divide
>     And burn in many places. On the topmast,
>     The yards and bowsprit would I flame distinctly,
>     Then meet and join.
>     ...
> PROSPERO. My brave spirit,
>     ...
> ARIEL.
>     ...
>     The King's son have I landed by himself,
>     Whom I left cooling of the air with sighs
>     In an odd angle of the isle, and sitting,
>     His arms in this sad knot. (1.2.193–201, 206, 221–24, TLN 305–13,
>     319, 338–41)

The culmination of the play's communitarian model of freedom through service brings matters home to the audience. The Epilogue focuses on playing and playgoing as forms of service. The actor playing Prospero has agreed as if by contract to "please" (Epilogue 13, TLN 2334) the audience, and the playgoers are expected to reciprocate by applauding, which is described as an activity able to save Prospero from isolation on the island and also able to free the actor playing Prospero from the "bands" of the role. "With the help of your good hands" (Epilogue 9–10, TLN 2330–2331) is perfect since it links the audience's liberating applause to the manual work performed by the sailors in the opening scene ("we will not hand a rope more," 1.1.20, TLN 30–31):

> ... Now, 'tis true
> I must be here confined by you
> Or sent to Naples; let me not,
> Since I have my dukedom got
> And pardoned the deceiver, dwell
> In this bare island by your spell,
> But release me from my bands
> With the help of your good hands. (Epilogue, 3–10, TLN 2324–31)

### Memory and Forgiveness

The play's adherence to the unity of time (i.e., the time it takes to perform is the same as the time that elapses in the story) requires an elaborate exposition in order to provide us with the information we need so we can follow the dramatic action. Shakespeare turns this potential weakness into a strength by showing us how it pains Prospero to remember his own history. His struggle with memory and his arguments with Ariel and Caliban about their shared past introduce the play's interest in memory as a crucial feature of identity and relations among people.

With his enemies about to land on the island, Prospero is at last ready to share his story with his daughter. But he hesitates. Before he begins, he asks her if she can remember a time before they came to the island. That is a normal conversational gambit, but there seems to be much at stake for him in her ability to remember, which he indicates by his surprise, as if remembering itself were a wondrous act:

PROSPERO. Canst thou remember
     A time before we came unto this cell?
     I do not think thou canst, for then thou wast not
     Out three years old.
MIRANDA. Certainly, sir, I can.
...
     'Tis far off—
     And rather like a dream than an assurance
     That my remembrance warrants. Had I not
     Four or five women once that tended me?
PROSPERO. Thou had'st, and more, Miranda. But how is it
     That this lives in thy mind? What see'st thou else
     In the dark backward and abysm of time? (1.2.38–41, 44–50,
     TLN 126–30, 134–40)

Prospero is encouraged by his daughter's ability to remember her
nursemaids in Milan because he understands how selective memory can
be. He knows that Antonio "[m]ade such a sinner of his memory" that
he believed "his own lie" that "[h]e was indeed the duke" (1.2.101–03,
TLN 198–200). In turn, Prospero floods with memory, suffering his
own emotional tempest as he recollects his overthrow and his and his
daughter's arduous journey to the island. He remembers those terrible
events in a way that tends to justify his actions, but he also tests the
accuracy of his memory by telling Miranda the story of his failure as a
ruler, even including the possibility that he was partly responsible for
this brother's treachery:

     I pray thee, mark me!
     I (thus neglecting worldly ends, all dedicated
     To closeness and the bettering of my mind
     With that which, but by being so retired,
     O'er-prized all popular rate) in my false brother
     Awaked an evil nature, and my trust,
     Like a good parent, did beget of him
     A falsehood in its contrary as great
     As my trust was, which had indeed no limit— (1.2.88–96, TLN 185–93)

Prospero challenges the other two creatures on the island who have lively recollections of their history with him. The justice of those relationships depends on recollection held in concert, but both encounters only exacerbate the problem of memory. When Ariel reminds Prospero about their agreement to shorten the length of his service by a full year, Prospero just changes the subject. It is remarkable that Prospero also seems keen to disagree with Ariel about the history of Sycorax, about which he can have no knowledge beyond what he has learned from Ariel. Things are little better in Prospero's next encounter. He and Caliban agree that their happy initial phase was shattered by the attack on Miranda. They each remember the event but disagree about its ethical character. Prospero, who describes it as the worst kind of treachery, seems to be superimposing on it Antonio's betrayal of his, Prospero's, parent-like trust, while Caliban remembers it with a strange animal chortling, as if it had little to do with the human categories of honor and trust. They disagree also about which of them has legitimate title to the island. Caliban argues that he inherited it from his mother. As in his previous argument with Ariel, Prospero simply ignores the claim, evidently because he thinks Caliban is not human enough to hold legal title to anything.

Memory underlies the characters' sense of who they are, what rights they can claim, and what acknowledgement of those rights is due to them from others. Prospero's failure to secure a shared recollection of what has happened on the island means that his rule can never be justified; he will always remain open to the charge that his rule of the island, like Antonio's usurpation of the dukedom, is an exercise of raw power rather than an instance of political justice. "I must obey," Caliban says, "his art is of such power / It would control my dam's god Setebos / And make a vassal of him" (1.2.375–77, TLN 515–17).

Prospero is unable to summon the kind of compliant recollections from his servants that would serve to confirm the justice of his rule on the island. He nevertheless seeks to stir up the memories of his old enemies, prompting them to acknowledge their violent abuse of him and his daughter, especially since he cannot forgive them unless they are sorry for their crimes. That is what the spectacle in 3.3 of the broken feast and the appearance of Ariel as a harpy are designed to achieve. In the scene, the famished courtiers are offered a banquet—a gesture of welcome and community. When they move toward the food, Ariel appears as a harpy, a classical figure symbolizing revenge for sin. After clapping his wings over the table and causing the food to disappear, he launches into a denunciation of the "three men of sin" for their crime against Prospero and his daughter:

> ... you three
> From Milan did supplant good Prospero,
> Exposed unto the sea (which hath requite it)
> Him and his innocent child, for which foul deed
> The powers (delaying, not forgetting) have
> Incensed the seas and shores (yea, all the creatures!)
> Against your peace. (3.3.69–75, TLN 1602–08)

Alonso takes the rebuke to heart. It organizes his past history and present loss into a coherent narrative of crime and punishment that is recounted to him by the deep music of sea, wind, and thunder:

> Oh, it is monstrous, monstrous!
> Methought the billows spoke and told me of it;
> The winds did sing it to me, and the thunder,
> That deep and dreadful organ pipe, pronounced
> The name of Prosper—it did bass my trespass.
> Therefore, my son i' th'ooze is bedded (3.3.95–100, TLN 1632–37)

In contrast, Antonio and Sebastian seem to grasp, not the meaning of Ariel's words, but only the threatening sound of his voice:

> SEBASTIAN. But one fiend at a time,
>     I'll fight their legions o'er.
> ANTONIO.                    I'll be thy second.
>                         (3.3.103–04, TLN 1640–42)

The spectacle's capacity to awaken memory in Alonso shows us how memory can bring sinners back to goodness; its failure to remind Antonio and Sebastian of their crimes, especially striking in Antonio's case since his sin ought to be easy to recall, tells us that memory cannot by itself create a political community. After all, as Stephano sings,

"Thought is free" (3.2.118, TLN 1479). People will remember what they want to remember; what "really happened" in the past will always remain a matter of dispute; and no one can be compelled to remember a past dictated by the powers-that-be.

The political limitations of memory are clear. Prospero might want to rebuild his rule of Milan by having everyone remember that he was a good ruler who was unlawfully removed from his dukedom and also by having the denizens of the island remember how "humane" his rule of them has been. But that desire is bound to remain frustrated since people and even spirits are individuals with their own recollections of the past. But that does not mean that Prospero's memory-work is pointless. Remembering the past allows Prospero to forgive his enemies rather than merely to repeat their violence against him, and it binds together the two former enemies on the strength of Alonso's apology and Prospero's pardon. That at least promises a fresh start for the political world of Italy.

## THE PLAY IN THE WORLD

*The Tempest* has had and continues to have a robust life in the theater and as a work of literature. It has also emerged in different forms such as music, painting, film, live-action TV, and animation. Indeed, it is a quality of great works of art that they—unlike the people who make them—grow younger, stronger, more various, and more influential as they grow older. While Shakespeare died in 1616, his play, then about five years old, has since traveled the world, been translated into many languages, and been adapted as opera, poem, novel, and film. It has inspired many other works of art (such as a painting by William Hogarth in the eighteenth century, poetry by Robert Browning in the nineteenth, and music by Jean Sibelius in the twentieth), and it has called forth a vast body of interpretive literature. The Russian critic and theorist Mikhail Bakhtin captured this dimension of the lives of works of art with his idea of "great time":

> Works break through the boundaries of their own time, they live in centuries, that is in *great time* and frequently (with great works, always) their lives there are more intense and fuller than are their lives within their own time. (4; emphasis in original)

Some critics have attributed the growth and dissemination of the play and of Shakespeare's works more generally to the expansion of British power in the eighteenth and nineteenth centuries. No doubt there is some truth in such arguments, especially since the play could not have achieved an international life at all if it had been unavailable outside England; but it is more important to consider the answerability of *The Tempest* to a range of artistic, social, and political situations and to see how the particular completeness and complexity of "the world in the play" has enabled it to light up so brightly in relation to the concerns of different communities in various places and at different times.

The life of the play in the modern age is hugely diverse. The most salient features of its fortunes in the twentieth and twenty-first centuries include the Americanization and globalization of the play, its growth as a form of social and political critique, and its entry into intermediality. As a play that has reached from England to the Americas, Europe, Africa, and China and in forms from live theater to print, film, pop music, and manga comics, *The Tempest* offers something of a textbook case of the public life of art in a globalized, mediatized age.

As we have seen, the play had an American dimension from the beginning, since it was occasioned by the remarkable story of an English ship that had run aground on a North American island, and also since it was responding to 100 years of writing about the European exploration and conquest of the Americas. But as Vaughan and Vaughan have pointed out, the American dimension was not prominent between the early modern period and the end of the nineteenth century, when a number of scholars began to take stock of the play's indebtedness to Renaissance travel literature and to re-assess its value for an understanding of the history of the Americas (118–43). In 1898, Sidney Lee reasoned that Shakespeare and his contemporaries would naturally have identified Prospero's island with the Bermudas since the miraculous recovery of the English sailors and colonists and the haunted but kindly Bermudas were the talk of the town in 1610. Lee also adduced several references in *The Tempest* to Renaissance travel literature in support of his argument; and he finished by suggesting that Caliban was "an imaginary portrait ... of the aboriginal savage of the New World, descriptions of whom abounded in contemporary travellers' speech and writings" (257). His work brought forward a dimension intrinsic to the play—its provocative interest in the Americas—and heralded the modern view of the play as a work implicated in the growth of colonialism.

A colonialist understanding of the play connected with the growth of the play into a powerful expressive register for late-nineteenth- and twentieth-century thinking about relations of domination between different classes and different races. Its power depended mostly on the characters of the master Prospero, the servant monster Caliban, and the complex relationship between them—a relationship that the play itself makes available for radical rethinking.

The emergence of the play as a key text of postcoloniality was complemented by the development of a socio-psychological theory of race and domination, much of it based on a reading of *The Tempest*. Prominent here was the work of Octave Mannoni (1899–1989), a French civil servant and psychoanalyst who spent twenty years in Madagascar. His model of a dependency complex between the colonizer and the colonized has been criticized by Frantz Fanon (1925–61), among others, in the 1960s and, more recently, by Chantal Zabus (b. 1955); and while Mannoni's racial politics have warranted the critique, his socio-psychological approach has had considerable influence over readings of the play.

Aimé Césaire (1913–2008) was one of Mannoni's most outspoken critics. But Césaire's important rewriting of the play as *Une Tempête* (1969), certainly the high point of the play as a text about race and colonialism, follows Mannoni by focusing on Caliban and Prospero. The ending of the play is all about the master and the servant and very much concerned with their emotionally charged relationship. Here, Caliban's rebellion is a process of inward self-discovery rather than an armed uprising; and, at the very end, his off-stage achievement of freedom is bound up with the imminent death of his erstwhile master. In this version, Caliban's defiance is powerfully stated—

> Understand what I say, Prospero:
> For years I bowed my head
> for years I took it, all of it—
> ...
> Prospero, you're a great magician:
> you're an old hand at deception.
> And you lied to me so much,

> about the world, about myself,
> that you ended up imposing on me
> an image of myself:
> underdeveloped, in your words, undercompetent
> that's how you made me see myself!
> And I hate that image ... and it's false!
> But now I know I know you, you old cancer,
> And I also know myself! (64)

—yet since, according to Césaire's conception, the two men are bound together, Caliban's liberation requires the passage of the time it takes Prospero to grow from angry adulthood to enfeebled old age. This is symbolized on stage by "the curtain's lowered halfway and reraised"; at the end of this hiatus, Prospero is near the end of his life, the island is overrun by "unclean nature," and the old man's helpless shouts for "Caliban" are answered only by a stage direction that reprises Caliban's populist anthem of liberation along with the sounds of a pure and enduring natural world:

> In the distance, above the sound of the surf and the chirping of birds,
> we hear snatches of Caliban's song:
> FREEDOM HI-DAY, FREEDOM HI-DAY! (68)

The focus on Prospero and Caliban has receded in many recent versions of the play. Often, as in two of the most prominent Canadian productions of the past twenty years, Caliban has become a far less important figure, and his relationship with Prospero has been displaced by the magician's relationship with his daughter and/or a feminized Ariel. In Robert Lepage's 1993 production at the Festival de théâtre des Amériques in Montreal, Caliban was a punk rocker whose colloquial "joual" French, set off against Prospero's formal diction, captured the persistence of class differences in modern Quebec and retained also something of the critical dimension of the postcolonialist *Tempest*. But, in general, this Prospero was a kind, loving, and somewhat stereotypical father to his daughter before he was anything else. In the Canadian Stratford Festival production of 2010, starring Christopher Plummer as Prospero, the figure of Caliban was a vestige of the previous century's engagement with the political meanings of the servant monster. The focus shifted to the girlish, blue Ariel, a witty and tender figure that held Prospero's heart just as he held hers.

The most renowned version of the play over the last thirty years is *Prospero's Books* (1991). Peter Greenaway's ravishingly beautiful cinematic reimagining of the play, at first an art-house film, has morphed and multiplied into a DVD, a book, an audio album, and a series of excerpts on YouTube. Like the original (also intermedial) play, the film is highly allusive: Shakespeare draws on Virgil and Ovid, among others, and Greenaway creates a pastiche of Renaissance and Baroque artists. Both put a premium on high-end entertainment—the playing company commissioned original songs by the King's lutenist, while Greenaway engaged composer Michael Nyman to write the score for the film; and both play and film used the latest special-effects technology of their respective ages. But whereas Shakespeare was able to incorporate allusiveness and entertainment into a work that could address social and political matters in formative ways, Greenaway's film brings to completion the makeover of the play into an almost pure spectacle of music, dance, and image that was begun with the Restoration adaptation, subtitled *The Enchanted Island* (see Appendix G). In Greenaway, tellingly, Caliban is transformed from a monstrously defiant orator into a grotesque naked dancer, a figure seemingly possessed by the "songs and sweet airs" of the island but without a song or a word of his own.

The depoliticization of *The Tempest* that is carried out by *Prospero's Books* does not mean that the film fails as art, but it certainly suggests that it fails as *theatrical* art, which is a kind of art that has traditionally been able to deploy a high degree of social as well as aesthetic creativity. The social creativity of Shakespeare's play has moved elsewhere— to local theatrical performances such as the collaborative Robert Lepage-Ex Machina / Huron-Wendat Nation performance of *La Tempête* (2011) with a mixed white and First Nations cast; niche films such as Derek Jarman's Gothic gay version (1979), in which Caliban, a "grimy-toothed lecher," has more than his fair share of screen time and a surprising degree of autonomy and authority; and musical adaptations such as the song "A New Kind of Freedom" (2001) by the German metal band Caliban. All of these are commercial artworks, each takes on matters of social concern in original ways, each is made at least partially available by way of the internet, each is addressed to a particular, limited constituency (as opposed to being marketed to a mass audience), and each is also able to attract larger and more various audiences. The social agency and aesthetic inventiveness of artists and artworks such as these, each addressed to *a* public rather than to *the* public, guarantees that Shakespeare's play will continue to enjoy, to quote Bakhtin again, a life in "great time" that is "more intense and fuller" than was its life in its own time (4).

## CONCLUSION:
### THE ENCHANTED ISLAND OF *THE TEMPEST*

Let us, finally, consider three of the play's principal sources—Virgil's *Aeneid*, Ovid's *Metamorphoses*, and Montaigne's "Of the Cannibals"— but not in the usual terms of source study. Source study is a critical approach that seeks to explain the specific uses that writers make of other works and/or how preceding works influence writers. The approach does not work well for *The Tempest* since, aside from a few clear-cut references to earlier works, Shakespeare's engagement with his three great predecessors is both deep and elusive—easy to feel but difficult to explain. In order to understand what Shakespeare did with Ovid, Virgil, and Montaigne, then, we will follow a clue offered by the play itself, unraveling that clue by way of the 1956 science-fiction film adaptation, *Forbidden Planet*. Taken together, the play and the sci-fi film show us that Shakespeare did not "use" his sources in any usual sense of the word; rather, the play and film suggest that Shakespeare lived in the earlier works as Prospero lives on the island. What we might call *The Tempest*'s archipelago of islands has become the source of the play's enduring literary power. It is the main island in an archipelagic sea, and Shakespeare is the chief island-hopper, someone who invites us to join him on his peregrinations and even to create islands of our own.

The island in *The Tempest* can be viewed as an actual island in the Mediterranean, a stand-in for the Bermudas, or an island of the imagi-nation (like Thomas More's Utopia). It is also a symbol of the playhouse in which the play was performed. Both the stage and the island are "desert" or bare. The island is the source of Prospero's power just as the theater is the source of Shakespeare's; they are places that stand apart from the normal world, places that offer ideal conditions for the conjuring of revelatory actions by highly talented performers able to give tangible form to the visions of magician-artists.

The playhouse is magic because of the talent of the performers, the beauty of the costumes, properties, and music, the frisson of the fireworks and claps of artificial thunder; and magic because of how the space is able to heighten the pleasure of the playgoers. It is also peopled by the great writers of the past. Someone like Shakespeare is able to achieve superhuman strength by harnessing their visions and voices. When Prospero says that "Graves at my command / Have waked their sleepers, oped, and let 'em forth" (5.1.48–49, TLN 1999–2000), he is as likely pointing to the literary practices of his creator as he is confessing to the practice of black magic.

The island is an emplacement of the cumulative power of the minds of the past. Another spatial version of the intellectual power of antiquity is the planet Altair IV in the film *Forbidden Planet*. The Prospero-figure here is Dr. Morbius, curiously enough a philologist, who came with an exploratory party from Earth twenty years before the action of the film begins. The other colonists are dead, torn to pieces by a fearsome monster, all except for Morbius's daughter, the Miranda-figure Altaira. Midway through the film, Morbius tells Captain Adams, the commander of the rescue ship, a fascinating story about the original inhabitants of the planet. (Morbius learned their history while he was mastering a tiny fraction of their technology.) The Krell were a brilliant race ("a million years ahead of humankind") that conquered disease, traveled the galaxy, and created a subterranean generating system so huge and powerful that it allowed them to create matter, machines, and creatures simply by thinking them (*Forbidden Planet* reel 4, p. 3). The generator was so durable that it survived the 200,000 years since the sudden destruction of the Krell civilization. As we learn, the almost infinite power they created undid the Krell in a single night because it gave instant form to the darkness that lay within even this highly evolved race; we learn also, and Morbius discovers to his horror, that the monster stalking the planet now is the creation of his jealous rage (his "Id monster") against anyone that would threaten to remove him or his daughter from Altair IV (reel 6, p. 10). In the end, as the Id monster is about to kill his daughter (she has fallen in love with Captain Adams), Morbius sacrifices his own life and so dissolves the monster. His dying instructions are to set the process in motion for planetary self-destruction and to flee the doomed Altair IV. In the last sequence, on board the home-bound spaceship, we witness the planet explode; then the Captain says,

Alta[ira], about a million years from now, the human race will have crawled up to where the Krell stood in their great moment of triumph and tragedy. And your father's name will shine again like a beacon in the galaxy—it's true, it will remind us that we are, after all, not God. (reel 6, p. 15)

*The Tempest*'s island is like Altair IV because both are gathering-places of huge stores of ancient knowledge-power. Magic alienates Prospero from others just as technology separates Morbius from humanity, but the two settings differ importantly because the planet enables only murder whereas the island is capable of procreation. It has the capacity to "bring forth more islands," issuing in a plethora of offspring, including *Forbidden Planet*. In keeping with the natural character of literary creation, moreover, the fertility of *The Tempest* is not wholly original to Shakespeare but is rather an outcome of his brilliant orchestration of already existing literary works.

For the Renaissance, the *Aeneid* was the most impressive work of Latin antiquity—the epic story of the destruction of Troy, the travels and suffering of the hero Aeneas, his tragic love affair with Dido, Queen of Carthage, and the victorious yet heartrending founding of Rome. It is a poem about the loss of one world and the creation of another, the relationship between the individual and the nation, the bonds between human action and destiny, and the severe costs of empire and of civilization itself, which is revealed to be inseparable from the violence that it is supposed to be able to prevent. There are a number of clear recollections of the poem in the play, including Ferdinand's reaction to his first sight of Miranda, "Most sure, the goddess" ("O dea certe"—*Aeneid*, 1.328), and the harpy scene in 3.3 (*Aeneid*, 3.209–77). For most Shakespeareans, however, Virgil's poem has been strangely there and not there in *The Tempest*. In 1954, Frank Kermode said he felt "that Shakespeare has Virgil in mind," but he took that intuition no further (xxxiv, n. 2). Robert Wiltenburg followed the intuition by arguing that Shakespeare developed a critical imitation of the poem's structure and theme. "Both works," he commented, "address the most fundamental questions raised by the enterprise of civilization: what is required to establish and to renew our life in common?" (168). But his very fine reading often claims strong parallels where there are merely broad resemblances, and it has to ignore much of the play, including Prospero's magic and the character Caliban.

We suggest that Shakespeare's approach to Virgil is threefold. One, he provides enough that is like the *Aeneid* (both works begin with a tempest and an interrupted sea voyage) to create a strong resonance and to arouse curiosity about how the play and the poem might speak to each other. Two, such engagement pays off because Shakespeare has indeed thought deeply about the key question asked by the *Aeneid*—what are the human costs of political power and of civilized life itself? The play answers this question generally by rejecting Virgilian ideals of law and justice and by embracing "kindness," the principle that couples benevolence toward others with the recognition of our shared life-experience as members of the same kind (i.e., species) (Wiltenburg 168). Three, the conversation between the play and the most famous poem of Latin antiquity, a conversation in which readers and critics have played a formative role, is of a piece with the elevation of *The Tempest* into the Western canon—that human-made constellation of texts that we are calling the archipelagic sea.

*The Tempest*'s relationship with the *Aeneid* helped give the play its entry into long-term thinking about exploration, conquest, and empire, making it an obvious choice for someone like Césaire when he undertook to write about the depredations of colonialism. In his book *Shakespeare and Ovid*, Jonathan Bate has tried to displace Virgil from his proximity to the play and replace him with Ovid (239–63). Bate has greatly enhanced our understanding of the play's Ovidian dimension, but his "one or the other" stance belongs to the practices of literary argument rather than to the practices of literature. Since works of literature are dynamic structures capable of ever-increasing complexity, a play like *The Tempest* can readily sponsor connections with Virgil as well as Ovid.

The most prominent instance of the play's Ovidianism is Prospero's renunciation speech in 5.1, which Shakespeare took from Arthur Golding's 1567 translation of Ovid's *Metamorphoses*. There it is spoken by the witch Medea, with an emphasis on the unnaturalness of her magic, which can cause streams to run backward, the noonday sun to grow dark, and the dead to rise from their graves (see Appendix B, p. 169). Shakespeare imports all these elements into the speech he gives Prospero. Bate rightly corrects the view that refuses to connect Medea's bad fame and black magic with Prospero (251–55). The magician is indeed acknowledging the dark potentialities of his magic by way of explaining why he is going to renounce it.

Prospero's renunciation speech deepens his characterization, showing that he grasps the limitations of his occult learning. It is no accident that the speech comes immediately after an exchange with Ariel in which he declares his intention not to take vengeance on those whose "high wrongs" injured him and his daughter, a decision that he takes in light of his recognition of natural fellowship with his enemies—that he is "[o]ne of their kind" (5.1.25, 23; TLN 1975, 1973). The speech also refers to the supernatural practices of Shakespeare himself, a greater and less harmful magician than either Prospero or Medea, a conjurer who can cause the dead poet Ovid to come forward at this moment and speak again.

Against Ovidian metamorphosis, however, Shakespeare articulates a Virgilian aspiration toward stability over time, the finding-out of one's life story in relation to the purposes of destiny. Neither classical predecessor is supplanted by the other; rather, the two great Roman poets serve the dialectical supremacy of a play that is able to include both Ariel's song of metamorphosis (1.2.400–08, TLN 539–47) and Gonzalo's awestruck speech about the gracious will of the gods and the happy fulfillment of destiny:

> ... look down, you gods,
> And on this couple drop a blessèd crown,
> For it is you that have chalked forth the way
> Which brought us hither. (5.1.203–06, TLN 2182–85)

*The Tempest* is peopled by ancient poets, who enjoy a second life in dialogue with each other and with Shakespeare. All their works are richer for the conversation. The islands of the archipelago include Shakespeare's contemporaries, too, chief among whom is Montaigne. Shakespeare shares with Montaigne an Ovidian awareness of the changefulness of the world, and he also shares a critical attitude toward civilization. In "Of the Cannibals," Montaigne upbraids Europeans for their prejudice against the Indigenous peoples of the Americas: "They are even savage, as we call those fruits wild which nature of herself ... hath produced: whereas indeed, they are those which ourselves have altered by our artificial devices ... we should rather term savage" (Appendix E, p. 185). Shakespeare, however, demurs from holding up "natural man" as an ideal to which we might aspire, and he challenges Montaigne, both by suggesting that human community, of whatever kind, must suffer the inborn flaws of the humans that constitute it and by developing a more balanced account of civilization, which is shown to be capable of good outcomes as well as bad.

To conclude, let us briefly reconsider the connection with another essay by Montaigne. Shakespeare takes from "Of Cruelty" Montaigne's idea of virtue as a capacity different from goodness and makes it key to Prospero's hard-won forgiveness of the men who betrayed him. This is Montaigne:

> Methinks virtue is another manner of thing and much *more noble than the inclinations unto goodness*, which in us are engendered. Minds well-born and directed by themselves follow one same path, and in their actions represent the same visage that the virtuous do. But virtue importeth and soundeth somewhat, I wot not, greater and more active than by a happy complexion, gently and peaceably, to suffer itself to be led or drawn to follow reason. He that through a natural facility and genuine mildness should neglect or condemn injuries received, should no doubt perform *a rare action* and worthy commendation; but he who being *stung to the quick* with any wrong or offence received, should arm himself with *reason against this furiously blind desire of revenge*, and in the end after a great conflict yield himself master over it, should doubtless do much more. (371–72; italics original)

In *The Tempest*, Montaigne's passage about virtue is subsumed in a conversation between Prospero and Ariel, which concludes with Prospero's declaration of his humanity in common with others:

> Hast thou, which art but air, a touch, a feeling
> Of their afflictions, and shall not myself,
> One of their kind, that relish all as sharply,
> Passion as they, be kindlier moved than thou art?
> Though with their high wrongs I am struck to th'quick,
> Yet with my nobler reason 'gainst my fury
> Do I take part. The rarer action is
> In virtue than in vengeance; ... (5.1.21–28, TLN 1971–78)

Have we caught Shakespeare reading here? There was evidently something appealing to Shakespeare in Montaigne's idea of virtue as something more noble than natural goodness, in virtue as a quality that the person makes actively and by struggle, and in the alignment of virtue and forgiveness. Yet aside from a few phrases, there is nothing here of Montaigne's book. Indeed, Shakespeare has rewritten his own reading as a scene pointedly without any book, where Prospero comes to feel his own humanity in the face of the fellow-feeling of the spirit Ariel.

On the strength of this admittedly questionable scene of reading (since we can't be sure about the connection with "Of Cruelty"), we might venture nevertheless to say that literary power is not instrumental but always deeply dialectical. We cannot make robots or monsters with it, or raise the dead from their graves, or create real islands. Literary power is the capacity of written language to arouse and sustain meaningful conversations; it does not make actual tempests but rather a play called *The Tempest* that can bring forth many more art works of all kinds. As we have seen, literary power can have real effects on the world, but these will always be indirect, mediated by the creativity and agency of readers, playgoers, writers, actors, filmmakers, and others. The social effects of works of literature such as *The Tempest* will always therefore retain the character of a conversation that is able to build human community, both in the here and now and also over long periods of time and across great distances.

# SHAKESPEARE'S LIFE

## by David Bevington

William Shakespeare was baptized on 26 April 1564, in Holy Trinity Church, Stratford-upon-Avon. He is traditionally assumed to have been born three days earlier, on 23 April, the feast day of St. George, England's patron saint. His father, John Shakespeare, prospering for years as a tanner, glover, and dealer in commodities such as wool and grain, rose to become city chamberlain or treasurer, alderman, and high bailiff, the town's highest municipal position. Beginning in 1577, John Shakespeare encountered financial difficulties, with the result that he was obliged to mortgage his wife's property and miss council meetings. Although some scholars argue that he was secretly a Catholic, absenting himself also from Anglican church services for that reason, the greater likelihood is that he stayed at home for fear of being prosecuted for debt. His wife, Mary, did come from a family with ongoing Catholic connections, but most of the evidence suggests that Shakespeare's parents were respected members of the Established Church. John's civic duties involved him in carrying out practices of the Protestant Reformation. John and Mary baptized all their children at the Anglican Holy Trinity Church and were buried there.

As a civic official, John must have sent his son William to the King Edward VI grammar school close to their house on Henley Street. Student records from the period have perished, but information about the program of education is plentifully available. William would have studied Latin grammar and authors, including Ovid, Virgil, Plautus, Seneca, and others that left an indelible mark on the plays he wrote in his early years.

Shakespeare did not, however, go to university. The reasons are presumably two: his father's financial difficulties, and, perhaps even more crucially, Shakespeare's own marriage at the age of eighteen to Anne Hathaway, since neither Oxford nor Cambridge would ordinarily admit married students. Anne was eight years older than William. She was also three months pregnant when they were married in November 1582. A special license had to be obtained from the Bishop of Worcester to allow them to marry quickly, without the customary readings on three successive Sundays in church of the banns, or announcements of intent to marry. The couple's first child, Susanna, was born in late May 1583. Twins, named Hamnet and Judith, the last of their children, followed in February 1585. Thereafter, evidence is scarce as to Shakespeare's whereabouts or occupation for about seven years. Perhaps he taught school, or was apprenticed to his father, or joined some company of traveling actors. At any event, he turns up in London in 1592. In that year, he was subjected to a vitriolic printed attack by a fellow dramatist, Robert Greene (1558–92), who seems to have been driven by professional envy to accuse Shakespeare of being an "upstart crow" who had beautified himself with the feathers of other writers for the stage, including Christopher Marlowe (1564–93), George Peele (1556–96), Thomas Nashe (1567–1601), and Greene himself.

Shakespeare was indeed well established as a playwright in London by the time of this incident in 1592. In the same year, Nashe paid tribute to the huge success of the tragic death of Lord Talbot in a play, and the only play we know that includes Talbot is Shakespeare's *1 Henry VI*. We do not know for what acting company or companies Shakespeare wrote in the years before 1594, or just how he got started, but he seems to have been an actor as well as a dramatist. Two other plays about the reign of Henry VI also belong to those early years, along with his triumphantly successful *Richard III*. These four plays, forming his first historical tetralogy, were instrumental in defining the genre of the English history play. Following shortly after the great defeat of the Spanish Armada in 1588, they celebrated England's ascent from a century of devastating civil wars to the accession in 1485 of the Tudor Henry VII, grandfather of Queen Elizabeth I. Shakespeare's early work also includes some fine ventures into comedy, including *The Comedy of Errors*, *The Two Gentlemen of Verona*, *Love's Labor's Lost*, and *The Taming of the Shrew*. He wrote only one tragedy at this time, *Titus Andronicus*, a revenge tragedy based on fictional early Roman history. Shakespeare also turned his hand to narrative poetry in these early years. *Venus and Adonis* in 1593 and *The Rape of Lucrece* in 1594, both dedicated to the Earl of Southampton, seem to show Shakespeare's interest in becoming a published poet, though ultimately he chose drama as more fulfilling and lucrative. He probably wrote some of his sonnets in these years, perhaps to the Earl of Southampton, though they were not published until 1609 and then without Shakespeare's authorization.

Shakespeare joined the newly formed Lord Chamberlain's Men, as an actor-sharer and playwright, in 1594, along with Richard Burbage (c. 1567–1619), his leading man. This group quickly became the premier acting company in London, in stiff competition with Edward Alleyn and the Lord Admiral's Men. For the Lord Chamberlain's group, Shakespeare wrote his second and more artistically mature tetralogy of English histories, including *Richard II* and the two *Henry IV* plays, centered on the Prince who then becomes the monarch and victor at Agincourt in *Henry V* (1599). He also wrote another history play, *King John*, in these years. Concurrently, Shakespeare achieved great success in romantic comedy, with *A Midsummer Night's Dream*, *The Merchant of Venice*, and *The Merry Wives of Windsor*. He hit the top of his form in romantic comedy in three plays of 1598–1600 with similar throw-away titles: *Much Ado About Nothing*, *As You Like It*, and *Twelfth Night, or What You Will*. Having fulfilled that amazing task, he set romantic comedy aside until some years later.

During this time Shakespeare lived in London, apart from his family in Stratford. He saw to it that they were handsomely housed and provided for; he bought New Place, one of the two finest houses in town. Presumably he went home to Stratford when he could. He was comfortably well off, owning one share among ten in an acting company that enjoyed remarkable artistic and financial success. He suffered a terrible tragedy in 1596 when his only son and heir, Hamnet, died at the age of eleven. In that year, Shakespeare applied successfully for a coat of arms for his father, so that John, and William too, could each style himself as a gentleman. John died in 1601, Shakespeare's mother in 1608.

Having set aside romantic comedy and patriotic English history at the end of the 1590s, Shakespeare turned instead to problematic plays such as *All's Well That Ends Well*, *Measure for Measure*, and *Troilus and Cressida*, the last of which is ambivalently a tragedy (with the death of Hector), a history play about the Trojan War, and a bleak existential drama about a failed love relationship. He also took up writing tragedies in earnest. *Romeo and Juliet*, in 1594–96, is a justly famous play, but in its early acts it is more a comedy than a tragedy, and its central figures are not tragic protagonists of the stature of those he created in plays from 1599 onward: *Julius Caesar*, *Hamlet*, *Othello*, *King Lear*, *Macbeth*, *Timon of Athens*, *Antony and Cleopatra*, and *Coriolanus*, this last play written in about 1608. Whether Shakespeare was moved to write these great tragedies by sad personal experiences, or by a shifting of the national mood in 1603 with the death of Queen Elizabeth and the accession to the throne of James VI of Scotland to become James I of England (when the Lord Chamberlain's Men became the King's Men), or by a growing skepticism and philosophical pessimism on his part, is impossible to say; perhaps he felt invigorated artistically by the challenge of excelling in the relatively new (for him) genre of tragedy.

Equally hard to answer with any certainty is the question of why he then turned, in his late years as a dramatist, to a form of comedy usually called romance, or tragicomedy. The genre was made popular by his contemporaries Francis Beaumont (1584–1616) and John Fletcher (1579–1625), and it is worth noting that the long indigenous tradition of English drama, comprising the cycles of mystery plays and the morality plays, was essentially tragicomic in form. The plays of this phase, from *Pericles* (c. 1606–08) to *Cymbeline*, *The Winter's Tale*, and *The Tempest* (c. 1608–11), would seem to overlap somewhat the late tragedies in dates of composition. These romances are like the early romantic comedies in many ways: young heroines in disguise, plots of adventure and separation leading to tearfully joyful reunions, comic highjinks, and so on. Yet these late romances are also tinged with the tragic vision that the dramatist had portrayed so vividly: death threatens or actually occurs in these plays, the emotional struggles of the male protagonists are nearly tragic in their psychic dimensions, and the restored happiness of the endings is apt to seem miraculous.

Shakespeare seems to have retired from London to Stratford-upon-Avon some time around 1611; *The Tempest* may have been designed as his farewell to the theater and his career as dramatist, after which he appears to have collaborated with Fletcher, his successor at the King's Men, in *Henry VIII* and *The Two Noble Kinsmen* (1613–14). His elder daughter, Susanna, had married the successful physician John Hall in 1607. In his last will and testament Shakespeare left various bequests to friends and colleagues, but to Anne, his wife, nothing other than his "second-best bed." Whether this betokens any estrangement between him and Anne, whom he had married under the necessity of her pregnancy and from whom he then lived apart during the two decades or so when he resided and worked in London, is a matter of hot debate. Divorce was impossible, whether contemplated or not. He did take good care of her and his family, and he did retire to Stratford. Anne lived on with Susanna and John until she died in 1623. Shakespeare was buried on 25 April 1616. Tradition assumes that he died on 23 April, since he would have left the world on the very feast day (of St. George, England's patron saint) that had probably witnessed his birth some 52 years earlier. He lies buried under the altar of Holy Trinity, next to his wife and other family members. A memorial bust, erected some time before 1623, is mounted on the chancel wall.

# SHAKESPEARE'S THEATER

## by David Bevington

Where Shakespeare's plays of the early 1590s were performed we do not know. When he joined the newly formed Lord Chamberlain's Men in 1594, with Richard Burbage as his leading man, most public performances of Shakespeare's plays would have been put on in a building called The Theatre, since, when it was erected in 1576 by Richard Burbage's father James Burbage (c. 1530–97), it was the only structure in London designed specifically for the performance of plays, and indeed the first such building in the history of English theater. Earlier, plays were staged by itinerant companies in inns and innyards, great houses, churchyards, public squares, and any other place that could be commandeered for dramatic presentation. In Shakespeare's time the professional companies still toured, but to a lesser extent, and several of them also derived part of their income from private performances at court.

The Theatre had been erected in Shoreditch (also called Moorfields), a short walking distance north of London's walls, in order to evade the too often censorious regulations of the city's governing council. There, spectators might have chosen to see *Romeo and Juliet*, *A Midsummer Night's Dream*, *The Merchant of Venice*, *King John*, or *Richard II*. They would also have seen some earlier Shakespeare plays that he had brought with him (perhaps as the price needed to pay for a share in the company) when he joined the Lord Chamberlain's Men: plays such as *Richard III* and *The Taming of the Shrew*. When in the late 1590s the Puritan-leaning owner of the land on which the building stood, Giles Allen, refused to renew their lease because he wished "to pull down the same, and to convert the wood and timber thereof to some better use," the Lord Chamberlain's Men performed for a while in the nearby Curtain Theatre. Eventually, in 1599, they solved their problem with the landlord by dismantling The Theatre and moving it across the River Thames to the shore opposite from London, just to the west of London Bridge, where audiences could reach the new theater—the Globe—by bridge or by water taxi, and where the players were still outside the authority of the city of London. At the time of this move, the River Thames was frozen over in an especially harsh winter, so possibly they slid the timbers of their theater across on the ice.

At any event, the Globe Theatre that they erected in Southwark, not far from the location of today's reconstructed Globe, was in the main the same building they had acted in before. Because timbers were all hand-hewn and fitted, the best plan was to reassemble them as much as was feasible. No doubt the company decided on some modifications, especially in the acting area, based on their theatrical experience, but the house remained essentially as before.

No pictures exist today of the interiors of the Theatre, the Curtain, or the Globe. We do have Visscher's View of London (1616) and other representations showing the exteriors of some theatrical buildings, but for the important matter of the interior design we have only a drawing of the Swan Theatre, copied by a Dutchman, Arend van Buchel (1565–1641), from a lost original by another Dutchman, Johannes de Witt, who visited London in about 1596–98. In many respects, the Swan seems to have been typical of such buildings. As seen in the accompanying illustration, the building appears to be circular or polygonal, with a thatched roof (called *tectum* in the illustration's labels) over the galleries containing seats and another roof over the stage, but leaving the space for standing spectators open to the heavens. (In the modern Globe, similarly constructed, spectators intending to stand in the yard for a performance can purchase a plastic rain poncho to ward off London's frequent rain showers.) From other kinds of information about Elizabethan playhouses, we can estimate a diameter of about 70 feet for the interior space. A large rectangular stage labeled the *proscaenium* (literally, "that which stands before the scene"), approximately 43 feet wide and 27 feet deep, juts out from one portion of the wall into the yard, or *planities siue arena* ("the plain place or arena"). The stage stands about 5 ½ feet above the surface of the yard. Two pillars support the roof over the stage, which in turn is surmounted by a hut. A flag is flying at the top, while a trumpeter at a door in the hut is presumably announcing the performance of a play. The spectators' seats are arrayed in three tiers of galleries. Stairway entrances (*ingressus*) are provided for spectators to gain access from the yard to the seats, labeled *orchestra* on the first level and nearest the stage, and *porticus* above.

The stage area is of greatest concern, and here the Swan drawing evidently does not show everything needed for performance in a theater

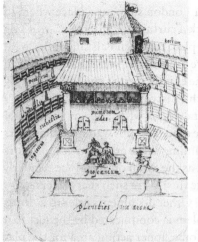

ABOVE, LEFT: This sketch of the Swan is the most complete we have of any theater of the time. The Swan was built in 1596; Shakespeare's company, The Chamberlain's Men, played there in the same year. RIGHT: This view of the first Globe by the Dutch engraver J.C. Visscher (1586–1652) was printed in 1625, but must be taken from an earlier drawing, since the first Globe burned to the ground in 1613 at the first performance of Shakespeare's *Henry VIII*. There is substantial evidence that Visscher simplified the appearance of the theater by portraying it as octagonal: most scholars now believe that it had twenty sides, thus making it seem more circular than in this engraving.

such as the Globe. No trapdoor is visible, though one is needed in a number of Renaissance plays for appearances by ghostly or diabolical visitations from the infernal regions imagined to lie beneath the earth. The underside of the stage roof is not visible in this drawing, but from the plays themselves and other sources of information we gather that this underside above the actors' heads, known as the "heavens," displayed representations of the sun, moon, planets, and stars (as in today's Globe in London). The back wall of the stage in the drawing, labeled *mimorum ades* or "housing for the actors," provides a visual barrier between the stage itself and what was commonly known as the "tiring house" or place where the actors could attire themselves and be ready for their entrances. The two doors shown in this wall confirm an arrangement evidently found in other theaters like the Globe, but the absence of any other means of access to the tiring house raises important questions. Many plays, by Shakespeare and others, seem to require some kind of "discovery space," located perhaps between the two doors, to accommodate a London shop, or a place where in *The Tempest* Prospero can pull back a curtain to "discover" Miranda and Ferdinand playing chess, or a place to which Falstaff, in the great tavern scene of *1 Henry IV*, can retire to avoid the Sheriff's visit and then be heard snoring offstage before he exits at scene's end into the tiring house. The modern Globe has such a discovery space.

Above the stage in the Swan drawing is what appears to be a gallery of six bays in which we can see seated figures watching the actors on the main stage, thereby surrounding those actors with spectators on all sides. But did theaters such as the Swan or the Globe regularly seat spectators above the stage like this? Were such seats reserved for dignitaries and persons of wealth? Other documents refer to a "lords' room" in such theaters. The problem is complicated by the fact that many Elizabethan plays require some upper acting area for the play itself, as when Juliet, in Act II of *Romeo and Juliet*, appears "above" at her "window" to be heard by Romeo and then converses with him, or later, when Romeo and Juliet are seen together "aloft" at her "window" before Romeo descends, presumably by means of a rope ladder in full view of the audience, to go to banishment (3.5). Richard II appears "*on the walls*" of Flint Castle when he is surrounded by his enemies and is obliged to descend (behind the scenes) and then enter on the main stage to Bolingbroke (*Richard II*, 3.3). Instances are numerous. The gallery above the stage, shown in the Swan drawing, must have provided the necessary acting area "above." On those many occasions when the space was needed for action of this sort, seemingly the acting company would not seat spectators there. It is unclear how spectators sitting above would have seen action in the "discovery space," since it may have been beneath them.

On stage, in the drawing, a well-dressed lady, seated on a bench and accompanied perhaps by her lady-in-waiting, receives the addresses of a courtier or soldier with a long-handled weapon or staff of office. Even though the sketch is rough and imperfect, it does suggest the extent to which the plays of Shakespeare and his contemporaries were acted on this broad, open stage with a minimum of scenic effects. The actors would identify their fictional roles and their location by their dialogue, their costumes, and their gestures. On other occasions, when, for example, a throne was needed for a throne scene, extras could bring on such large objects and then remove them when they were no longer needed. Beds, as in the final scene of *Othello*, were apparently thrust on stage from the tiring house. The building itself was handsomely decorated and picturesque, such that the stage picture was by no means unimpressive, yet the visual effects were not designed to inform the audience about setting or time of the action. The play texts and the actors took care of that.

We have a verbal description of the Globe Theatre by Thomas Platter, a visitor to London in 1599, on the occasion of a performance of *Julius Caesar*. The description unfortunately says little about the stage, but it is otherwise very informative about the London playhouses:

> The playhouses are so constructed that they play on a raised platform, so that everyone has a good view. There are different galleries and places, however, where the seating is better and more comfortable and therefore more expensive. For whoever cares to stand below pays only one English penny, but if he wishes to sit, he enters by another door and pays another penny, while if he desires to sit in the most comfortable seats, which are cushioned, where he not only sees everything well but can also be seen, then he pays yet another English penny at another door. And during the performance food and drink are carried around the audience, so that for what one cares to pay one may also have refreshment.

Shakespeare's company may have included ten or so actor-sharers, who owned the company jointly and distributed important roles among themselves. Richard Burbage was Shakespeare's leading man from 1594 until Shakespeare's retirement from the theater. Other actor-sharers, such as John Heminges (1566–1630) and Henry Condell (d. 1627), who would edit the First Folio collection of Shakespeare's plays in 1623, were his longtime professional associates. The quality of performance appears to have been high. Hired men generally took minor roles of messengers, soldiers, and servants. The women's parts were played by boys, who were trained by the major actors in a kind of apprenticeship and remained as actors of women's parts until their voices changed. Many went on in later years to be adult actors.

# WILLIAM SHAKESPEARE AND *THE TEMPEST*: A BRIEF CHRONOLOGY

(Some dates are approximate, notably those of the plays)

| | |
|---|---|
| 1509–47 | Reign of Henry VIII. |
| 1534 | Act of Supremacy, declaring Henry VIII head of the Church of England. |
| 1547–53 | Reign of Edward VI. |
| 1553–58 | Reign of Mary I; England returns to Catholicism. |
| 1558–1603 | Reign of Elizabeth I. |
| 1563 | Adoption of the Thirty-Nine Articles, establishing Anglicanism as a middle path between Roman Catholicism and more fundamentalist Protestantism. |
| 1564 | William Shakespeare born, c. 23 April. |
| 1569 | Suppression of Northern Rebellion of Catholic earls. |
| 1576 | James Burbage builds The Theatre. |
| 1582 | Shakespeare's marriage to Anne Hathaway, late November. |
| 1583 | Birth of daughter Susanna, 26 May. English translation published of Bartholomew de las Casas, *The Spanish colonie*. |
| 1583–84 | Plots against Elizabeth on behalf of Mary Queen of Scots. |
| 1585 | Births of Shakespeare's twins, Hamnet and Judith, 2 February. Earl of Leicester sent to aid the Dutch against the Spanish. |
| 1587 | Execution of Mary Queen of Scots, 8 February. |
| 1588 | At some point, Shakespeare moves to London; family remains in Stratford. War with Spain; the Spanish Armada fleet destroyed in July. |
| 1588–94 | Shakespeare writes his early comedies and histories, and his early tragedy *Titus Andronicus*. |
| 1590 | Philip Sidney, *Arcadia*; Edmund Spenser, *The Faerie Queene*, Books 1–3. |
| 1592 | Shakespeare attacked in print by Robert Greene. |

| | |
|---|---|
| 1593 | *Venus and Adonis.* |
| 1593–1609 | *The Sonnets.* |
| 1594 | Shakespeare joins the Lord Chamberlain's Men; *The Rape of Lucrece.* |
| 1594–95 | *A Midsummer Night's Dream, Richard II, Romeo and Juliet.* |
| 1596 | Spenser, *Faerie Queene*, complete poem. |
| 1596–98 | *The Merchant of Venice, Henry IV Parts 1 and 2.* |
| 1597 | Earl of Essex sent to Ireland to put down a rebellion led by the Earl of Tyrone. |
| 1598 | Ben Jonson, *Every Man in His Humor.* |
| 1598–99 | *Much Ado About Nothing, The Merry Wives of Windsor.* |
| 1599 | Shakespeare's company moves to the Globe; *As You Like It, Henry V, Julius Caesar.* Prohibition and public burning of satires. |
| 1600–02 | *Twelfth Night, Troilus and Cressida, Hamlet, All's Well That Ends Well.* |
| 1601 | Shakespeare's father dies. Essex's abortive rebellion and subsequent execution; Thomas Dekker, *Satiromastix*; Jonson, *Poetaster*; the Poet's War, a literary feud among Dekker, Jonson, and Marston. |
| 1603 | Death of Elizabeth I; coronation of James I, 24 March. Shakespeare's company the Lord Chamberlain's Men is renamed the King's Men; Michel de Montaigne, *The Essayes*, English translation. |
| 1603–04 | *Measure for Measure, Othello.* |
| 1604 | James's confrontation with the Puritans at the Hampton Court Conference. Peace with Spain. |
| 1605 | The Gunpowder Plot foiled, 5 November. |
| 1605–06 | *King Lear.* |
| 1606–07 | *Macbeth, Timon of Athens, Antony and Cleopatra, Pericles.* |
| 1608 | *Coriolanus.* |
| 1609 | *Shakespeares Sonnets.* English ship the *Sea Venture* disappears en route to Jamestown, Virginia; assumed lost. |

| | |
|---|---|
| 1610 | News reaches London of the survival of the *Sea Venture* crew and passengers. |
| 1609–11 | *Cymbeline, The Winter's Tale, The Tempest.* |
| 1611 | *The Tempest* performed at court at Whitehall, 1 November. |
| 1613–14 | *Henry VIII, The Two Noble Kinsmen*; Globe burns down, soon rebuilt. Shakespeare in retirement, living in Stratford. |
| 1614 | Jonson, *Bartholomew Fair.* |
| 1616 | Death of Shakespeare, 23 April. |
| 1623 | Publication of First Folio—*Mr. William Shakespeare's Comedies, Histories, & Tragedies*; *The Tempest* featured as first play in the volume. |

In 1623, seven years after Shakespeare's death, a very large book, entitled *Mr. William Shakespeares Comedies, Histories, & Tragedies. Published according to the True Originall Copies*, was issued from the printing house of Isaac Jaggard and went on sale at Edward Blount's bookshop near St. Paul's (Smith 1). Prospective book-buyers browsing the latest releases would have been greeted by a handsome, unbound volume with the face of the author looking out at them from the title page.

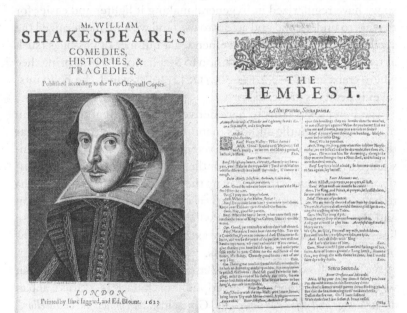

If they turned over the first few pages, they would have found the usual gathering of prefatory epistles and dedicatory poems, a few other preliminary pages, and then the opening scene of the play that appeared first among the thirty-six plays included in the volume. The first play in the Folio is *The Tempest*.

Many have thought that *The Tempest* has pride of place in the Folio because it somehow addresses Shakespeare's own thinking about his life and art. W.W. Greg argued long ago that the publisher put it first because it was one of the plays that had not been published previously and would therefore be more likely to induce shoppers to buy the book (80). That is a cogent argument, and it is true that Jaggard took unusual care with the printing of the play and especially with the first page. The printers stopped and corrected the proofs four times—a time-consuming and costly interruption in their work (Hinman 2: 347). It evidently mattered a great deal to the publisher to get the presentation of the play right.

Since the 1623 Folio *Tempest* is the only early printed version of the play, it has served as the copy-text for this edition. While the Folio text is excellent, it is not without its challenges. The punctuation is erratic, so we have regularized it, in general making it lighter and easier for readers to understand and actors to use, and we have modernized the spelling throughout. We have emended a number of passages (such as Caliban's sweet, poetic invitation to Stephano—"let me bring thee where crabs grow"—2.2.145–50, TLN 1212–17), which the Folio mistakenly prints as prose.

The Folio text seems to have derived from a scribal transcription made either from the author's manuscript or from a copy. It is clear that the scribe was Ralph Crane, a veteran legal scrivener who also transcribed a number of other plays for the Folio project (Howard-Hill *passim*). Crane did more than clean up the text for the printers. He seems to have set out to improve it, by way of his often quirky punctuation and also by his tendency to elide syllables in order to regularize verse lines. We have emended the Folio text in places where we believe it has been misshaped by Crane's efforts.

We have followed the *Dramatis Personae* as it appears in the Folio, but we caution readers about the descriptions of characters such as Caliban as "*a saluage and deformed slaue*" and Gonzalo as "*an honest old Councellor,*" since these descriptions might have been added to Shakespeare's text by Crane (Vaughan and Vaughan 127).

We follow another major feature that might have derived from Crane's imagination as much as from Shakespeare's (Greg 419–20). The Folio text is unusual in the number of stage directions that read like narrative descriptions of stage action rather than like instructions to the players who are putting on the play. There are, of course, plenty of the usual kind, such as "*Enter PROSPERO, FERDINAND, and MIRANDA*" at the start of Act 4. But 150 lines later, the text says this: "*Enter certain reapers, properly habited; they join with the nymphs in a graceful dance, towards the end whereof* PROSPERO *starts suddenly and speaks, after which,* to a strange, hollow, and confused noise, they heavily vanish." This is oddly literary—not something a theatrical practitioner such as Shakespeare would have included in his manuscript but rather like someone recollecting a performance he had seen. This remarkable aspect of the Folio text, and of our edition too, attests to the fact that while Shakespeare is indeed the author of *The Tempest*, the text as it has come down to us is the work of more than the author's hands alone.

Finally, a brief note concerning line numbers: This edition provides the traditional act.scene.line numbers, as well as the Through Line Numbers (TLNs), used by the Internet Shakespeare Editions and originally created by Charlton Hinman for *The Norton Facsimile: The First Folio of Shakespeare* (Norton, 1968). The latter appear at the top of each page.

# THE TEMPEST

[CHARACTERS IN THE PLAY

PROSPERO, *the right Duke of Milan*
ANTONIO, *his brother, the usurping Duke of Milan*
MIRANDA, *daughter to Prospero*
ALONSO, *King of Naples*
SEBASTIAN, *his brother*
FERDINAND, *son to the King of Naples*
GONZALO, *an honest old counselor*
ADRIAN and FRANCISCO, *lords*

TRINCULO, *a jester*
STEPHANO, *a drunken butler*
MASTER of a ship
BOATSWAIN
MARINERS

CALIBAN, *a savage and deformed slave*
ARIEL, *an airy spirit*
IRIS
CERES
JUNO
Nymphs
Reapers]

## [1.1]

*A tempestuous noise of thunder and lightning heard.*[1] *Enter a Shipmaster and a Boatswain.*

SHIPMASTER. Boatswain![2]
BOATSWAIN. Here, master. What cheer?

---

1 The sound of thunder was produced by beating a drum or by rolling cannon balls through a wooden trough; the effect of lightning was created with fireworks.
2 Pronounced *bosun*; the shipmaster's officer in charge of the crew and equipment.

---

1.1.1–7:               A SHIP IN A TEMPEST
                          (TLN 1–14)

In *A True Reportory of the Wracke*, Shakespeare's source for this scene of shipwreck (see Introduction, pp. 12–13, and Appendix F), the sailors and their noble passengers work together to try to save the ship. "Euery man came duely vpon his watch," writes William Strachey, "tooke the Bucket, or Pumpe for one houre, and rested another. Then men might be seene to labour, I may well say, for life, and the better sort, euen our Gouernour, and Admirall themselues, not refusing their turne, and to spell each the other, to giue example to other." On the ship in *The Tempest*, in contrast, while the mariners work "yarely" and skillfully to try to save the ship, the noble passengers don't lift a finger to help. In their terror and anger, they actually hamper the efforts of the sailors.

Shakespeare's scene emphasizes the practical knowledge and the ability of the sailors. What the Boatswain is trying to do is to use the storm wind itself to push the ship past the rocks that loom ahead. In *Shakespeare and the Sea*, the historian A.F. Falconer tells us that "[t]he manoeuvres described are difficult and some would be attempted only in an emergency. Quickness and resource are needed, and a level of skill.... Shakespeare could not have written a scene of this kind without taking great pains to grasp completely how a ship beset with these difficulties would have to be handled. He has not only worked out a series of manoeuvres, but has made exact use of the professional language of seamanship" (37–39).

SHIPMASTER. Good.[1] Speak to the mariners. Fall to it yarely[2] or we run ourselves aground. Bestir! Bestir!

*Exit [Shipmaster].*

*Enter Mariners.*

---

1 Either "good cheer" (in response to the Boatswain's question, "What cheer?") or "an expression of satisfaction at the boatswain's presence" (Orgel).
2 Readily, promptly.

"Ships running aground in a storm" (1690s), by Ludolf Bakhuizen. Wikimedia Commons.

The changes he made to the scene as he found it in Strachey show us how Shakespeare loves to incite debate about the relative strengths and weaknesses of different kinds and ranks of people. The scene also exemplifies Shakespeare's respect for artisanal skill and skillful collaborative action—a feature equally important for those sailing a ship or those—like Shakespeare, his fellow actors, musicians, and sound and fireworks artificers—who worked together to stage plays such as *The Tempest*.

5    BOATSWAIN. Heigh, my hearts! Cheerly, cheerly, my hearts! Yare,
     yare. Take in the topsail! Tend to the master's whistle. [*To the
     storm*] Blow till thou burst thy wind if room enough![1]

     *Enter ALONSO, SEBASTIAN, ANTONIO, FERDINAND, GONZALO, and
     others.*
     ALONSO. Good boatswain, have care. Where's the master? Play the
     men.[2]
10   BOATSWAIN. I pray now, keep below.
     ANTONIO. Where is the master, boatswain?
     BOATSWAIN. Do you not hear him? You mar our labor. Keep your
     cabins! You do assist the storm.
     GONZALO. Nay, good, be patient.
15   BOATSWAIN. When the sea is. Hence! What cares these roarers[3] for
     the name of King? To cabin! Silence: trouble us not.
     GONZALO. Good, yet remember whom thou hast aboard.
     BOATSWAIN. None that I more love than myself. You are a coun-
     selor—if you can command these elements to silence and work
20   the peace of the present,[4] we will not hand a rope more. Use your
     authority; if you cannot, give thanks you have lived so long, and
     make yourself ready in your cabin for the mischance of the hour
     if it so hap. [*To Mariners*] Cheerly, good hearts! [*To Courtiers*] Out
     of our way, I say!

                                                      *Exit [Boatswain].*

25   GONZALO. I have great comfort from this fellow. Methinks he hath
     no drowning mark upon him; his complexion is perfect gallows.
     Stand fast, good Fate, to his hanging. Make the rope of his des-
     tiny[5] our cable, for our own doth little advantage. If he be not
     born to be hanged, our case[6] is miserable.

                              *Exit [SEBASTIAN, ANTONIO, and GONZALO].*

---

1    As long as the ship has clear passage. The sailors are attempting to ride out a
strong onshore wind by making for the island and then sailing past it.
2    Directed at the sailors: "act like men."
3    Violent winds and waves, with a suggestion of roaring, riotous people.
4    "Make the present moment peaceful" (Mowat and Werstine).
5    The rope he is destined to hang from. Gonzalo's use of rope recalls the ropes
and cables the sailors are handling to try to save the ship.
6    Predicament.

*Enter Boatswain.*

BOATSWAIN. Down with the topmast! Yare: lower, lower. Bring her   30
to try with main-course!¹

*A cry within. Enter SEBASTIAN, ANTONIO, and GONZALO.*

BOATSWAIN. A plague upon this howling; they are louder than the
weather or our office.² Yet again? What do you here? Shall we give
over and drown? Have you a mind to sink?

SEBASTIAN. A pox on your throat, you bawling, blasphemous,   35
uncharitable dog!

BOATSWAIN. Work you, then!

ANTONIO. Hang, cur. Hang, you whoreson,³ insolent noisemaker!
We are less afraid to be drowned than thou art.

GONZALO. I'll warrant him for drowning, though the ship were no   40
stronger than a nutshell and as leaky as an unstanched wench.⁴

BOATSWAIN. Lay her ahold, ahold: set her two courses off to sea
again. Lay her off!

*Enter Mariners, wet.*

MARINERS. All lost! To prayers, to prayers! All lost!

BOATSWAIN. What, must our mouths be cold?⁵   45

GONZALO. The King and prince at prayers. Let's assist them, for
our case is as theirs.

SEBASTIAN. I am out of patience.

ANTONIO. We are merely cheated of our lives by drunkards. This
wide-chopped rascal!
[*To Boatswain*] Would thou mightst lie drowning the washing of
ten tides.⁶

GONZALO. He'll be hanged yet,   50
Though every drop of water swear against it

---

1   Taking down the topmast sail will make the ship less top-heavy and reduce its
roll toward shore. The "main-course" is the main sail. The Boatswain is still intent
on riding the onshore wind past the rocky island and out to open sea again.
2   Business.
3   Son of a whore.
4   A young woman who is menstruating or who is sexually incontinent.
5   To be cold in the mouth means to be dead.
6   Pirates were hanged at the edge of the sea and their bodies left to be "washed"
by the tides.

And gape at wid'st to glut him.[1]

*A confused noise within.*

MARINERS. Mercy on us!
　　We split, we split! Farewell, my wife and children!
55　　Farewell, brother! We split,[2] we split, we split!
ANTONIO. Let's all sink wi'th' King.
SEBASTIAN. Let's take leave of him.

*Exit [with ANTONIO].*

GONZALO. Now would I give a thousand furlongs[3] of sea for an acre
　　of barren ground—long heath, brown furze, anything. The wills
60　　above be done, but I would fain die a dry death.

*Exit.*

## [1.2]

*Enter PROSPERO and MIRANDA.*
MIRANDA. If by your art, my dearest father, you have
　　Put the wild waters in this roar, allay them.
　　The sky, it seems, would pour down stinking pitch°　　*a kind of tar*
　　But that the sea, mounting to th'welkin's° cheek,　　*the sky's*
5　　Dashes the fire out. Oh! I have suffered
　　With those that I saw suffer. A brave vessel,
　　Who had no doubt some noble creature in her,
　　Dashed all to pieces. Oh, the cry did knock
　　Against my very heart. Poor souls, they perished.
10　　Had I been any god of power, I would
　　Have sunk the sea within the earth, or ere°　　*before*
　　It should the good ship so have swallowed and
　　The fraughting souls[4] within her.
PROSPERO.　　　　　　　　　　Be collected.
　　No more amazement; tell your piteous heart

---

1　Swallow him; the seas seems on the verge of swallowing up the ship.
2　The ship has been torn asunder and is now sinking.
3　Square of ten acres.
4　Anxious people; also refers to a cargo of souls.

There's no harm done.
MIRANDA.                    Oh, woe the day!
PROSPERO.                              No harm!                              15
  I have done nothing but in care of thee—
  Of thee my dear one, thee my daughter—who
  Art ignorant of what thou art, not knowing
  Of whence I am, nor that I am more better
  Than Prospero, master of a full poor cell,°     *very bare dwelling-place*     20
  And thy no greater father.
MIRANDA.                    More to know
  Did never meddle with my thoughts.
PROSPERO.                              'Tis time
  I should inform thee farther. Lend thy hand
  And pluck my magic garment from me. So
  Lie there, my art.[1] Wipe thou thine eyes; have comfort.              25
  The direful spectacle of the wreck, which touched
  The very virtue of compassion in thee,
  I have, with such provision in mine art,
  So safely ordered that there is no soul
  (No, not so much perdition as an hair!)                              30
  Betide to° any creature in the vessel     *suffered by*
  Which thou heard'st cry, which thou saw'st sink. Sit down,
  For thou must now know farther.
MIRANDA.                              You have often
  Begun to tell me what I am, but stopped
  And left me to a bootless° inquisition,     *fruitless or useless*     35
  Concluding, "Stay—not yet."
PROSPERO.                              The hour's now come.
  The very minute bids thee ope thine ear:
  Obey and be attentive. Canst thou remember
  A time before we came unto this cell?
  I do not think thou canst, for then thou wast not              40
  Out three years old.
MIRANDA.                    Certainly, sir, I can.
PROSPERO. By what? By any other house or person?
  Of anything the image tell me that

---

1   Prospero addresses his magic robe directly.

Hath kept with thy remembrance.

MIRANDA.          'Tis far off—

45    And rather like a dream than an assurance
      That my remembrance warrants.° Had I not     *my memory confirms*
      Four or five women once that tended me?

PROSPERO. Thou had'st, and more, Miranda. But how is it
      That this lives in thy mind? What see'st thou else

50    In the dark backward and abysm of time?[1]
      If thou remember'st aught° ere thou cam'st here,     *anything*
      How thou cam'st here, thou mayst.

MIRANDA.          But that I do not.

PROSPERO. Twelve years since, Miranda, twelve years since,
      Thy father was the Duke of Milan and
      A prince of power.

55    MIRANDA.        Sir, are not you my father?

PROSPERO. Thy mother was a piece of virtue,° and    *exemplar of virtue*
      She said thou wast my daughter; and thy father
      Was Duke of Milan—and his only heir
      And princess no worse issued.[2]

MIRANDA.          Oh, the heavens!

60    What foul play had we that we came from thence—
      Or blessèd was't we did?

PROSPERO.        Both, both, my girl.
      By foul play (as thou say'st) were we heaved thence,
      But blessedly holp hither.°         *brought here*

MIRANDA.          Oh, my heart bleeds
      To think o'th' teen that I have turned you to,[3]

65    Which is from my remembrance. Please you, farther.

PROSPERO. My brother and thy uncle, called Antonio—
      I pray thee, mark me, that a brother should
      Be so perfidious!°—he whom, next thyself,     *treacherous*
      Of all the world I loved, and to him put

70    The manage of my state[4] as, at that time,

---

1   Backward is an adjective used as a noun. Abysm combines "abyss" and
"chasm." The phrase evokes the vast spaces of past time.
2   Of no lesser birth than a noblewoman.
3   The sorrow that I have caused you.
4   Administration of the government.

Through all the seigniories,° it was the first,      *feudal lordships*
And Prospero, the prime duke, being so reputed
In dignity, and for the liberal arts[1]
Without a parallel (those being all my study),
The government I cast upon my brother,          75
And to my state grew stranger, being transported
And rapt in secret studies.[2] Thy false uncle—
Dost thou attend me?
MIRANDA.          Sir, most heedfully—
PROSPERO. Being once perfected how to grant suits[3]
  (How to deny them, who t'advance, and who      80
  To trash for over-topping[4]), new created
  The creatures that were mine,[5] I say, or changed 'em,
  Or else new formed them; having both the key
  Of officer and office, set all hearts i'th' state
  To what tune pleased his ear, that now he was     85
  The ivy which had hid my princely trunk
  And sucked my verdure out on't[6]—thou attend'st not.
MIRANDA. O good sir, I do.
PROSPERO.          I pray thee, mark me!
  I (thus neglecting worldly ends, all dedicated
  To closeness[7] and the bettering of my mind      90
  With that which, but by being so retired,
  O'er-prized all popular rate[8]) in my false brother
  Awaked an evil nature, and my trust,

---

1    Areas of study appropriate for a free gentleman, as opposed to a laborer. The liberal arts comprised the trivium (grammar, logic, rhetoric) and the quadrivium (arithmetic, geometry, music, and astronomy).
2    Became alienated from the work of government on account of my obsession with the magic arts.
3    Having perfected his ability to grant petitions from suitors at court.
4    Curb for going beyond proper limits. To trash is to pull back sharply on the leash of an excited hound.
5    Made over the men who had served me into his servants. "Creatures" suggests the degree to which members of the court are made what they are by the favor of the ruler.
6    The one who enjoyed the powers and perquisites of my dukedom by usurping them; verdure means lush green vegetation.
7    Withdrawal from society.
8    With what ordinary people could not value correctly because it was hidden from them.

Like a good parent, did beget of him
95      A falsehood in its contrary as great
        As my trust was, which had indeed no limit—
        A confidence sans bound.° He being thus lorded,          *without limit*
        Not only with what my revenue yielded
        But what my power might else exact like one
100     Who, having into truth by telling of it,
        Made such a sinner of his memory
        To credit his own lie, he did believe
        He was indeed the duke[1] out o'th' substitution[2]
        And executing the outward face of royalty
105     With all prerogative; hence, his ambition growing—
        Dost thou hear?
MIRANDA.              Your tale, sir, would cure deafness.
PROSPERO. To have no screen between this part he played
        And him he played it for—he needs will be
        Absolute Milan.° Me (poor man), my library          *absolute ruler of Milan*
110     Was dukedom large enough. Of temporal royalties°    *political power*
        He thinks me now incapable. Confederates
        (So dry he was for sway[3]) wi'th' King of Naples
        To give him annual tribute, do him homage,
        Subject his coronet to his crown,[4] and bend
115     The dukedom, yet unbowed (alas, poor Milan!),
        To most ignoble stooping.
MIRANDA.                        Oh, the heavens!
PROSPERO. Mark his condition and th'event, then tell me
        If this might be a brother.
MIRANDA.                        I should sin
        To think but nobly of my grandmother:
        Good wombs have born bad sons.
120 PROSPERO.                        Now the condition:
        This King of Naples, being an enemy

---

1   Like a man who tells lies to himself so effectively that his memory itself
becomes corrupt and he believes the lie.
2   By virtue of acting as the substitute.
3   So thirsty he was for power.
4   Make the dukedom of Milan a subject state of the kingdom of Naples.

To me inveterate,° hearkens my brother's suit,[1]    *long-established*
Which was that he (in lieu o'th' premises°  *in return for the agreed terms*
Of homage and I know not how much tribute)
Should presently extirpate me and mine[2]            125
Out of the dukedom, and confer fair Milan,
With all the honors, on my brother—whereon,
A treacherous army levied, one midnight
Fated to the purpose, did Antonio open
The gates of Milan, and i'th' dead of darkness       130
The ministers for the purpose hurried thence
Me and thy crying self.
MIRANDA.            Alack, for pity!
I, not remembering how I cried out then,
Will cry it o'er again; it is a hint
That wrings mine eyes° to't.           *makes me weep*
PROSPERO.          Hear a little further,    135
And then I'll bring thee to the present business
Which now's upon's, without the which this story
Were most impertinent.
MIRANDA.          Wherefore did they not
That hour destroy us?
PROSPERO.         Well demanded, wench.[3]
My tale provokes that question. Dear, they durst not,   140
So dear the love my people bore me, nor set
A mark so bloody on the business, but
With colors fairer, painted their foul ends.
In few,° they hurried us aboard a bark,[4]    *in a few words*
Bore us some leagues to sea,[5] where they prepared   145
A rotten carcass of a butt;[6] not rigged,
Nor tackle, sail, nor mast. The very rats

---

1   Looks favorably on my brother's plan.
2   Remove me and Miranda without delay. Extirpate means "pull or pluck up by the roots" (*OED* 2.a).
3   Young woman; often pejorative, but here used as a term of endearment.
4   A small sailing ship.
5   Milan is not a port city; Shakespeare's geography is often a bit shaky, but perhaps Prospero and Miranda were taken downriver to be put out to sea.
6   A "butt" is literally a tub or barrel; the boat they were forced into was small and unseaworthy.

Instinctively have quit it. There they hoist us
To cry to th'sea that roared to us, to sigh
150    To th'winds, whose pity, sighing back again,
Did us but loving wrong.

MIRANDA.                Alack, what trouble
Was I then to you?

PROSPERO.            Oh, a cherubin°        *heavenly angel*
Thou wast that did preserve me. Thou didst smile,
Infusèd with a fortitude from heaven
155    (When I have decked the sea with drops full salt[1]
Under my burden groaned), which raised in me
An undergoing stomach° to bear up          *courage*
Against what should ensue.

MIRANDA. How came we ashore?

PROSPERO.              By providence divine.
160    Some food we had and some fresh water that
A noble Neapolitan,[2] Gonzalo,
Out of his charity (who being then appointed
Master of this design°) did give us, with     *person in charge*
Rich garments, linens, stuffs, and necessaries,
165    Which since have steaded much.[3] So of his gentleness,
Knowing I loved my books, he furnished me
From mine own library with volumes that
I prize above my dukedom.[4]

MIRANDA.             Would I might
But ever see that man.

PROSPERO.           Now I arise.[5]
170    Sit still and hear the last of our sea-sorrow.
Here in this island we arrived, and here
Have I, thy schoolmaster, made thee more profit
Than other princes can that have more time

---

1    Added more saltwater, by my tears, to the sea.
2    As a counselor to Alonso, King of Naples, Gonzalo directed the small military force that carried out the abduction of Prospero and Miranda.
3    Been very useful.
4    Prospero's shift to present tense is striking. Even after his twelve-year exile, he still seems to prefer a life of learning to the life of a duke.
5    Both an implied stage direction and a claim that his fortunes are rising.

For vainer hours, and tutors not so careful.[1]

MIRANDA. Heavens thank you for't! And now I pray you, sir,   175
    For still 'tis beating in my mind: your reason
    For raising this sea-storm?

PROSPERO.                    Know thus far forth:
    By accident most strange, bountiful Fortune
    (Now, my dear lady!) hath mine enemies
    Brought to this shore, and by my prescience°   *foreknowledge*   180
    I find my zenith[2] doth depend upon
    A most auspicious star, whose influence
    If now I court not, but omit, my fortunes
    Will ever after droop. Here cease more questions.
    Thou art inclined to sleep; 'tis a good dullness,   185
    And give it way.[3] I know thou canst not choose.
    Come away, servant, come, I am ready now.
    Approach, my Ariel,[4] come.

*Enter ARIEL.*

ARIEL. All hail, great master! Grave sir, hail! I come
    To answer thy best pleasure, be't to fly,   190
    To swim, to dive into the fire, to ride
    On the curlèd clouds. To thy strong bidding, task
    Ariel and all his quality![5]

PROSPERO.                    Hast thou, spirit,
    Performed to point[6] the tempest that I bade thee?

ARIEL. To every article.   195
    I boarded the King's ship—now on the beak,
    Now in the waist,[7] the deck, in every cabin,

---

1   I have provided a better education to you because you have not had the kinds
of distractions that other princes have and because I have been an exceptionally
careful tutor.
2   The highest point of a star's orbit, hence the peak of Prospero's good fortune.
3   Prominent among Prospero's powers is the ability to render others uncon-
scious, as he does here, or incapable of movement.
4   Common name for a spirit, meaning "lion of God."
5   His abilities and/or his fellow spirits.
6   Carried out in perfect detail (as I instructed you).
7   Now at the bow of the ship, now amidships.

I flamed amazement.[1] Sometime I'd divide
And burn in many places. On the topmast,
200    The yards and bowsprit would I flame distinctly,
Then meet and join.[2] Jove's lightning, the precursors
O'th' dreadful thunderclaps, more momentary
And sight out-running were not.[3] The fire and cracks
Of sulphurous[4] roaring, the most mighty Neptune
205    Seemed to besiege and made his bold waves tremble—
Yea, his dread trident shake![5]

PROSPERO.                        My brave spirit,
Who was so firm, so constant, that this coil°            *confusion, turmoil*
Would not infect his reason?

ARIEL.                              Not a soul
But felt a fever of the mad, and played
210    Some tricks of desperation. All but mariners
Plunged in the foaming brine and quit the vessel;
Then all afire with me, the King's son, Ferdinand,
With hair up-staring (then like reeds, not hair![6])
Was the first man that leapt, cried, "Hell is empty,
And all the devils are here!"

215    PROSPERO.                        Why, that's my spirit!
But was not this nigh shore?

ARIEL.                              Close by, my master.

PROSPERO. But are they, Ariel, safe?

ARIEL.                              Not a hair perished;

---

1    Blazed, causing fear and awe. For ideas about ball lightning see Appendix F.
2    I appeared as flame in distinct places in the ship's rigging and also over the whole ship.
3    My fiery movements were as sudden and as hard to track with the eye as lightning is.
4    Sulphur was used in making explosives; hence it was commonly associated with lightning and thunder.
5    Ariel boasts playfully that the fiery commotion he made on the ship seemed to attack the god of the sea himself, making the waves tremble and causing Neptune's trademark trident to shake from fear.
6    Ariel's metaphor suggests how Ferdinand's hair was standing straight up from terror. Since they are fragile and also hard to kill, reeds are also a symbol of both human frailty and resilience.

On their sustaining garments,[1] not a blemish,
But fresher than before. And as thou bad'st me,
In troops I have dispersed them 'bout the isle.          220
The King's son have I landed by himself,
Whom I left cooling of the air with sighs
In an odd angle of the isle, and sitting,
His arms in this sad knot.[2]
PROSPERO.                    Of the King's ship,
The mariners—say how thou hast disposed,          225
And all the rest o'th' fleet.
ARIEL.                         Safely in harbor
Is the King's ship, in the deep nook, where once
Thou called me up at midnight to fetch dew
From the still-vexed Bermudas,[3] there she's hid.
The mariners all under hatches stowed,°     *confined below deck*  230
Who, with a charm joined to their suffered labor,
I have left asleep; and for the rest o'th' fleet,
Which I dispersed, they all have met again
And are upon the Mediterranean float,
Bound sadly home for Naples,                       235
Supposing that they saw the King's ship wracked°     *wrecked*
And his great person perish.
PROSPERO.                      Ariel, thy charge
Exactly is performed—but there's more work.
What is the time o'th' day?
ARIEL.                     Past the mid season.
PROSPERO. At least two glasses[4]—the time 'twixt six and now—   240
Must by us both be spent most preciously.
ARIEL. Is there more toil? Since thou dost give me pains,
Let me remember° thee what thou hast promised,          *remind*

---

1    Ariel might mean that the courtiers' clothing held them up somehow when
they dove into the sea.
2    With crossed arms, a posture associated with melancholy. The line is an
invitation to the actor playing Ariel to make fun of the shipwrecked Ferdinand by
crossing his own arms.
3    The tempestuous climate of the Bermudas and its dangerous reefs were general knowledge by this time. The islands were also often associated with devilish
powers.
4    Two turnings of an hourglass; i.e., it is 2 p.m.

Which is not yet performed me.°         *not yet done for me*
PROSPERO.               How now? Moody?
What is't thou canst demand?
245  ARIEL.                 My liberty.
PROSPERO. Before the time be out? No more!
ARIEL.                        I prithee,
Remember I have done thee worthy service,
Told thee no lies, made thee no mistakings, served
Without or grudge or grumblings. Thou did promise
To bate me a full year.[1]
250  PROSPERO.           Dost thou forget
From what a torment I did free thee?
ARIEL.                     No.
PROSPERO. Thou dost, and think'st it much to tread the ooze
Of the salt deep,
To run upon the sharp wind of the north,
255  To do me business in the veins o' th'earth
When it is baked with frost.
ARIEL.                 I do not, sir.
PROSPERO. Thou liest, malignant thing! Hast thou forgot
The foul witch Sycorax, who with age and envy
Was grown into a hoop?[2] Hast thou forgot her?
260  ARIEL. No, sir.
PROSPERO. Thou hast. Where was she born? Speak: tell me.
ARIEL. Sir, in Algiers.[3]
PROSPERO.         Oh, was she so? I must
Once in a month recount what thou hast been,
Which thou forget'st. This damned witch Sycorax,
265  For mischiefs manifold and sorceries terrible
To enter human hearing, from Algiers
Thou know'st was banished. For one thing she did,[4]
They would not take her life. Is not this true?
ARIEL. Ay, sir.

---

1   Ariel reminds Prospero about his promise to reduce his time of service by a full year.
2   With old age and envy was bent over. It is curious that a woman bent almost into a hoop by old age could nevertheless become pregnant.
3   Capital of Algeria and a significant North African port.
4   This line seems to refer to Sycorax's pregnancy. Women accused of capital crimes could obtain a stay of execution if they were pregnant.

# SYCORAX AND MEDEA
## (TLN 391)

*Medea* by Frederick Sandys (1866–68). Wikimedia Commons.

A drawing of Sycorax from *The Tempest* by Robert Anning Bell (c. 1900). Wikimedia Commons.

Although alternative sources have been mentioned over the years, Sycorax—her name derived from the Greek words *sus* (pig) and *korax* (raven)—is generally thought to have been inspired by the classical figure of Medea. In Greek mythology, Medea was a sorceress and granddaughter of the sun god Helios (as well as being Circe's niece). Some sources see her as a goddess, others as a mortal, but her magical abilities seem to be her most important trait. She is often linked to Hecate, the goddess of magic. She was believed to control the moon and tides, among a slew of other powers. She most notably appears in the myth of Jason and the Argonauts and in Euripides' play *Medea* (430 BCE). Through the various iterations of her story, she appears as a powerful magician, vulnerable to her emotions and capable of horrendous vengeful acts.

Shakespeare likely encountered Medea in Ovid. She appears in *Heroides* and *Tristia* (as well as a now-lost tragedy called *Medea*) but most prominently features in *Metamorphoses* (vii, 1–450). Though Sycorax never appears in *The Tempest*, her great powers are often referenced and, like Medea, she comes across as somewhat inhuman (or more than human) and cruel (for instance, in imprisoning Ariel). Prospero's magic is also reminiscent of the story of Medea, in particular his control over the elements (moon and oceans especially) and over the island's natural world generally. Prospero's farewell speech to his powers in the last act echoes such a connection (5.1.33–58, TLN 1984–2008). For more on Medea, see Appendix B.

270 PROSPERO. This blue-eyed[1] hag was hither brought, with child,
    And here was left by th'sailors. Thou, my slave,
    As thou report'st thyself, was then her servant;
    And, for° thou wast a spirit too delicate         *because*
    To act her earthy and abhorred commands,
275   Refusing her grand hests, she did confine thee,
    By help of her more potent ministers
    And her most unmitigable rage,
    Into a cloven[2] pine, within which rift
    Imprisoned, thou didst painfully remain
280   A dozen years, within which space she died
    And left thee there, where thou didst vent thy groans
    As fast as millwheels strike.[3] Then was this island
    (Save for the son that she did litter here,
    A freckled whelp, hag-born) not honored with
    A human shape.[4]
285 ARIEL.             Yes—Caliban, her son.
    PROSPERO. Dull thing, I say so—he, that Caliban,
    Whom now I keep in service. Thou best know'st
    What torment I did find thee in: thy groans
    Did make wolves howl, and penetrate the breasts
290   Of ever-angry bears; it was a torment
    To lay upon the damned, which Sycorax
    Could not again undo. It was mine art,
    When I arrived and heard thee, that made gape°    *caused to open*
    The pine and let thee out.[5]
    ARIEL.              I thank thee, master.
295 PROSPERO. If thou more murmur'st, I will rend an oak
    And peg thee in his knotty entrails till
    Thou hast howled away twelve winters.
    ARIEL.                   Pardon, master.

---

1    This could refer to Sycorax's eye color or the shade of her eyelids.
2    A pine that was split in the past so that it has grown up with two trunks.
3    Very frequently: as fast as the blades of a millwheel strike the water.
4    These lines suggest Caliban's human appearance, but Prospero's choice of words, especially litter and whelp (puppy), suggests an animal rather than a human birth.
5    Prospero claims that his power was greater than Sycorax's.

I will be correspondent° to command           *compliant*
And do my spriting gently.°       *perform my magic quietly, softly*

PROSPERO.           Do so, and after two days
  I will discharge thee.

ARIEL.           That's my noble master!            300
  What shall I do? Say what. What shall I do?

PROSPERO. Go take thyself like a nymph o'th' sea.
  Be subject to no sight but thine and mine, invisible[1]
  To every eyeball else. Go take this shape
  And hither come in't. Go, hence with diligence.       305

                          *Exit* [*ARIEL*].

Awake, dear heart, awake, thou hast slept well,
Awake.

MIRANDA. The strangeness of your story put
  Heaviness in me.

PROSPERO.         Shake it off. Come on,
  We'll visit Caliban, my slave, who never          310
  Yields us kind answer.

MIRANDA. 'Tis a villain, sir,
  I do not love to look on.

PROSPERO. But as 'tis,
  We cannot miss him; he does make our fire,        315
  Fetch in our wood, and serves in offices
  That profit us. What ho! Slave Caliban!
  Thou earth,[2] thou, speak!

CALIBAN.           (*Within*)[3] There's wood enough within.

PROSPERO. Come forth, I say, there's other business for thee.
  Come, thou tortoise,[4] when!

---

1   Often in productions Prospero gives Ariel a robe or cloak that indicates his
change from sprite to sea nymph. When the audience members see Ariel in this
costume, they know that he is invisible to all others onstage (except for Prospero).
2   Caliban is earthy, in contrast to the airy Ariel.
3   The stage direction "within" suggests that in early productions, Caliban's cave
was located in a discovery space at the back of the stage (see Shakespeare's Theater,
pp. 53–54); more modern productions sometimes place his cave below the stage,
accessible through a trapdoor.
4   Prospero upbraids Caliban for his slowness.

*Enter* ARIEL *like a water nymph.*

320                         Fine apparition, my quaint Ariel:
        Hark in thine ear.

ARIEL.            My Lord, it shall be done.

                                    *Exit* [ARIEL].

PROSPERO. Thou poisonous slave, got by the devil himself
        Upon thy wicked dam,[1] come forth!

*Enter* CALIBAN.

CALIBAN. As wicked dew as e'er my mother brushed
325     With raven's feather from unwholesome fen[2]
        Drop on you both! A southwest blow on ye
        And blister you all over.[3]
PROSPERO. For this be sure: tonight thou shalt have cramps,
        Side-stitches that shall pen thy breath up; urchins
330     Shall, for that vast of night that they may work,
        All exercise on thee.[4] Thou shalt be pinched
        As thick as honeycomb,[5] each pinch more stinging
        Than bees that made 'em.
CALIBAN.                    I must eat my dinner.
        This island's mine by Sycorax, my mother,[6]
335     Which thou tak'st from me. When thou cam'st first,
        Thou strok'st me and made much of me, wouldst give me
        Water with berries[7] in't, and teach me how

---

1   I.e., the devil fathered you; "dam" is contemptuous because it generally means
an animal's mother. Prospero's invective is based on widespread stories about
sexual congress between witches and the devil.
2   Ravens are associated with Sycorax ("korax" is "raven" in Greek); a "fen" is a
swamp, associated with bad air and thus with disease.
3   Winds from the south were thought to be moist and unhealthy.
4   Prospero threatens Caliban with urchins (goblins in the prickly shape of
hedgehogs) that will torture him through the night.
5   Bees were thought to form honeycomb cells by pinching them. The implica-
tion is that Caliban will receive as many bruises from pinching as there are cells in
a honeycomb.
6   Caliban's claim of sovereignty over the island based on inheritance from his
mother.
7   Strachey's letter recounts how the castaways soaked cedar berries in water to
produce "a kind of pleasant drink" (1737).

To name the bigger light and how the less
That burn by day and night.[1] And then I loved thee
And showed thee all the qualities° o' th'isle:                    *features*      340
The fresh springs, brine-pits, barren place and fertile.
Cursed be I that did so! All the charms
Of Sycorax—toads, beetles, bats light on you!
For I am all the subjects that you have,
Which first was mine own King; and here you sty me                     345
In this hard rock[2] whiles you do keep from me
The rest o' th'island.

PROSPERO.                    Thou most lying slave,
  Whom stripes may move,[3] not kindness—I have used thee
  (Filth as thou art) with human[4] care, and lodged thee
  In mine own cell till thou didst seek to violate                    350
  The honor of my child.

CALIBAN. Oh ho! Oh ho! Would't had been done!
  Thou didst prevent me. I had peopled else
  This isle with Calibans.[5]

MIRANDA.                    Abhorrèd slave,
  Which any print of goodness wilt not take,                         355
  Being capable of all ill! I pitied thee,
  Took pains to make thee speak, taught thee each hour
  One thing or other when thou didst not, savage,
  Know thine own meaning, but wouldst gabble like
  A thing most brutish. I endowed thy purposes                       360

---

1   Caliban's description of the sun and moon echoes Genesis (1.16) in the *Geneva Bible* (1599): "God then made two great lights: the greater light to rule the day, and the lesser light to rule the night."
2   Pen me up (i.e., like an animal) in this stone cell.
3   May be subdued by lashes from a whip.
4   "Human" and "humane" were used interchangeably in Shakespeare's time. The first spelling contrasts Prospero's humanity with Caliban's supposed bestial nature; the second spelling suggests that Prospero has treated Caliban with compassion.
5   With its mix of the word "peopled" and image of multiple births (usually associated with animals), Caliban's language draws our attention again to the question of his humanity.

With words that made them known, but thy vile race[1]
(Though thou didst learn) had that in't which good natures
Could not abide to be with; therefore wast thou
Deservedly confined into this rock,
365   Who hadst deserved more than° a prison.       *worse than*
CALIBAN. You taught me language, and my profit on't
   Is—I know how to curse. The red plague[2] rid you
   For learning° me your language.       *teaching*
PROSPERO.                Hag-seed, hence!
   Fetch us in fuel, and be quick. Thou'rt best
370   To answer other business. Shrug'st thou, malice?
   If thou neglect'st or dost unwillingly
   What I command, I'll rack thee with old cramps,
   Fill all thy bones with aches, make thee roar
   That beasts shall tremble at thy din.
CALIBAN.                No, pray thee.
375   [*Aside*] I must obey; his art is of such power
   It would control my dam's god Setebos[3]
   And make a vassal° of him.       *slave, serf*
PROSPERO.            So, slave, hence.

                              *Exit CALIBAN.*


*Enter FERDINAND, and ARIEL invisible, playing [music] and singing.*
ARIEL
*Song.*
   Come unto these yellow sands,
     And then take hands;
380   Curtsied when you have, and kissed,
     The wild waves whist;°       *quiet, still*
   Foot it featly° here and there,       *dance elegantly*
   And, sweet sprites, bear the burden.[4]
   Hark, hark!

---

1   "Race" could suggest natural qualities passed along by way of a family blood-
line. It could also designate collective, ethnic differences, though it did not take on
a full sense of biological categorization until the nineteenth century.
2   This describes either the red boils produced by the plague (which could surface
in yellow or black sores too) or any disease that causes bloody skin eruptions.
3   A reputedly devilish Patagonian god, mentioned in Antonio Pigafetta's narrative of Magellan's 1519–22 expedition.
4   Sing the song's refrain.

[*Burden, dispersedly, within*].[1]

Bow-wow.                                                                    385

The watchdogs bark!

[*Burden, dispersedly, within.*]

Bow-wow.

Hark, hark! I hear

The strain of strutting Chanticleer:[2]

Cry cock-a-diddle-dow!                                                      390

FERDINAND. Where should this music be? I' th'air or th'earth?

It sounds no more, and sure it waits upon

Some god o' th'island. Sitting on a bank,

Weeping again the King my father's wrack,

This music crept by me upon the waters,                                     395

Allaying both their fury and my passion

With its sweet air; thence I have followed it

(Or it hath drawn me, rather), but 'tis gone.

No, it begins again!

ARIEL

*Song.*

Full fathom five[3] thy father lies,                                        400

Of his bones are coral made;

Those are pearls that were his eyes.

Nothing of him that doth fade

But doth suffer a sea-change

Into something rich and strange.                                            405

Sea nymphs hourly ring his knell.

[*Burden.*] Ding dong.

Hark, now I hear them, ding-dong bell!

FERDINAND. The ditty does remember[4] my drowned father.

This is no mortal business, nor no sound                                    410

That the earth owes.° I hear it now above me.[5]                    owns

PROSPERO. [*To MIRANDA*] The fringèd curtains of thine eye

advance,

---

1   The refrain is sung by singers in different positions offstage.

2   A fabled singing rooster, as in Chaucer's "Nun's Priest's Tale."

3   A "fathom" is a nautical measurement; five fathoms equal 30 feet.

4   Song reminds me of.

5   Perhaps Ariel moves to an upper stage or the music comes from musicians in the gallery (Orgel).

And say what thou seest yond.

MIRANDA.                              What is't, a spirit?
Lord, how it looks about. Believe me, sir,
415    It carries a brave form, but 'tis a spirit.

PROSPERO. No, wench, it eats and sleeps, and hath such senses
As we have such. This gallant which thou see'st
Was in the wrack, and but he's something stained
With grief[1] (that's beauty's canker[2]), thou mightst call him
420    A goodly person. He hath lost his fellows,
And strays about to find 'em.

MIRANDA.                        I might call him
A thing divine, for nothing natural
I ever saw so noble.

PROSPERO. [Aside] It goes on, I see,
425    As my soul prompts it. [To ARIEL] Spirit, fine spirit, I'll free
        thee
Within two days for this.

FERDINAND.                        Most sure, the goddess[3]
On whom these airs attend. [To MIRANDA] Vouchsafe my prayer
May know if you remain upon this island,
And that you will some good instruction give
430    How I may bear° me here. My prime request,          conduct, comport
Which I do last pronounce, is (O you wonder!)
If you be maid or no?[4]

MIRANDA.                        No wonder, sir,
But certainly a maid.

FERDINAND.                        My language! Heavens!
I am the best of them that speak this speech,
Were I but where 'tis spoken.

435 PROSPERO.                                How? The best?
What wert thou if the King of Naples heard thee?

FERDINAND. A single thing, as I am now, that wonders

---

1    With red eyes and downcast features from weeping.
2    The cankerworm, which eats shrubs and trees, destroying the buds.
3    This is a paraphrase of "O dea certe," a line in Virgil's *Aeneid*, where Aeneas meets his mother Venus.
4    Ferdinand is using the word "goddess" loosely, especially given his question about Miranda's maidenhood (a human rather than a divine attribute).

To hear thee speak of Naples; he does hear me,
And that he does, I weep. Myself am Naples,[1]
Who with mine eyes (never since at ebb[2]) beheld 440
The King my father wracked.

MIRANDA.                 Alack, for mercy!

FERDINAND. Yes, faith, and all his lords, the Duke of Milan
And his brave son[3] being twain.

PROSPERO.               [*Aside*] The Duke of Milan
And his more braver daughter[4] could control thee
If now 'twere fit to do't. At the first sight 445
They have changed eyes.[5] [*To* ARIEL] Delicate Ariel,
I'll set thee free for this. [*To* FERDINAND] A word good, sir—
I fear you have done yourself some wrong. A word.

MIRANDA. [*Aside*] Why speaks my father so ungently? This
Is the third man that e'er I saw, the first 450
That e'er I sighed for; pity move my father
To be inclined my way.

FERDINAND.           Oh, if a virgin
And your affection not gone forth, I'll make you
The Queen of Naples!

PROSPERO.            Soft, sir, one word more.
[*Aside*] They are both in either's powers, but this swift business 455
I must uneasy make, lest too light winning
Make the prize light.[6] [*To* FERDINAND] One word more: I
   charge thee
That thou attend me. Thou dost here usurp
The name thou ow'st not, and hast put thyself
Upon this island as a spy to win it 460

---

1   I.e., the King of Naples. Ferdinand means that he is all alone and that, his
father being dead, he is himself now king. Therefore, "he" in "he does hear me" is
Ferdinand himself.
2   The tide of Ferdinand's tears has never ebbed.
3   Antonio's son is not mentioned anywhere else in the play; the line suggests
that Shakespeare had intended at some point to include such a character.
4   "Brave" means both courageous and beautiful; Shakespeare adds "more" to
give the comparison greater emphasis.
5   Exchanged affections or affectionate looks. Contemporary love poetry often
figured strong emotion as entering through the eyes.
6   Simple, cheap. The second use carries the suggestion of promiscuity (sexual
"lightness").

From me, the Lord on't.

FERDINAND. No, as I am a man.

MIRANDA. There's nothing ill can dwell in such a temple.
If the ill spirit have so fair a house,
Good things will strive to dwell with't.

PROSPERO. [*To* FERDINAND] Follow
me.

465 [*To* MIRANDA] Speak not you for him; he's a traitor. [*To*
FERDINAND] Come,
I'll manacle thy neck and feet together;
Sea water shalt thou drink; thy food shall be
The fresh-brook mussels,[1] withered roots, and husks
Wherein the acorn cradled. Follow.

FERDINAND. No.

470 I will resist such entertainment° till                    *Treatment*
Mine enemy has more power.

*He draws [a sword] and is charmed from moving.*

MIRANDA. O dear father,
Make not too rash a trial of him, for
He's gentle and not fearful.°                    *inspiring fear*

PROSPERO. What, I say?
My foot, my tutor?[2] [*To* FERDINAND] Put thy sword up, traitor,

475 Who mak'st a show, but dar'st not strike. Thy conscience
Is so possessed with guilt. Come from thy ward,[3]
For I can here disarm thee with this stick
And make thy weapon drop.

MIRANDA. Beseech you, father!

PROSPERO. Hence! Hang not on my garments.

MIRANDA. Sir, have pity—
I'll be his surety.°                    *guarantor*

480 PROSPERO. Silence! One word more
Shall make me chide thee if not hate thee. What,

---

1 An inedible kind of mussel.
2 A proverbial phrase meaning "shall my meanest appendage tell me what to
do?"
3 Defensive position.

An advocate for an impostor? Hush.
Thou think'st there is no more such shapes as he,
Having seen but him and Caliban. Foolish wench,
To th'most of men this is a Caliban,                    485
And they to him are angels.

MIRANDA.                      My affections
Are then most humble; I have no ambition
To see a goodlier man.

PROSPERO.                   [*To FERDINAND*] Come on, obey!
Thy nerves are in their infancy again
And have no vigor in them.

FERDINAND.                   So they are.              490
My spirits, as in a dream, are all bound up:
My father's loss, the weakness which I feel,
The wrack of all my friends, nor this man's threats
To whom I am subdued, are but light to me.
Might I, but through my prison, once a day            495
Behold this maid, all corners else o' th'earth
Let liberty make use of—space enough
Have I in such a prison.

PROSPERO.                   [*Aside*] It works! [*To FERDINAND*] Come on!
[*To ARIEL*] Thou hast done well, fine Ariel; follow me:
Hark what thou else shalt do me.

MIRANDA.                      [*To FERDINAND*] Be of comfort—  500
My father's of a better nature, sir,
Than he appears by speech. This is unwonted°          *atypical*
Which now came from him.

PROSPERO.                   [*To ARIEL*] Thou shalt be as free
As mountain winds, but then° exactly do              *until then*
All points of my command.

ARIEL.                       To th'syllable.            505

PROSPERO. [*To FERDINAND*] Come, follow. [*To MIRANDA*] Speak
    not for him!

                                        *Exeunt.*

The spell that Prospero casts on Ferdinand, which makes him unable to move except in obedience to Prospero's commands, reflects early modern ideas about how the body and mind work, ideas that originated in Antiquity and stayed active and influential well into the seventeenth century. According to seventeenth-century thinkers such as Francis Bacon (1561–1626) and René Descartes (1596–1650), the "animal spirits" run through all the conduits of the body. The word "animal" derives from "anima," Latin for "soul." Animal spirits *animate* the body. They do that by connecting the mind or the soul with the body, thereby making possible the kind of willed, purposeful movement that Ferdinand finds himself incapable of when he is brought under the magical influence of his future father-in-law. The illustration on this page, from Descartes's *L'Homme*, shows one of these bodily conduits, which carry the animal spirits back and forth from the limb to the mind (by way, according to Descartes, of the pineal gland). As David Lindley explains in the Cambridge edition of *The Tempest*: "The animal, vital and natural spirits, deriving from the brain, heart and liver, were carried respectively through the body by the sinews (nerves), arteries and veins. The meaning here, as elsewhere in the play, is primarily physiological, and 'psychological' as a consequence of the bodily effect" (1.2.485n).

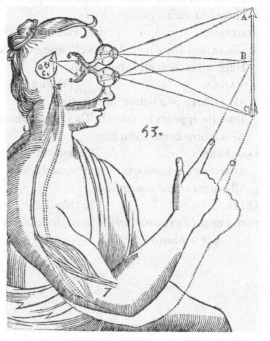

From *L'Homme de René Descartes* (Paris, 1664), 27. Wikimedia Commons.

## [2.1]

*Enter ALONSO, SEBASTIAN, ANTONIO, GONZALO, ADRIAN,*
*FRANCISCO, and others.*

GONZALO. [*To ALONSO*] Beseech you, sir: be merry. You have
    cause—
  So have we all—of joy, for our escape
  Is much beyond° our loss. Our hint of woe         *far outweighs*
  Is common: every day, some sailor's wife,
  The masters of some merchant, and the merchant[1]     5
  Have just our theme of woe—but for the miracle
  (I mean our preservation), few in millions
  Can speak like us. Then wisely, good sir, weigh
  Our sorrow with our comfort.
ALONSO. Prithee, peace.         10
SEBASTIAN. [*To ANTONIO*] He receives comfort like cold porridge.[2]
ANTONIO. The visitor[3] will not give him o'er so.
SEBASTIAN. Look, he's winding up the watch of his wit;[4]
  By and by it will strike.
GONZALO. Sir—
SEBASTIAN.     One. Tell.°         *the clock has struck one o'clock*
GONZALO.         When every grief is entertained     15
  That's offered, comes to th'entertainer—
SEBASTIAN.         A dollar.
GONZALO. Dolor comes to him indeed—you have spoken truer than
  you purposed.[5]
SEBASTIAN. You have taken it wiselier than I meant you should.
GONZALO. Therefore, my Lord—     20

---

1    The owners or officers of a merchant vessel and the owner of the cargo.
2    Sebastian puns on Alonso's "peace." "Pease porridge" is a spiced pudding
made with peas.
3    A church official who comforts ailing parish members.
4    Striking pocket watches (invented around 1510) needed to be wound. The
ongoing joke in these lines is that Gonzalo's method of comforting Alonso is as
predictable as a striking watch.
5    Sebastian takes Gonzalo's word "entertainer" in its usual sense to mean someone who puts on a show for money. Gonzalo actually means that people who take
every little sad occasion too much to heart will suffer "dolor" (i.e., sorrow).

ANTONIO. Fie, what a spendthrift[1] is he of his tongue.

ALONSO. [To GONZALO] I prithee, spare.

GONZALO. Well, I have done. But yet—

SEBASTIAN. He will be talking.

25 ANTONIO. Which of he or Adrian, for a good wager, first begins to crow?

SEBASTIAN. The old cock.

ANTONIO. The cockerel.[2]

SEBASTIAN. Done. The wager?

30 ANTONIO. A laughter.[3]

SEBASTIAN. A match!

ADRIAN. Though this island seem to be desert—

ANTONIO. Ha, ha, ha!

SEBASTIAN. [To ANTONIO] So, you're paid.

35 ADRIAN. Uninhabitable and almost inaccessible—

SEBASTIAN. Yet—

ADRIAN. Yet—

ANTONIO. He could not miss't.[4]

ADRIAN. It must needs be of subtle, tender, and delicate temperance.

40 ANTONIO. Temperance was a delicate wench.

SEBASTIAN. Ay, and a subtle, as he most learnedly delivered.[5]

ADRIAN. The air breathes upon us here most sweetly.

SEBASTIAN. As if it had lungs—and rotten ones.

ANTONIO. Or as 'twere perfumed by a fen.

45 GONZALO. Here is everything advantageous to life.

ANTONIO. True, save means to live.

SEBASTIAN. Of that there's none or little.

GONZALO. How lush and lusty the grass looks. How green!

ANTONIO. The ground indeed is tawny.[6]

---

1   Extravagant spender.

2   The joke involves imagining Gonzalo as an old rooster (cock) and Adrian as a young rooster (cockerel; also used figuratively as "young man"). The wager is on who will speak (crow) first.

3   Both the act of laughing and the term for the eggs laid by a hen before she is ready to sit on the nest. The term continues the cock/cockerel joke of the earlier lines.

4   He was bound to reply that way.

5   Adrian uses the term to mean "mild." Antonio and Sebastian interpret Adrian's use of "temperance" as the name of a woman who is "delicate" (i.e., prone to sexual pleasure) and "subtle" (i.e., cunning).

6   Orange or yellowish brown.

SEBASTIAN. With an eye° of green in it.                                    *tinge*    50

ANTONIO. He misses not much.

SEBASTIAN. No, he doth but mistake the truth totally.

GONZALO. But the rarity of it is, which is indeed almost beyond
     credit°—                                                              *belief*

SEBASTIAN. As many vouched rarities[1] are.                                         55

GONZALO. That our garments, being as they were drenched in the
     sea, hold notwithstanding their freshness and glosses, being
     rather new-dyed than stained with salt water.

ANTONIO. If but one of his pockets could speak, would it not say
     he lies?[2]                                                                    60

SEBASTIAN. Ay, or very falsely pocket up° his report.                      *conceal*

GONZALO. Methinks our garments are now as fresh as when we put
     them on first in Africa at the marriage of the King's fair daughter
     Claribel to the King of Tunis.[3]

SEBASTIAN. 'Twas a sweet marriage, and we prosper well in our             65
     return.

ADRIAN. Tunis was never graced before with such a paragon to their
     queen.

GONZALO. Not since widow Dido's[4] time.

ANTONIO. Widow? A pox on that! How came that widow in? Widow          70
     Dido!

SEBASTIAN. What if he had said "widower Aeneas" too? Good Lord,
     how you take it!

ADRIAN. "Widow Dido," said you? You make me study of that: she
     was of Carthage,[5] not of Tunis.                                             75

GONZALO. This Tunis, sir, was Carthage.

ADRIAN. Carthage?

GONZALO. I assure you—Carthage.

ANTONIO. His word is more than the miraculous harp.

---

1   Unlikely circumstances that are sworn to be true.
2   Antonio jokes that Gonzalo's clothes might look clean on the outside but are
dirty right through to the pockets.
3   A city-state in northern Africa (now the capital of Tunisia).
4   In ancient tradition and in Virgil's *Aeneid*, Dido, the lover of Aeneas, was the
widow of Sychaeus and the founder of Carthage. Dido committed suicide when
Aeneas abandoned her and sailed to Italy to found Rome.
5   After the fall of Carthage, Tunis took that city's place as the area's political and
mercantile center. The cities were closely associated in early modern political and
cartographic writing.

80 SEBASTIAN. He hath raised the wall and houses too.[1]

ANTONIO. What impossible matter will he make easy next?

SEBASTIAN. I think he will carry this island home in his pocket and
give it his son for an apple.

ANTONIO. And sowing the kernels[2] of it in the sea, bring forth more
85 islands.

GONZALO. Ay—

ANTONIO. Why, in good time.

GONZALO. [To ALONSO] Sir, we were talking that our garments seem
now as fresh as when we were at Tunis at the marriage of your
90 daughter, who is now queen.

ANTONIO. And the rarest that e'er came there.

SEBASTIAN. Bate,° I beseech you, widow Dido.                    except

ANTONIO. Oh, widow Dido? Ay, widow Dido!

GONZALO. [To ALONSO] Is not, sir, my doublet[3] as fresh as the first
95 day I wore it—I mean, in a sort?

ANTONIO. That sort[4] was well fished for.

GONZALO. When I wore it at your daughter's marriage?

ALONSO. You cram these words into mine ears against
The stomach of my sense.[5] Would I had never
100 Married my daughter there, for coming thence
My son is lost; and, in my rate,° she too,          in my judgment
Who is so far from Italy removed,
I ne'er again shall see her. O thou mine heir
Of Naples and of Milan,[6] what strange fish
Hath made his meal on thee?

105 FRANCISCO.                          Sir, he may live.
I saw him beat the surges under him
And ride upon their backs; he trod the water,
Whose enmity he flung aside, and breasted

---

1  Antonio and Sebastian ridicule Gonzalo's inaccurate story-telling, suggesting that Gonzalo's miraculous harp (like the one Amphion used to build Thebes)
metaphorically rebuilt Carthage, which was destroyed by the Romans in 146 BCE.

2  Seeds.

3  Jacket.

4  Gonzalo's "in a sort" means "in a way." Antonio's "That sort" means "that
kind of claim."

5  Alonso complains that he has no stomach or appetite for the lords' words of
consolation; it goes against his mood.

6  This refers to the deal Alonso has made with Antonio that Ferdinand will
inherit both city-states.

The surge most swoll'n that met him. His bold head
'Bove the contentious waves he kept, and oared                    110
Himself with his good arms in lusty stroke
To th'shore that o'er his wave-worn basis[1] bowed
As stooping to relieve him—I not doubt
He came alive to land.

ALONSO.                  No, no, he's gone!

SEBASTIAN. Sir, you may thank yourself for this great loss,       115
That would not bless our Europe with your daughter,
But rather loose her to an African,
Where she at least is banished from your eye,
Who hath cause to wet the grief on't.

ALONSO.                              Prithee, peace.

SEBASTIAN. You were kneeled to and importuned otherwise          120
By all of us, and the fair soul herself
Weighed between loathness and obedience, at
Which end o'th' beam should bow.[2] We have lost your son,
I fear, forever; Milan and Naples have
More widows in them of this business' making                     125
Than we bring men to comfort them—
The fault's your own.

ALONSO.                  So is the dear'st o'th' loss.

GONZALO. My Lord Sebastian,
The truth you speak doth lack some gentleness
And time to speak it in; you rub the sore                         130
When you should bring the plaster.°          *curative ointment or bandage*

SEBASTIAN.                        Very well.

ANTONIO. And most chirurgeonly.°            *like a surgeon*

GONZALO. [*To ALONSO*] It is foul weather in us all, good sir,
When you are cloudy.

SEBASTIAN.            Foul weather?

ANTONIO.                            Very foul.

GONZALO. Had I plantation[3] of this isle, my Lord—              135

---

1   The base of the cliffs eroded by the sea.
2   Alonso's daughter Claribel, as if on a balance beam, was forced to decide
between a sense of duty toward her father and her unwillingness to enter the
arranged marriage.
3   Colonization rights. Antonio and Sebastian quibble on the term's agricultural
sense.

ANTONIO. He'd sow't with nettle-seed.°                    *prickly weed*

SEBASTIAN.                              Or docks or mallows.[1]

GONZALO. And were the King on't, what would I do?

SEBASTIAN. 'Scape being drunk for want of wine.

GONZALO. I'th' commonwealth[2] I would by contraries[3]

140    Execute all things, for no kind of traffic°                    *trade*
       Would I admit: no name of magistrate;
       Letters° should not be known; riches, poverty,          *the Liberal Arts*
       And use of service,° none; contract, succession,[4]    *keeping servants*
       Bourne, bound of land,[5] tilth, vineyard, none;

145    No use of metal, corn, or wine, or oil;
       No occupation°—all men idle all,                           *employment*
       And women too, but innocent and pure;
       No sovereignty[6]—

SEBASTIAN.                    Yet he would be King on't!

ANTONIO. The latter end of his commonwealth forgets the beginning.

150    GONZALO. All things in common nature should produce
       Without sweat or endeavor. Treason, felony,
       Sword, pike, knife, gun, or need of any engine[7]
       Would I not have; but nature should bring forth
       Of its own kind all foison,° all abundance,              *plenty*

155    To feed my innocent people.

SEBASTIAN. No marrying 'mong his subjects?

ANTONIO. None, man, all idle[8]—whores and knaves.

GONZALO. I would, with such perfection, govern, sir,
       T'excel the Golden Age.

SEBASTIAN.                              'Save his majesty.

ANTONIO. Long live Gonzalo!

---

1   Docks are medicinal weedy herbs; mallows are purple wildflowers with hairy
stems.
2   A self-administering community or state.
3   Contrary to usual practices.
4   System of inheritance.
5   Land enclosure, a practice that caused a great deal of social unrest in the
sixteenth and seventeenth centuries.
6   Gonzalo's speech closely mirrors a passage in Montaigne's "Of the Cannibals"
in Florio's 1603 translation. See Appendix E.
7   Machinery, especially for use in war.
8   Gonzalo earlier used the word "idle" to mean unemployed (2.1.146, TLN 831).
Antonio intends it to mean lustful or frivolous.

# THE GOLDEN AGE
## (TLN 846)

Gonzalo's description of his vision of a utopian common-wealth directly references Ovid's Golden Age. "The Ages of Man" was a widespread concept in Antiquity going as far back as Hesiod's descrip-tion of the Five Ages of Man in *Works and Days* (750–650 BCE). It detailed the various epochs of mankind throughout their fall from grace (thus suggest-ing that the current age was the least desirable one). The Golden Age, popularized by

*The Golden Age* by Lucas Cranach the Elder (c. 1530). From Wikimedia Commons.

Ovid in *Metamorphoses* (8 CE) was thought to be the first (and ideal) age of man, in which there was sexual freedom and an absence of discord, where men and gods mingled, food was plentiful, and there was no need for rule of law or military power. Men in the Golden Age were said not to know of such things as navigation, tool making, or any other art save agriculture. The idea of a Golden Age also occurs in Christian and Hindu mythologies, among others, as a paradise such as the Garden of Eden that man can never reclaim.

Gonzalo's assertion that his dream commonwealth would "excel" (exceed) the Golden Age would have undoubtedly channeled Ovid for early modern audiences, since Ovid's description of the Golden Age was the epitome of such a utopian concept in the period. With this reference, Shakespeare furthers his depiction of the island as a magical non-place in which the rules and scientific knowledge of man is useless in the face of Prospero's magic. Sebastian and Antonio's deriding of the counselor as he speaks (as well as the play's focus on navigation and colonial impe-rialism) also agrees with the general perception of mankind within the "Ages of Man" model as increasingly degraded: the more knowledge and skills we acquire, the further away we move from such an ideal state. For more on Ovid's depiction of the Golden Age, see Appendix B.

GONZALO.                                        [*To ALONSO*] And—do
160      you mark¹ me, sir?

ALONSO. Prithee, no more: thou dost talk nothing to me.

GONZALO. I do well believe your highness, and did it to minister
      occasion to these gentlemen, who are of such sensible² and nim-
      ble lungs that they always use to laugh at nothing.

165  ANTONIO. 'Twas you we laughed at.

GONZALO. Who, in this kind of merry fooling, am nothing to you;
      so you may continue and laugh at nothing still!

ANTONIO. What a blow was there given!

SEBASTIAN. And° it had not fallen flat-long.³                    *if*

170  GONZALO. You are gentlemen of brave metal; you would lift the
      moon out of her sphere if she would continue in it five weeks⁴
      without changing.

*Enter ARIEL [invisible], playing solemn music.*

SEBASTIAN. We would so, and then go a-bat-fowling.⁵

ANTONIO. Nay, good my lord, be not angry.

175  GONZALO. No, I warrant you; I will not adventure my discretion so
      weakly.⁶ Will you laugh me asleep, for I am very heavy?

ANTONIO. Go sleep, and hear us.

[*All sleep, except ALONSO, SEBASTIAN, and ANTONIO.*]

ALONSO. What, all so soon asleep? I wish mine eyes
      Would with themselves shut up my thoughts;
180      I find they are inclined to do so.

SEBASTIAN. Please you, sir,
      Do not omit the heavy offer of it.⁷

---

1   Pay attention to.
2   Lungs that are sensitive to laughter and are provoked by very little.
3   The relatively harmless part of a sword; the flat side. Antonio and Sebastian
mean that Gonzalo's gibe is ineffective.
4   The moon is as likely to stop changing phases as your joking is to be effective.
5   Killing roosting birds at night with a club. Sebastian picks up from Gonzalo's
remark about lifting the moon out of her sphere. He imagines using the moon as a
torch to surprise nesting birds, making them easier to kill.
6   Risk losing my equanimity for such a weak reason.
7   Do not ignore the invitation to sleepiness.

It seldom visits sorrow; when it doth, it is a comforter.

ANTONIO. We two, my Lord, will guard your person

   While you take your rest, and watch your safety.                    185

ALONSO. Thank you—wondrous heavy—

   [*ALONSO sleeps. Exit ARIEL.*]

SEBASTIAN. What a strange drowsiness possesses them.

ANTONIO. It is the quality o'th' climate.

SEBASTIAN.                              Why

   Doth it not then our eyelids sink? I find

   Not myself disposed to sleep.                                       190

ANTONIO. Nor I. My spirits are nimble.

   They fell together all, as by consent.

   They dropped as by a thunder-stroke. What might,

   Worthy Sebastian? Oh, what might—? No more—

   And yet methinks I see it in thy face,                              195

   What thou shouldst be—th'occasion speaks thee,[1] and

   My strong imagination sees a crown

   Dropping upon thy head.

SEBASTIAN.                        What, art thou waking?

ANTONIO. Do you not hear me speak?

SEBASTIAN.                              I do, and surely

   It is a sleepy language, and thou speak'st                          200

   Out of thy sleep. What is it thou didst say?

   This is a strange repose, to be asleep

   With eyes wide open—standing, speaking, moving,

   And yet so fast asleep.

ANTONIO.                      Noble Sebastian,

   Thou let'st thy fortune sleep (die rather); wink'st                 205

   Whiles thou art waking.[2]

SEBASTIAN.                        Thou dost snore distinctly—

   There's meaning in thy snores.

ANTONIO. I am more serious than my custom; you

   Must be so too, if heed me,° which to do       *if you heed me*

   Trebles thee o'er.°                      *makes you three times more powerful*

---

1  The present situation offers you a new self-definition.

2  Closing your eyes in sleep while you are conscious. Antonio accuses Sebastian of refusing to see the opportunity before him.

210   SEBASTIAN.          Well, I am standing water.
     ANTONIO. I'll teach you how to flow.
     SEBASTIAN.                 Do so; to ebb
     Hereditary sloth instructs me.[1]
     ANTONIO.               Oh,
     If you but knew how you the purpose cherish
     Whiles thus you mock it, how in stripping it
215     You more invest it![2] Ebbing men indeed
     Most often do so near the bottom run
     By their own fear or sloth.[3]
     SEBASTIAN.             Prithee, say on—
     The setting of thine eye and cheek proclaim
     A matter from thee and a birth indeed,
220     Which throes thee much to yield.[4]
     ANTONIO. Thus, Sir,
     Although this Lord of weak remembrance,[5] this
     Who shall be of as little memory
     When he is earthed, hath here almost persuaded
225     (For he's a spirit of persuasion, only
     Professes to persuade) the King his son's alive,
     'Tis as impossible that he's undrowned
     As he that sleeps here, swims.
     SEBASTIAN.                I have no hope
     That he's undrowned.
     ANTONIO.           Oh, out of that "no hope"
230     What great hope have you! No hope that way is,
     Another way, so high a hope that even
     Ambition cannot pierce a wink beyond

---

1   Teach me how to take action since I am lazy by nature.
2   If you only realized how much you cherish the proposed action you are mocking. This is also a clothing metaphor that compares Sebastian's desire for the throne with a ritual robing (i.e., investing).
3   Powerless, inactive men remain at the bottom of the political order on account of their own fear or laziness.
4   You look like you have something of consequence to say and as if what you have to say were as hard to deliver as a baby. The word "throes" was associated with the pain of giving birth.
5   Gonzalo (who, in Antonio's view, isn't important enough to be remembered).

But doubt discovery there.¹ Will you grant with me
That Ferdinand is drowned?
SEBASTIAN. He's gone.                                                    235
ANTONIO. Then tell me,
  Who's the next heir of Naples?
SEBASTIAN. Claribel.
ANTONIO. She that is Queen of Tunis, she that dwells
  Ten leagues beyond man's life, she that from Naples          240
  Can have no note unless the sun were post²
  (The man I'th' moon's too slow) till newborn chins
  Be rough and razorable; she that from whom
  We all were sea-swallowed, though some cast again,³
  And by that destiny to perform an act                        245
  Whereof what's past is prologue,⁴ what to come
  In yours and my discharge.⁵
SEBASTIAN. What stuff is this? How say you?
  'Tis true my brother's daughter's Queen of Tunis;
  So is she heir of Naples, 'twixt which regions                250
  There is some space.
ANTONIO.          A space whose every cubit°      *about 18–20 inches*
  Seems to cry out, "how shall that Claribel
  Measure us⁶ back to Naples? Keep in Tunis
  And let Sebastian wake." Say this were death
  That now hath seized them—why, they were no worse            255
  Than now they are. There be that can rule Naples
  As well as he that sleeps, lords that can prate°              *chatter*
  As amply and unnecessarily
  As this Gonzalo. I myself could make

---

1   The general sense of these lines is that there is no hope of advancement in the
way Sebastian is thinking, but the highest ambition—the goal of becoming king—
nevertheless is realizable: "doubt discovery" here means "but you are uncertain
about discovering the ambitious pathway I am showing you."
2   She lives at a distance farther than could be traveled in a lifetime; she could get
news from Italy only if the sun itself were the messenger.
3   On our return from Claribel's wedding, we were swallowed by the ocean but
some, the survivors, were vomited up again (cast again).
4   A theatrical metaphor: everything up to this moment has been preparation for
what we are about to do; what we do will be the real action of the play.
5   What is about to happen is up to us to perform.
6   Follow us (i.e., the cubits).

260      A chough of as deep chat.[1] Oh, that you bore
        The mind that I do—what a sleep were this
        For your advancement. Do you understand me?
        SEBASTIAN. Methinks I do.
        ANTONIO.            And how does your content
        Tender your own good fortune?
        SEBASTIAN.            I remember
        You did supplant your brother Prospero.
265      ANTONIO.            True—
        And look how well my garments sit upon me
        Much feater° than before. My brother's servants     *more fittingly*
        Were then my fellows, now they are my men.
        SEBASTIAN. But for your conscience?
270      ANTONIO. Ay, sir, where lies that? If 'twere a kibe,°    *a sore on the heel*
        'Twould put me to my slipper. But I feel not
        This deity in my bosom. Twenty consciences
        That stand 'twixt me and Milan, candied be they
        And melt ere they molest.[2] Here lies your brother,
275      No better than the earth he lies upon.
        If he were that which now he's like, that's dead
        (Whom I, with this obedient steel,° three inches of it,     *dagger*
        Can lay to bed forever), whiles you, doing thus,
        To the perpetual wink for aye,° might put     *close Gonzalo's eyes forever*
280      This ancient morsel, this Sir Prudence, who
        Should not upbraid our course.° For all the rest,    *criticize our action*
        They'll take suggestion as a cat laps milk;
        They'll tell the clock to any business that
        We say befits the hour.°     *the lords will agree with whatever we propose*
        SEBASTIAN.            Thy case, dear friend,
285      Shall be my precedent. As thou got'st Milan,
        I'll come by Naples. Draw thy sword: one stroke

---

1   I could instruct a jackdaw (a noisy bird of the crow family) to chatter as much as Gonzalo does.
2   Antonio is saying, "let's say that twenty consciences stood between me and the dukedom; if they did, they'd all be candy and would melt away before they could get in my way."

Shall free thee from the tribute[1] which thou payest,
And I, the King, shall love thee.

ANTONIO.                              Draw together,
And when I rear my hand, do you the like
To fall it on Gonzalo.

SEBASTIAN.              Oh, but one word——                        290

*[They talk apart.] Enter* ARIEL, *[invisible,] with music and song.*

ARIEL. My master, through his art, foresees the danger
    That you, his friend, are in, and sends me forth
    (For else his project dies) to keep them living.
    *Sings in* GONZALO'S *ear*
    While you here do snoring lie,
    Open-eyed conspiracy                                         295
    His time doth take.
    If of life you keep a care,
    Shake off slumber, and beware:
    Awake, awake!

ANTONIO. Then let us both be sudden.                             300

GONZALO. Now, good angels, preserve the King!

ALONSO. Why, how now, ho! Awake! Why are you drawn?
    Wherefore this ghastly° looking?         *fearful, inspiring terror*

GONZALO.                        What's the matter?

SEBASTIAN. Whiles we stood here securing your repose,
    Even now we heard a hollow burst of bellowing               305
    Like bulls, or rather lions—did't not wake you?
    It struck mine ear most terribly.

ALONSO.                        I heard nothing.

ANTONIO. Oh, 'twas a din to fright a monster's ear,
    To make an earthquake! Sure it was the roar
    Of a whole herd of lions.

ALONSO.                        Heard you this, Gonzalo?         310

GONZALO. Upon mine honor, sir, I heard a humming,
    And that a strange one too, which did awake me.
    I shook you, sir, and cried. As mine eyes opened,

---

1   Antonio struck a deal with Alonso to pay annual tribute to Naples to ensure its
support of the deposition of Prospero.

I saw their weapons drawn. There was a noise,
315 That's verily. 'Tis best we stand upon our guard
Or that we quit this place. Let's draw our weapons.
ALONSO. Lead off this ground, and let's make further search
For my poor son.
GONZALO.　　　　　Heavens keep him from these beasts,
For he is sure i' th'island.
ALONSO.　　　　　　　　Lead away.
320 ARIEL. [Aside] Prospero my Lord shall know what I have done:
So, King, go safely on to seek thy son.

*Exeunt.*

[2.2]

*Enter CALIBAN with a burden of wood; a noise of thunder heard.*
CALIBAN. All the infections[1] that the sun sucks up
From bogs, fens, flats on Prosper fall and make him
By inchmeal° a disease! His spirits hear me,　　*gradually, inch by inch*
And yet I needs must curse. But they'll nor° pinch,　　*neither*
5 Fright me with urchin-shows,[2] pitch me i'th' mire,
Nor lead me like a firebrand[3] in the dark
Out of my way, unless he bid 'em; but
For every trifle are they set upon me—
Sometimes like apes that mow[4] and chatter at me
10 And after bite me; then like hedgehogs,° which　　*goblins*
Lie tumbling in my barefoot way and mount
Their pricks at my foot-fall. Sometime am I
All wound with adders, who with cloven tongues
Do hiss me into madness. Lo, now lo—

*Enter TRINCULO.*
15 Here comes a spirit of his, and to torment me

---

1　It was believed that the sun was able to draw contagion out from the earth.
2　Goblin shows; they were said to appear in the form of hedgehogs.
3　Literally, a piece of burning wood, a torch; possibly the will o' the wisp, a phosphorescent flame that appears in marshes at night.
4　Make faces or grimaces.

For bringing wood in slowly. I'll fall flat;[1]
Perchance he will not mind me.

TRINCULO. Here's neither bush nor shrub to bear off[2] any weather
at all—and another storm brewing! I hear it sing in the wind. Yon
same black cloud, yon huge one, looks like a foul bombard[3] that      20
would shed his liquor. If it should thunder as it did before, I know
not where to hide my head; yon same loud cannot choose but fall
by pailfuls. What have we here—a man or a fish? Dead or alive?
A fish. He smells like a fish—a very ancient and fish-like smell, a
kind of not-of-the-newest poor-John.[4] A strange fish. Were I in      25
England now, as once I was, and had but this fish painted, not a
holiday-fool there but would give a piece of silver.[5] There would
this monster make a man. Any strange beast there makes a man.[6]
When they will not give a doit[7] to relieve a lame beggar, they ill lay
out ten to see a dead Indian.[8] Legged like a man, and his fins like    30
arms. Warm o'my troth—I do now let loose my opinion, hold it
no longer: this is no fish but an islander that hath lately suffered
by a thunderbolt. Alas, the storm is come again—my best way
is to creep under his gaberdine; there is no other shelter here-
about. Misery acquaints a man with strange bedfellows. I will       35
here shroud till the dregs of the storm be past.

[*TRINCULO crawls under* CALIBAN's *cloak.*] *Enter* STEPHANO, *singing*
[*and drinking*].

STEPHANO. I shall no more to sea, to sea; here shall I die ashore.
This is a very scurvy[9] tune to sing at a man's funeral. Well, here's
my comfort.

---

1  Caliban flattens himself under his cloak or "gabardine," a rough, thick cotton
cloth usually worn by poorer folk.
2  Protect from.
3  Leather jug or bottle.
4  Dried fish.
5  He would attract souvenir-buying holiday travelers.
6  Make a man his fortune; pass for a man.
7  Small coin, worth half a farthing.
8  It was fairly common practice for the bodies of dead Native Americans to be
displayed for a paying audience. Occasionally the Native people reached Europe
alive, but few survived the journey across the ocean.
9  Inappropriate.

*Drinks.*
*Sings.*

40  The master, the swabber,[1] the boatswain, and I,
     The gunner, and his mate,
     Loved Mall, Meg, and Marian, and Margery,
     But none of us cared for Kate;
     For she had a tongue with a tang,[2]
45   Would cry to a sailor, "go hang!"
     She loved not the savor of tar nor of pitch,
     Yet a tailor might scratch her where'er she did itch:[3]
     Then to sea, boys, and let her go hang!
     This is a scurvy tune too, but here's my comfort.

*Drinks.*

50  CALIBAN. [*To STEPHANO*] Do not torment me, oh!
     STEPHANO. What's the matter? Have we devils here? Do you put
       tricks upon us with savages and men of Ind?[4] Ha! I have not
       escaped drowning to be afeard now of your four legs,[5] for it
       hath been said, "As proper a man as ever went on four legs can-
55     not make him give ground," and it shall be said so again while
       Stephano breathes at nostrils.[6]
     CALIBAN. The spirit torments me, oh!
     STEPHANO. This is some monster of the isle with four legs, who hath
       got, as I take it, an ague.[7] Where the devil should he learn our
60     language? I will give him some relief if it be but for that. If I can

---

1  The sailor who mops the deck of a ship.
2  Sting; i.e., sharp-tongued, or possibly with an unpleasant tone.
3  Women's tailors were often considered unmanly because of their close proximity to women, or else lecherous. The line suggests that the tailor has sexually
satiated Kate.
4  Men of India or the West Indies.
5  In production, Trinculo hides under the gabardine so that four legs are partially showing. Stephano alters the proverbial phrase "as good a man as goes on
two legs" to reflect his observation of this four-legged creature.
6  At the nostrils.
7  A shivering fever.

recover[1] him, and keep him tame, and get to Naples with him,
he's a present for any emperor that ever trod on neat's-leather.[2]

CALIBAN. Do not torment me, prithee. I'll bring my wood home
faster!

STEPHANO. He's in his fit now and does not talk after[3] the wisest.    65
He shall taste of my bottle; if he have never drunk wine afore, it
will go near to remove his fit. If I can recover him and keep him
tame, I will not take too much for him—he shall pay for him that
hath him, and that soundly.[4]

CALIBAN. Thou dost me yet but little hurt; thou wilt anon—I know    70
it by thy trembling.[5] Now Prosper works upon[6] thee.

STEPHANO. Come on your ways. Open your mouth—here is that
which will give language to you, cat.[7] Open your mouth—this will
shake your shaking, I can tell you, and that soundly. You cannot
tell who's your friend. Open your chops[8] again.                      75

[CALIBAN drinks.]

TRINCULO. I should know that voice. It should be—but he is
drowned, and these are devils. O defend me!

STEPHANO. Four legs and two voices?—a most delicate monster!
His forward voice now is to speak well of his friend; his backward
voice is to utter foul speeches and to detract. If all the wine in my    80
bottle will recover him, I will help his ague. Come: amen, I will
pour some in thy other mouth.

TRINCULO. Stephano?

---

1    Restore, heal.
2    A proverbial saying: "as good a man as ever trod on neat's leather." Neat's
leather refers to a fine shoe made from cowhide.
3    Like.
4    If I can revive him and keep him docile, I will not accept less than the high
price he is worth. These lines continue what Trinculo has already said about making Caliban a marketable commodity.
5    Caliban feels Trinculo's fearful shaking and mistakes it for one of Prospero's
tormenting agents.
6    Through.
7    This refers to a proverbial phrase: "ale that would make a cat speak."
8    Jaw.

STEPHANO. Doth thy other mouth call me? Mercy, mercy! This is a
85    devil and no monster! I will leave him—I have no long spoon.[1]

TRINCULO. Stephano, if thou be'st Stephano, touch me and speak
to me, for I am Trinculo. Be not afeard, thy good friend Trinculo.

STEPHANO. If thou be'st Trinculo, come forth. I'll pull thee by the
lesser legs. If any be Trinculo's legs, these are they. Thou art
90    very Trinculo indeed! How cam'st thou to be the siege[2] of this
mooncalf?[3] Can he vent Trinculos?[4]

TRINCULO. I took him to be killed with a thunderstroke—but art
thou not drowned, Stephano? I hope now thou art not drowned.
Is the storm overblown? I hid me under the dead mooncalf's gab-
95    erdine for fear of the storm. And art thou living, Stephano? O
Stephano, two Neapolitans 'scaped!

STEPHANO. Prithee, do not turn me about; my stomach is not
constant.

CALIBAN. [Aside] These be fine things, an if they be not sprites. That's
100    a brave god, and bears celestial liquor. I will kneel to him.

STEPHANO. How didst thou 'scape? How cam'st thou hither? Swear
by this bottle how thou cam'st hither—I escaped upon a butt of
sack[5] which the sailors heaved o'erboard—by this bottle, which
I made of the bark of a tree with mine own hands since I was
105    cast ashore.

CALIBAN. I'll swear upon that bottle to be thy true 130 subject, for
the liquor is not earthly.

STEPHANO. Here: swear then how thou escaped.

TRINCULO. Swam ashore, man, like a duck; I can swim like a duck,
110    I'll be sworn.

STEPHANO. Here, kiss the book.[6] Though thou canst swim like a
duck, thou art made like a goose.

TRINCULO. O Stephano, hast any more of this?

---

1    This refers to a proverbial phrase: "he must have a long spoon that will eat
with the devil."
2    Seat, rear end.
3    A natural fool; a monstrosity produced by the ill influence of the moon.
4    Excrete Trinculos.
5    Cask of white wine.
6    Kissing the Bible was a sign of loyalty. Stephano uses it as a metaphor for
drinking from the bottle.

STEPHANO. The whole butt, man! My cellar is in a rock by the sea-
side, where my wine is hid. [*To* CALIBAN] How now mooncalf?  115
How does thine ague?

CALIBAN. Hast thou not dropped from heaven?

STEPHANO. Out of the moon, I do assure thee.[1] I was the man in
the moon when time was.[2]

CALIBAN. I have seen thee in her, and I do adore thee! My mistress  120
showed me thee, and thy dog and thy bush.[3]

STEPHANO. Come, swear to that: kiss the book. I will furnish it anon
with new contents. Swear!

TRINCULO. [*To* STEPHANO] By this good light, this is a very shallow monster. I afeared of him? A very weak monster. The man in  125
the moon? A most poor, credulous[4] monster. [*To* CALIBAN, *who is
drinking*] Well drawn, monster, in good sooth.[5]

CALIBAN. [*To* STEPHANO] I'll show thee every fertile inch of the
island, and I will kiss thy foot. I prithee be my god.

TRINCULO. By this light, a most perfidious and drunken monster—  130
when his god's asleep, he'll rob his bottle.

CALIBAN. I'll kiss thy foot; I'll swear myself thy subject.

STEPHANO. Come on then: down and swear.

TRINCULO. I shall laugh myself to death at this puppy-headed[6] monster, a most scurvy monster. I could find in my heart to beat him.  135

STEPHANO. Come, kiss.[7]

TRINCULO. But that the poor monster's in drink. An abominable
monster.

CALIBAN. I'll show thee the best springs, I'll pluck thee berries, I'll
fish for thee and get thee wood enough! A plague upon the tyrant  140
that I serve! I'll bear him no more sticks, but follow thee, thou
wondrous man.

---

1   These lines possibly refer to the belief that New World natives thought that
European conquerors were gods descended from the heavens.
2   Once upon a time.
3   According to folk legend, the man in the moon (with his dog) was banished to
the moon for collecting firewood on the Sabbath.
4   Gullible.
5   Well drunk, indeed.
6   Stupid, ridiculous-looking. Some Calibans are portrayed as having dog-like
ears because of this line, but Trinculo is merely insulting Caliban's intelligence.
7   Take another swig.

TRINCULO. A most ridiculous monster, to make a wonder of a poor
` drunkard.
145 CALIBAN. I prithee let me bring thee where crabs[1] grow,
And I with my long nails will dig thee pignuts,[2]
Show thee a jay's nest, and instruct thee how
To snare the nimble marmoset.[3] I'll bring thee
To clustering filberts,[4] and sometimes I'll get thee
150 Young scamels from the rock. Wilt thou go with me?
STEPHANO. Ay prithee now lead the way without any more talking.
Trinculo, the King and all our company else being drowned, we
will inherit here. Here, bear my bottle, fellow Trinculo; we'll fill
him[5] by and by again.

*CALIBAN sings drunkenly.*

155 CALIBAN. Farewell, master, farewell, farewell!
TRINCULO. A howling monster, a drunken monster!
CALIBAN. No more dams[6] I'll make for fish,
Nor fetch in firing at requiring,[7]
Nor scrape trenchering,[8] nor wash dish:
160 'Ban 'Ban Ca-Caliban
Has a new master. Get a new man![9]
Freedom, high-day,[10] high-day, freedom, freedom, high-day,
freedom!
STEPHANO. O brave monster, lead the way!

*Exeunt.*

---

1   Shellfish or crabapples. Crabapples are inedible by themselves. What Caliban
considers delicious food is at odds with conventional taste.
2   An edible wild tuber.
3   A small monkey from Central and South America, considered edible.
4   Hazelnuts or hazelnut trees.
5   Caliban, the bottle, or both.
6   Damming rivers in order to catch fish was a common practice both in the New
World and in England.
7   I won't gather firewood at Prospero's behest.
8   Crockery, either wooden or earthenware.
9   Caliban proclaims that Prospero will need to get a new servant.
10  Holiday, day of celebration.

What are scamels? They must be, in Caliban's estimation, very good to eat since they are the very last item on his list of appetizing comestibles—a foodstuff so irresistible that it will be able to secure Stephano's willingness to become Caliban's god and to take part in the overthrow of Prospero. But what are scamels? Although *The Tempest* is the most carefully printed text in the 1623 First Folio, and despite the clarity of

> A plague vpon the Tyrant that I ſerue ;
> I'le beare him no more Stickes, but follow thee, thou wondrous man.
>
>    *Tri.* A moſt rediculous Monſter, to make a wonder of a poore drunkard.
>
>    *Cal.* I'prethee let me bring thee where Crabs grow; and I with my long nayles will digge thee pig-nuts; ſhow thee a Iayes neſt, and inſtruct thee how to ſnare the nimble Marmazet : I'le bring thee to cluſtring Philbirts, and ſometimes I'le get thee young Scamels from the Rocke : Wilt thou goe with me ?

the printed word as shown above, most editors since the eighteenth century have tried to emend it so that it and every other word spoken by Caliban is perfectly clear and understandable. In his 1733 edition, Lewis Theobald changed it to "Shamois" which, he explained in his gloss, are young goats. In their 1793 edition, Johnson and Stevens printed "sea-mels," which is a kind of gull, and they chided Theobald for preferring young goats to sea birds. Most scholarly twenty-first-century editions leave the word as it is in the Folio but nevertheless undertake to explain its mystery, glossing it as a fish, a shellfish, or a seabird. Of course, there is nothing at all wrong in an editor trying to make sense of enigmatic parts of texts: that is part of an editor's job. But in a play in which Shakespeare seems keen to make up new personal names, such as Sycorax, Setebos, and, yes, Caliban, it might be worth considering that Shakespeare made up the name of one of Caliban's favorite things to eat—the mysterious "young scamels from the rock."

[3.1]

*Enter* FERDINAND, *bearing a log.*

FERDINAND. There be some sports are painful, and their labor
　　Delight in them set off.[1] Some kinds of baseness
　　Are nobly undergone, and most poor matters
　　Point to rich ends; this, my mean° task,　　　　　*undignified, crude*
5　　Would be as heavy° to me, as odious, but　　　*laborious, wearisome*
　　The mistress which I serve quickens° what's dead　　*restores life to*
　　And makes my labors pleasures. Oh, she is
　　Ten times more gentle than her father's crabbed,[2]
　　And he's composed of harshness. I must remove
10　　Some thousands of these logs and pile them up
　　Upon a sore injunction.° My sweet mistress　　*on an onerous command*
　　Weeps when she sees me work, and says such baseness
　　Had never like executor.[3] I forget—
　　But these sweet thoughts do even refresh my labors
　　Most busiliest[4] when I do it.

*Enter* MIRANDA *and* PROSPERO [*he, at a distance, unseen*].

15　MIRANDA.　　　　　　　　　Alas, now pray you,
　　Work not so hard. I would the lightning had
　　Burnt up those logs that you are enjoined to pile.
　　Pray, set it down and rest you—when this burns,
　　'Twill weep[5] for having wearied you. My father
20　　Is hard at study; pray now, rest yourself.
　　He's safe° for these three hours.　　　*occupied, safely apart from us*
FERDINAND.　　　　　　　　O most dear mistress,
　　The sun will set before I shall discharge
　　What I must strive to do.

---

1　I.e., though some pastimes are painful, the actual performance of them, their
labor, engenders delight.
2　Ill-tempered, churlish. From the sixteenth century on, the adjective also
became "a frequent epithet of old age" (*OED*).
3　"Such base labour was never performed by one so noble" (Orgel).
4　Most busily. Ferdinand's sweet thoughts about Miranda renew his energy
most actively, especially when he is performing the tasks assigned to him.
5　Miranda suggests that sap seeping from the burning firewood will appear to
be tears.

MIRANDA.                    If you'll sit down,
   I'll bear your logs the while. Pray, give me that;
   I'll carry it to the pile.
FERDINAND.               No, precious creature;                           25
   I had rather crack my sinews,° break my back        *tendons, ligaments*
   Than you should such dishonor undergo
   While I sit lazy by.
MIRANDA.            It would become me
   As well as it does you, and I should do it
   With much more ease, for my good will is to it,                        30
   And yours it is against.
PROSPERO.            [*Aside*] Poor worm, thou art infected;
   This visitation shows it.[1]
MIRANDA.               You look wearily.
FERDINAND. No, noble mistress, 'tis fresh morning with me
   When you are by at night. I do beseech you
   (Chiefly that I might set it in my prayers),                           35
   What is your name?
MIRANDA.            Miranda. [*Aside*] O my father,
   I have broke your hest° to say so!              *bidding, command*
FERDINAND.                    Admired Miranda,
   Indeed the top of admiration, worth
   What's dearest to the world: full many a lady
   I have eyed with best regard,[2] and many a time                      40
   Th'harmony of their tongues hath into bondage
   Brought my too diligent ear.[3] For several virtues
   Have I liked several women—never any
   With so full soul, but some defect in her
   Did quarrel with the noblest grace she owed                           45
   And put it to the foil.[4] But you, O you

---

1   Prospero means that Miranda has caught love as if it were a disease.
"Visitation" was a term frequently associated with the plague, referring either to
the charitable action of visiting the sick or to the spread of the disease itself.
2   Both "gaze" and "esteem."
3   Ferdinand says that he has fallen in love with the lovely voices of many ladies.
4   "Put to the foil" refers to the jewelry-making practice of putting silver- or gold-
colored foil around a diamond to set it off advantageously. Ferdinand is saying that
the women he previously loved all had admirable qualities that were set off by their
less desirable traits.

So perfect and so peerless, are created
Of every creature's best.

MIRANDA.          I do not know
One of my sex, no woman's face remember—
50     Save, from my glass,° mine own. Nor have I seen      *mirror*
More that I may call men than you, good friend,
And my dear father. How features are abroad
I am skilless° of, but by my modesty        *not knowledgeable*
(The jewel in my dower[1]), I would not wish
55     Any companion in the world but you,
Nor can imagination form a shape,
Besides yourself, to like of—but I prattle°      *speak triflingly*
Something too wildly, and my father's precepts
I therein do forget.

FERDINAND.        I am, in my condition,
60     A prince, Miranda, I do think a King
(I would not so[2]), and would no more endure
This wooden slavery than to suffer
The flesh-fly blow[3] my mouth. Hear my soul speak:
The very instant that I saw you did
65     My heart fly to your service, there resides
To make me slave to it, and for your sake
Am I this patient log man.

MIRANDA.          Do you love me?

FERDINAND. O heaven, O earth, bear witness to this sound,
And crown what I profess with kind event°      *favorable result*
70     If I speak true; if hollowly, invert
What best is boded me to mischief.[4] I,
Beyond all limit of what else i'th' world,
Do love, prize, honor you.

MIRANDA.          I am a fool

---

1   Miranda's virginity is the most precious thing she owns, the most valuable item in her marriage dowry (dower).
2   I wish it were not the case.
3   A "flesh fly" is a type of insect that lays its eggs in rotting flesh (also called a "blow-fly"). "To blow" refers to insects depositing or filling up a space with their eggs.
4   Promised me into misfortune. Ferdinand asks the heavens to plague him with misfortune if he is not speaking honestly.

To weep at what I am glad of.

PROSPERO.                    [*Aside*] Fair encounter
   Of two most rare affections! Heavens rain grace                    75
   On that which breeds between 'em.¹

FERDINAND.                              Wherefore weep you?

MIRANDA. At mine unworthiness, that dare not offer
   What I desire to give, and much less take
   What I shall die to want.° But this is trifling,        *perish for lack of*
   And all the more it seeks to hide itself,                         80
   The bigger bulk it shows. Hence, bashful cunning,
   And prompt me, plain and holy innocence:
   I am your wife if you will marry me—
   If not, I'll die your maid.² To be your fellow
   You may deny me, but I'll be your servant                         85
   Whether you will or no.

FERDINAND.                  My mistress dearest,
   And I thus humble ever.

MIRANDA.                    My husband then?

FERDINAND. Ay, with a heart as willing
   As bondage e'er of freedom:³ here's my hand.

MIRANDA. And mine, with my heart in't; and now, farewell        90
   Till half an hour hence.

FERDINAND.              A thousand, thousand.°       *a million (goodbyes)*

                    *Exit* [MIRANDA *and* FERDINAND].


PROSPERO. So glad of this as they I cannot be,
   Who are surprised with all,⁴ but my rejoicing
   At nothing can be more. I'll to my book,
   For yet ere suppertime must I perform                            95
   Much business appertaining.

                                        *Exit.*

---

1   Prospero blesses the love that springs between Miranda and Ferdinand.
2   Maid means both "virgin" and "servant."
3   As desirous of Miranda as a slave is of freedom.
4   By everything that they are experiencing.

[3.2]

*Enter CALIBAN, STEPHANO, and TRINCULO.*

STEPHANO. [*To TRINCULO*] Tell not me! When the butt is out,[1] we
   will drink water, not a drop before: therefore bear up and board
   'em.[2] [*To CALIBAN*] Servant monster, drink to me!

TRINCULO. Servant monster?[3] The folly of this island! They say[4]
5   there's but five upon this isle; we are three of them. If the other
   two be brained like us,[5] the state totters.

STEPHANO. Drink, servant monster, when I bid thee; thy eyes are
   almost set in thy head.[6]

TRINCULO. Where should they be set else? He were a brave[7] monster
10   indeed if they were set in his tail.

STEPHANO. My man-monster hath drowned his tongue in sack. For
   my part, the sea cannot drown me. I swam, ere I could recover
   the shore, five and thirty leagues[8] off and on.[9] By this light, thou
   shalt be my lieutenant monster—or my standard.

15 TRINCULO. Your lieutenant, if you list; he's no standard.[10]

STEPHANO. We'll not run,[11] Monsieur Monster.

TRINCULO. Nor go,[12] neither—but you'll lie like dogs and yet say
   nothing, neither.

STEPHANO. Mooncalf: speak once in thy life, if thou be'st a good
20   mooncalf.

---

1   The cask is empty.

2   Terms used in naval warfare (i.e., "advance and attack"), here meaning "drink
up."

3   This is the phrase Ben Jonson makes reference to in *Bartholomew Fair* as a
critique of Shakespeare's play (Induction, 130–35). See the Introduction, p. 10.

4   Stephano and Caliban say.

5   As drunk as we are.

6   Colloquial expression meaning "you're drunk."

7   Impressive, fine.

8   A league is roughly equal to three miles. Stephano claims to have swum about
100 miles to get to shore. This story contradicts what Stephano reported earlier
about how he reached the shore (2.2.102–05, TLN 1164–68).

9   At intervals, intermittently.

10   Ensign, flag-bearer. Trinculo puns on "stander," suggesting that none of them
is in any condition to stand up straight.

11   Run away from battle.

12   Walk. The line is proverbial: "he may ill run that cannot go."

CALIBAN. How does thy honor? Let me lick thy shoe. I'll not serve
  him; he is not valiant.
TRINCULO. Thou liest, most ignorant monster. I am in case to jostle
  a constable.[1] Why, thou deboshed[2] fish thou, was there ever man
  a coward that hath drunk so much sack as I today? Wilt thou tell   25
  a monstrous lie, being but half a fish and half a monster?
CALIBAN. Lo, how he mocks me! Wilt thou let him, my Lord?
TRINCULO. "Lord," quoth he!—that a monster should be such a
  natural.[3]
CALIBAN. Lo, lo, again! Bite him to death, I prithee.   30
STEPHANO. Trinculo: keep a good tongue in your head.[4] If you
  prove a mutineer, the next tree![5] The poor monster's my subject,
  and he shall not suffer indignity.
CALIBAN. I thank my noble Lord. Wilt thou be pleased to hearken
  once again to the suit I made to thee?   35
STEPHANO. Marry[6] will I: kneel and repeat it. I will stand and so
  shall Trinculo.

*Enter ARIEL, invisible.*
CALIBAN. As I told thee before, I am subject to a tyrant,
  A sorcerer, that by his cunning hath
  Cheated me of the island.   40
ARIEL. [*In TRINCULO's voice*] Thou liest.
CALIBAN. [*To TRINCULO*] Thou liest, thou jesting monkey thou!
  I would my valiant master would destroy thee.
  I do not lie.
STEPHANO. Trinculo, if you trouble him any more in's tale, by this   45
  hand I will supplant° some of your teeth.                    *root up*
TRINCULO. Why, I said nothing.
STEPHANO. Mum,° then, and no more. Proceed.              *be quiet*
CALIBAN. I say, by sorcery he got this isle.

---

1  Ready to push or knock down a constable (i.e., someone in a position of
  authority).
2  Debauched.
3  Idiot, simpleton. Trinculo quibbles on the meaning of "unnatural," meaning
  "monstrous."
4  Speak politely.
5  I will hang you at the next tree.
6  A mild oath meaning "by the Virgin Mary."

50   From me he got it. If thy greatness will
     Revenge it on him—for I know thou dar'st,
     But this thing° dare not—                                    *Trinculo*
     STEPHANO. That's most certain.
     CALIBAN. Thou shalt be lord of it, and I'll serve thee.
55   STEPHANO. How now shall this be compassed?[1] Canst thou bring
     me to the party?
     CALIBAN. Yea, yea, my Lord; I'll yield him thee asleep,
     Where thou mayst knock a nail into his head.
     ARIEL. [*In TRINCULO's voice*] Thou liest: thou canst not.
60   CALIBAN. What a pied ninny's this! Thou scurvy patch![2]
     I do beseech thy greatness, give him blows
     And take his bottle from him. When that's gone,
     He shall drink nought but brine, for I'll not show him
     Where the quick freshes° are.                    *freshwater springs*
65   STEPHANO. Trinculo, run into no further danger. Interrupt the
     monster one word further, and by this hand I'll turn my mercy
     out of doors and make a stockfish[3] of thee.
     TRINCULO. Why, what did I? I did nothing. I'll go farther off.
     STEPHANO. Didst thou not say he lied?
70   ARIEL. Thou liest.
     STEPHANO. Do I so? Take thou that! As you like this, give me the
     lie[4] another time!
     TRINCULO. I did not give the lie! Out of your wits and hearing too?
     A pox on your bottle—this can sack and drinking do. A murrain
75   on your monster, and the devil take your fingers![5]
     CALIBAN. Ha ha ha!
     STEPHANO. Now, forward with your tale. [*To TRINCULO*] Prithee,
     stand further off!
     CALIBAN. Beat him enough! After a little time, I'll beat him too.
80   STEPHANO. Stand farther. Come, proceed.
     CALIBAN. Why, as I told thee, 'tis a custom with him

---

1   Contrived, achieved.
2   Both insults peg Trinculo as a worthless fool, referring to the multicolored
costume of the court jester (pied and patch).
3   Beaten, dried fish.
4   Accuse me of being a liar.
5   Both expressions are commonplace early-modern curses referring to infec-
tious diseases (most frequently the plague). Murrain is the dead flesh of diseased
animals.

I' th'afternoon to sleep: there thou mayst brain him,
Having first seized his books, or with a log
Batter his skull, or paunch° him with a stake,            *to stab the stomach*
Or cut his weasand° with thy knife. Remember            *windpipe*   85
First to possess his books, for without them
He's but a sot,° as I am, nor hath not                              *idiot*
One spirit to command; they all do hate him
As rootedly° as I. Burn but his books;                    *firmly, deeply*
He has brave utensils, for so he calls them,                              90
Which, when he has a house, he'll deck withal.
And that most deeply to consider is
The beauty of his daughter—he himself
Calls her a nonpareil.° I never saw a woman            *one without equal*
But only Sycorax, my dam, and she,                                       95
But she as far surpasseth Sycorax
As great'st does least.
STEPHANO. Is it so brave a lass?
CALIBAN. Ay, Lord, she will become[1] thy bed, I warrant,
    And bring thee forth brave brood.°        *splendid, strong children*   100
STEPHANO. Monster, I will kill this man. His daughter and I will be
    King and Queen, save our graces, and Trinculo and thyself shall
    be viceroys.[2] Dost thou like the plot,° Trinculo?             *plan*
TRINCULO. Excellent.
STEPHANO. Give me thy hand. I am sorry I beat thee; but while thou   105
    liv'st, keep a good tongue in thy head.
CALIBAN. Within this half hour will he be asleep.
    Wilt thou destroy him then?
STEPHANO. Ay, on mine honor.
ARIEL. [*Aside*] This will I tell my master.                                110
CALIBAN. Thou mak'st me merry; I am full of pleasure.
    Let us be jocund! Will you troll the catch[3]
    You taught me but whilere?°                        *just a moment ago*
STEPHANO. At thy request, monster, I will do reason,[4] any reason.
    Come on, Trinculo, let us sing.                                      115

---

1   Be suitable for.
2   Nobles appointed to rule in the stead of a king.
3   Sing the musical round boisterously.
4   Act reasonably.

*Sings*
Flout 'em and cout 'em; and skout 'em and flout 'em:[1]
Thought is free.

CALIBAN. That's not the tune!

ARIEL *plays the tune on a tabor[2] and pipe.*

STEPHANO. What is this same?

120 TRINCULO. This is the tune of our catch, played by the picture of
Nobody.

STEPHANO. If thou be'st a man, show thyself in thy likeness; if thou
be'st a devil, take't as thou list.[3]

TRINCULO. O forgive me my sins!

125 STEPHANO. He that dies pays all debts.[4] I defy thee! Mercy upon us![5]

CALIBAN. Art thou afeard?

STEPHANO. No, monster, not I.

CALIBAN. Be not afeard, the isle is full of noises,
Sounds, and sweet airs[6] that give delight and hurt not.

130 Sometimes a thousand twangling[7] instruments
Will hum about mine ears, and sometimes voices—
That if I then had waked after long sleep,
Will make me sleep again—and then, in dreaming,
The clouds methought would open and show riches

135 Ready to drop upon me, that when I waked
I cried to dream again.

STEPHANO. This will prove a brave kingdom to me, where I shall
have my music for nothing!

CALIBAN. When Prospero is destroyed.

---

1    Flout and skout both mean to insult or deride someone; cout is presumably a
slang version of these words.

2    Small drum played simultaneously with a pipe. Each could be played with one
hand. They are associated with popular merry-making.

3    This line is proverbial: "take as you list [please]," meaning "if you are the devil,
do what you want; we cannot prevent you."

4    Proverbial: "Death pays all debts"; i.e., those who die do not have to pay debts.

5    Terrified, Stephano first puts on a brave face and then implores the invisible
powers to have mercy.

6    Lyric songs, often accompanied by a lute.

7    Refers to the sounds produced by string instruments.

Title page of *Nobody and Somebody* (c. 1592),
printed by John Trundel in 1606. Wikimedia
Commons.

Trinculo's reference to Ariel's invisibility also constitutes a popular reference to an early modern play, *Nobody and Somebody*, whose title page reprinted to the left was widely known by the time Shakespeare wrote *The Tempest*. It also echoes a stock figure with a long history throughout Europe: the scapegoat Nobody, meant to take on the ills and follies of mankind. Such a figure, the naive fool being mistakenly blamed for everyone's faults, was found in French, German, and Dutch literature and was often associated with lower-class individuals such as household servants. Its popularity in early-modern England was bolstered by the pun its name suggested (a nobody, as someone with literally *no body*). Here, the figure appears to have no body to speak of, as its legs seemingly begin at its head. It remained a popular figure throughout English history. The famed nineteenth-century British illustrator George Cruikshank (1792–1878) is said to have drawn inspiration from it for several of his political caricatures.

Having the play's lower-class characters bring up the "Picture of Nobody" echoes its usual associations with bumbling servants and comedic undertones.

140 STEPHANO. That shall be by and by; I remember the story.

TRINCULO. The sound is going away. Let's follow it, and after do our work.

STEPHANO. Lead, monster: we'll follow. I would I could see this taborer; he lays it on.[1]

145 TRINCULO. [*To* CALIBAN] Wilt come? [*To* STEPHANO] I'll follow, Stephano.

*Exeunt.*

---

1   Plays the tabor well.

---

### 3.2.128–36:   "BE NOT AFEARD: THE ISLE IS FULL OF NOISES" (TLN 1492–1500)

*The Tempest* is the most musical of Shakespeare's plays. The company commissioned Robert Johnson (c. 1583–1633), lutenist to King James, to write two original songs for the play—"Full Fathom Five" and "Where the Bee Sucks." The play is also filled with musical imagery. There seems to be music in the air, water, and land. Alonso, the King of Naples, grieving deeply for his son Ferdinand, whom he believes has drowned, is brought face to face with his own sin and its just punishment by a massive natural symphony of judgment that seems to issue from the sea, the wind, and the storm. "[T]he thunder," he says, "That deep and dreadful organ pipe, pronounced / The name of Prosper—it did bass my trespass. / Therefore, my son i' th'ooze is bedded" (3.3.97–100, TLN 1634–37).

In this scene, in which Caliban reassures the two Italian servants that the weirdly invisible music is harmless, music changes from an instrument of justice to something like an agent of healing, even a power able to make a person whole. In her essay "Dynamic Conversions: Grief and Joy in George Herbert's Musical Verse," Anna Lewton-Brain describes a common belief about music in Shakespeare's time—an idea about how music could heal the souls of those who listened to it and could move people toward the grace of salvation. Lewton-Brain quotes the Elizabethan theologian Richard Hooker (1554–1600): "the very harmony of sounds being framed in due sort and carried from the ear to the spiritual faculties of our souls, is by a native puissance and efficacy greatly available to bring to a perfect temper whatsoever is there troubled." The music

## [3.3]

*Enter ALONSO, SEBASTIAN, ANTONIO, GONZALO, ADRIAN,*
*FRANCISCO, and others.*

GONZALO. By'r lakin,[1] I can go no further, sir;
My old bones aches. Here's a maze trod[2] indeed

---

1  An abbreviation of "by our Ladykin," the Virgin Mary.
2  We're in a virtual labyrinth; i.e., we are lost.

of the Island seems similarly carried from Caliban's ear to his soul. Its "native puissance" makes him sleep and dream of the clouds opening and showing riches ready to drop upon him. Are the riches from the heavens a metaphor for the divine gift of grace? If that is what music can bring to Caliban, it is no wonder he cried to dream again.

"The Lute Player" (1596), by Michelangelo Merisi da Caravaggio, from Wikimedia Commons.

Through forthrights and meanders.[1] By your patience,
I needs must rest me.°                                   *I have to rest*

ALONSO.                    Old lord, I cannot blame thee,
5    Who am myself attached with° weariness              *seized by*
To th'dulling of my spirits. Sit down and rest.
Even here I will put off my hope and keep it
No longer for my flatterer.[2] He is drowned
Whom thus we stray to find, and the sea mocks
10   Our frustrate[3] search on land. Well, let him go.
ANTONIO. [*Aside to* SEBASTIAN] I am right glad that he's so out of
        hope.
Do not for one repulse° forgo the purpose            *setback*
That you resolved t'effect.
SEBASTIAN.                    [*Aside to* ANTONIO] The next advantage
Will we take thoroughly.
ANTONIO.                    [*Aside to* SEBASTIAN] Let it be tonight,
15   For now they are oppressed with travail;° they     *extreme effort*
Will not nor cannot use such vigilance
As when they are fresh.
SEBASTIAN.                    [*Aside to* ANTONIO] I say tonight. No more.

*Solemn and strange music, and* PROSPERO *on the top* [*i.e., on an upper
playform*], *invisible. Enter several strange shapes bringing in a banquet,
and dance about it with gentle actions of salutations, and, inviting the
King* [*and others*] *to eat, they depart.*

ALONSO. What harmony is this, my good friends? Hark!
GONZALO. Marvelous sweet music!
20   ALONSO. Give us kind keepers, heavens! What were these?
SEBASTIAN. A living drollery![4] Now I will believe
That there are unicorns, that in Arabia
There is one tree, the phoenix's[5] throne—one phoenix
At this hour reigning there.

---

1    Straight and twisted pathways.
2    Now I will no longer allow Hope to flatter me with his comforts (about my son
Ferdinand). Here hope is personified as a courtier.
3    Fruitless, unsuccessful.
4    A comic puppet show put on by human actors; a living caricature.
5    A mythological bird known for being resurrected from its own funeral ashes.

ANTONIO.                          I'll believe both—
  And what does else want credit,° come to me,          *lack believability*   25
  And I'll be sworn 'tis true. Travelers ne'er did lie,[1]
  Though fools at home condemn 'em.
GONZALO.                                    If in Naples
  I should report this now, would they believe me?
  If I should say I saw such islanders
  (For certes,° these are people of the island),          *certainly*   30
  Who, though they are of monstrous shape, yet note
  Their manners are more gentle, kind, than of
  Our human generation[2] you shall find
  Many—nay, almost any.
PROSPERO.                          [*Aside*] Honest Lord,
  Thou hast said well, for some of you there present          35
  Are worse than devils.
ALONSO.                  I cannot too much muse
  Such shapes, such gesture, and such sound expressing
  (Although they want the use of tongue) a kind
  Of excellent dumb° discourse.                              *silent*
PROSPERO.                      [*Aside*] Praise in departing.[3]
FRANCISCO. They vanished strangely.
SEBASTIAN.                      No matter, since          40
  They have left their viands[4] behind, for we have stomachs.[5]
  Will't please you taste of what is here?
ALONSO.                          Not I.
GONZALO. Faith, sir, you need not fear. When we were boys,
  Who would believe that there were mountaineers
  Dewlapped[6] like bulls, whose throats had hanging at 'em          45
  Wallets[7] of flesh? Or that there were such men
  Whose heads stood in their breasts, which now we find

---

1  This line contradicts the proverb "a traveler may lie with authority." In "Of the Cannibals," Montaigne wishes that travelers would stick to what they know and not make up stories about places they'd never visited. See Appendix E, pp. 184–85.
2  Human species, though connotations of nation and race are possible.
3  Proverbial: "keep your praise till the end."
4  Food.
5  We have appetites.
6  Dewlaps are the loose flesh hanging from the throats of cattle.
7  Wattles, hanging flaps of flesh.

Each putter-out of five for one[1] will bring us
Good warrant of?

ALONSO.          I will stand to and feed,

50    Although my last. No matter, since I feel
The best is past. Brother, my Lord the Duke:
Stand to[2] and do as we.

---

1    One who bets at odds of five to one. In Jonson's *Every Man Out of His Humour*
(1599), Puntarvolo makes a bet with Fastidious Brisk that he can return safely
from a voyage to Constantinople. Through a notary, he pays Brisk a sum of money,
to be repaid fivefold upon his safe return.

2    Set to work, start eating.

---

3.3.46–49:    "MEN WHOSE HEADS STOOD
IN THEIR BREASTS" (TLN 1575–76)

Gonzalo's mention of men with heads in their chests, echoed in Othello's
allusion to "men whose heads / Do grow beneath their shoulders"
(1.3.145–46, TLN 489–90), as a recent factual discovery, gestured toward
a longstanding history of mythical, monstrous creatures permeating

the geographical, narrative,
and cultural spheres of the
western worlds. The creature
depicted to the left, often mistakenly identified as a member of a mythical cannibal
race called Anthropophagi
due to Othello's lines, is
known as a "Blemmye," a
being with facial features
on its torso (eyes on either
its shoulders or upper torso,
mouth and nose on its chest).

Detail from Hartmann Schedel's *World History* or
*Nuremberg Chronicle* (*Schedelsche Welchronik, 1493*),
p. 12. From Wikimedia Commons.

Blemmyes appear as far back
as Herodotus's *Histories* (440
BCE).

*Thunder and lightning. Enter* ARIEL *like a harpy,*[1] *claps his wings upon the table, and with a quaint device,*[2] *the banquet vanishes.*

ARIEL. You are three men of sin,[3] whom Destiny
  (That hath to instrument° this lower world,           *command*
  And what is in't) the never surfeited sea                 55

---

1   A mythical bird with the head of a woman, hands like talons, and the body of a vulture. Harpies are associated with divine retribution; the scene alludes visually to an episode in Book 3 of the *Aeneid*, in which Aeneas and his men are interrupted when they attempt to feast.
2   This could be any stage machinery that would make the banquet "disappear." In many productions, the table top flips or swivels to reveal an empty surface.
3   Ariel speaks to Alonso, Antonio, and Sebastian.

Blemmyes were believed to inhabit various regions of the globe that would appear as foreign and exotic to an English audience (India, Egypt, South America, and so on). The fact that they shared a name with an actual nomadic tribe in Nubia (c. 660 BCE) might have contributed to a general belief of their actual existence. They subsequently appeared in *The Alexander Romance*, on medieval maps, and in *The Travel of Sir John Mandeville* (c. 1360). Likewise, they were a staple of early-modern travel writing, mentioned in Richard Hakluyt's *Principal Navigations, Voyages, Traffiques and Discoveries of the English Nation* (1589) and Sir Walter Raleigh's *Discovery of Guiana* (1595). While gathering the qualities usually ascribed to urban legends, its association with documents thought to be of historical (non-fiction) accounts contributed to the potency of the myth.

Gonzalo's mention of them in the wake of the banquet, as an example of fantastical stories that were eventually proven to be true, is part of a larger ethnocentric tradition in the period which characterized non-European nations as monstrous. It echoes the characters' perception and treatment of Caliban throughout *The Tempest* (as a non-human creature). It also serves as a prime example of the ways in which purely fantastical stories would be gradually woven into the historical and cultural fabrics over time. Gonzalo and the other men have likely never encountered a Blemmye, but they take their existence at face value given written reports of them. The exotic nature of the island in the play would signal to audiences a similar realm of mythical possibilities.

Hath caused to belch up you; and on this island,
Where man doth not inhabit, you 'mongst men,
Being most unfit to live, I have made you mad.
And even with such-like valor,[1] men hang and drown
Their proper selves.°                                        *themselves*

[*ALONSO, SEBASTIAN, and others draw their swords.*]

60      You fools! I and my fellows
Are ministers of Fate. The elements
Of whom your swords are tempered may as well
Wound the loud winds, or with bemocked-at° stabs  *derided*
Kill the still-closing waters,[2] as diminish
65 One dowl that's in my plume.[3] My fellow ministers
Are like° invulnerable; if you could hurt,   *similarly*
Your swords are now too massy° for your strengths *heavy*
And will not be uplifted. But remember,
For that's my business° to you, that you three  *purpose*
70 From Milan did supplant good Prospero,
Exposed unto the sea (which hath requite° it) *repaid, avenged*
Him and his innocent child, for which foul deed
The powers (delaying, not forgetting) have
Incensed the seas and shores (yea, all the creatures!)
75 Against your peace. Thee of thy son, Alonso,
They have bereft, and do pronounce by me:
Ling'ring perdition, worse than any death
Can be at once, shall step by step attend
You and your ways; whose wraths to guard you from
80 (Which here, in this most desolate isle, else falls
Upon your heads) is nothing but heart's sorrow
And a clear life ensuing.[4]

*He vanishes in thunder; then, to soft music, enter the shapes again and
dance with mocks and mows[5] and carrying out the table.*

---

1 Misguided courage that pushes men to acts of desperation.
2 You can't wound the air or the water with swords.
3 One fiber of my plumage.
4 The powers above, not forgetting your crime, have stirred up nature and all the
animals against you, killed your son, Alonso, and now impose by me a sentence of
suffering that will dog you through your whole lives unless you summon remorse
in your hearts and commit to a virtuous life for the rest of your days.
5 Macabre gestures.

PROSPERO. Bravely the figure of this harpy hast thou
    Performed, my Ariel. A grace it had, devouring![1]
    Of my instruction hast thou nothing bated°       *neglected, left out*  85
    In what thou hadst to say; so with good life
    And observation strange, my meaner ministers
    Their several kinds have done. My high charms' work,
    And these, mine enemies, are all knit up
    In their distractions. They now are in my power,       90
    And in these fits I leave them while I visit
    Young Ferdinand (whom they suppose is drowned)
    And his and mine loved darling.
GONZALO. I'th' name of something holy, sir, why stand you
    In this strange stare?
ALONSO.           Oh, it is monstrous, monstrous!    95
    Methought the billows° spoke and told me of it;    *waves*
    The winds did sing it to me, and the thunder,
    That deep and dreadful organ pipe, pronounced
    The name of Prosper—it did bass my trespass.[2]
    Therefore, my son i' th'ooze is bedded; and      100
    I'll seek him deeper than e'er plummet[3] sounded,
    And with him there lie mudded.
                                 *Exit [ALONSO].*

SEBASTIAN. But one fiend at a time,
    I'll fight their legions o'er.
ANTONIO.            I'll be thy second.
         *Exit [SEBASTIAN, ANTONIO, and FRANCISCO].*

GONZALO. All three of them are desperate. Their great guilt    105
    (Like poison given to work a great time after)
    Now 'gins to bite the spirits.[4] I do beseech you,
    That are of suppler joints, follow them swiftly,

---

1    This suggests that Ariel "devoured" the banquet in making it disappear. In the
*Aeneid*, Book 3, the harpies both eat and befoul the Trojans' feast.
2    Underscore my transgressions. The metaphor is musical: "bass" here means to
form the musical basis (of a song).
3    A lead weight used to measure the depth of water.
4    Decrease their vital forces.

And hinder them from what this ecstasy°    *insanity*
May now provoke them to.

110 ADRIAN.      [*To remaining others*] Follow, I pray you.
                   *Exeunt omnes.*

## [4.1]

*Enter* PROSPERO, FERDINAND, *and* MIRANDA.

PROSPERO. If I have too austerely punished you,
 Your compensation makes amends, for I
 Have given you here a third¹ of mine own life,
 Or that for which I live, who once again
5 I tender to thy hand. All thy vexations
 Were but my trials of thy love, and thou
 Hast strangely² stood the test. Here, afore heaven,
 I ratify this my rich gift. O Ferdinand,
 Do not smile at me that I boast of her,
10 For thou shalt find she will outstrip all praise
 And make it halt° behind her.      *limp*
FERDINAND.      I do believe it
 Against an oracle.°    *despite an oracle's prediction*
PROSPERO. Then as my gift, and thine own acquisition
 Worthily purchased, take my daughter. But
15 If thou dost break her virgin knot° before  *virginity*
 All sanctimonious° ceremonies may    *sacred*
 With full and holy rite be ministered,
 No sweet aspersion³ shall the heavens let fall
 To make this contract grow; but barren hate,
20 Sour-eyed disdain, and discord shall bestrew
 The union of your bed with weeds so loathly
 That you shall hate it both. Therefore take heed
 As Hymen's lamp⁴ shall light you.
FERDINAND.      As I hope

---

1 Prospero means that Miranda is especially important to him.
2 Surpassingly, marvelously.
3 Rain-like sprinkling of divine grace.
4 As the god of marriage in Greek and Roman mythology, Hymen carried a
lamp whose brightness predicted the fate of the couple's union.

For quiet days, fair issue,[1] and long life
With such love as 'tis now, the murkiest den,°    *lair of a wild beast*  25
The most opportune place, the strong'st suggestion
Our worser genius can,[2] shall never melt
Mine honor into lust to take away
The edge of that day's celebration
When I shall think or° Phoebus' steeds are foundered,    *either*  30
Or night kept chained below.[3]
PROSPERO.                Fairly spoke.
Sit then and talk with her; she is thine own.
What,[4] Ariel! My industrious servant Ariel!

*Enter ARIEL.*

ARIEL. What would my potent master? Here I am.
PROSPERO. Thou and thy meaner fellows, your last service    35
Did worthily perform, and I must use you
In such another trick: go bring the rabble[5]
(O'er whom I give thee power) here to this place.
Incite them to quick motion, for I must
Bestow upon the eyes of this young couple    40
Some vanity of mine art;[6] it is my promise,
And they expect it from me.
ARIEL.              Presently?°    *immediately*
PROSPERO. Ay, with a twink.°    *in the wink of an eye*
ARIEL. Before you can say "come" and "go,"
And breathe twice and cry "so, so,"    45
Each one, tripping° on his toe,    *moving nimbly*
Will be here with mop and mow.°    *making grotesque faces*
Do you love me, master, no?
PROSPERO. Dearly, my delicate Ariel. Do not approach

---

1    Offspring.
2    The largest temptation the worst of our evil spirits can suggest.
3    Ferdinand imagines his wedding day when it seems that night will never come, either because the horses drawing the chariot of the sun have gone lame (leaving the sun stuck up in the sky) or because night is imprisoned somewhere below the horizon.
4    An exclamation used to gain someone's attention.
5    A derogatory term for a group of lowly people (in this case, the spirits over which Ariel has power).
6    A minor or trivial display of Prospero's powers.

Till thou dost hear me call.

50 ARIEL.                    Well I conceive.°                    *comprehend*

*Exit* [ARIEL].

PROSPERO. [*To* FERDINAND] Look thou be true: do not give
    dalliance
Too much the rein.[1] The strongest oaths are straw
To th'fire i'th' blood. Be more abstemious,
Or else good night your vow.

---

1    Do not give your passions too much freedom.

---

4.1.60–139:    THE WEDDING MASQUE
(TLN 1717–1809)

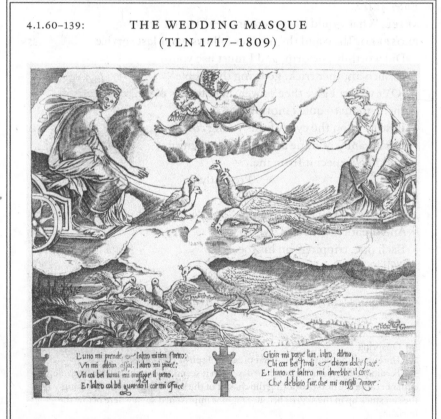

*Allegory of* Love and Marriage; *Juno in a chariot drawn by peacocks at left,* Venus *in a chariot drawn by doves at the right,* by Raphael. From Wikimedia Commons.

FERDINAND.                                 I warrant you, sir,
The white-cold virgin snow upon my heart                          55
Abates the ardor of my liver.[1]
PROSPERO.                                  Well.
Now come, my Ariel. Bring a corollary
Rather than want a spirit:[2] appear, and pertly!
*Soft music*
No tongue—all eyes—be silent!

---

1  The liver was considered the seat of physical desire.
2  Ariel should bring in reinforcements from the spirit world rather than resort to his own devices.

---

Among Shakespeare's plays, *The Tempest* is most aligned with the theatrical tradition of spectacle. Be it the storm at sea that opens the play, the banquet with which Prospero instructs Ariel to torture his foes, or the wedding masque that they conjure up for Miranda and Ferdinand, the play's reliance on visual (and auditory) spectacle suggests that it certainly was conceived for an indoor theater capable of delivering such artifices (such as Blackfriars). Though we remain uncertain of how some of them were achieved on the early-modern stage, practical effects, such as the "quaint device" used to make the banquet suddenly disappear (3.3.52, TLN 1584), undoubtedly added to the play's overall exploration of magic and divinity.

In the wedding masque, figures from Roman mythology come down and bless Miranda and Ferdinand's union. Iris is the messenger of the gods, in the form of a rainbow, directing the course of the weather; Ceres is a god representing the earth's robust fertility; and Juno, Jove's wife and sister, embodies light and birth. This scene represents Shakespeare's most overt gesture to the style of courtly masque popularized by the writer Ben Jonson (1572–1637) and scenic designer Inigo Jones (1573–1652). The lavish spectacle of Juno, the queen of the gods, descending in her chariot drawn by peacocks, provides an exclamation point to the interlude that the masque creates between Prospero's interactions with his enemies. The emphasis on music, singing, and spectacle helps to foster the sense of wonder that the play generally evokes, by drawing on easily recognizable mythological figures and by dazzling the audience with clever mechanical contraptions such as the vanishing banquet.

*Enter* IRIS.

60 IRIS. Ceres, most bounteous lady, thy rich leas°       *grassy fields*
    Of wheat, rye, barley, vetches,[1] oats, and peas;
    Thy turfy mountains where live nibbling sheep,
    And flat meads° thatched with stover,[2] them to keep;   *meadows*
    Thy banks with pionèd and twillèd brims,°    *gentle slopes and terraces*
65   Which spongy April at thy hest betrims
    To make cold nymphs chaste crowns; and thy broomgroves,[3]
    Whose shadow the dismissèd bachelor loves,
    Being lass-lorn; thy pole-clipped vineyard[4]
    And thy sea-marge,° sterile and rocky-hard,       *shore*
70   Where thou thyself dost air: the Queen o'th' sky,[5]
    Whose wat'ry arch and messenger am I,
    Bids thee leave these,[6] and with her sovereign grace
    JUNO *descends* [*slowly in her chariot*].
    Here on this grass-plot, in this very place,
    To come and sport. Here peacocks[7] fly amain.°   *with full speed*
75   Approach, rich Ceres, her to entertain.°    *welcome as a guest*

*Enter* CERES.

CERES. Hail, many-colored messenger, that ne'er
    Dost disobey the wife of Jupiter;
    Who, with thy saffron wings,[8] upon my flowers
    Diffusest honey-drops, refreshing showers,
80   And with each end of thy blue bow dost crown
    My bosky[9] acres and my unshrubbed down,°   *pasture land*
    Rich scarf[10] to my proud earth: why hath thy queen

---

1   Crops used for animal feed.
2   Grass.
3   Broom is a shrub associated with love-charms. A broomgrove is an ideal place for a young "lass-lorn" man (a man without a female beloved)—a place where he might find the means to attract a lass.
4   Either "surrounded by poles" or "pruned short."
5   Referring to Juno, who enters three lines later.
6   Iris refers to the places Ceres frequents and that are mentioned throughout the speech.
7   Juno's sacred birds; the peacock's opulent plumage is appropriate for the Queen of the Sky. In myth, the birds pull the goddess's carriage.
8   Kermode notes that "saffron wings" is likely an allusion to the *Aeneid* (Book 4, line 700).
9   Covered in bushes or thickets.
10   Referring to Iris's rainbows adorning the earth.

Summoned me hither to this short-grassed green?
IRIS. A contract of true love to celebrate,
  And some donation freely to estate°        *gift freely given*  85
  On the blessed lovers.
CERES.             Tell me, heavenly bow,
  If Venus or her son,[1] as thou dost know,
  Do now attend the queen? Since they did plot
  The means that dusky° Dis my daughter got,[2]  *dark and melancholy*
  Her and her blind boy's scandaled° company      *scandalous*  90
  I have forsworn.
IRIS.           Of her society
  Be not afraid—I met her deity
  Cutting the clouds towards Paphos,[3] and her son
  Dove-drawn with her. Here thought they to have done
  Some wanton charm upon this man and maid,           95
  Whose vows are that no bed-right shall be paid
  Till Hymen's torch be lighted;[4] but in vain,
  Mars' hot minion[5] is returned again;
  Her waspish-headed° son has broke his arrows,   *petulant, irritable*
  Swears he will shoot no more but play with sparrows[6]  100
  And be a boy right out.°          *outright, thoroughly*

[*JUNO alights.*]

CERES.          Highest Queen of state,
  Great Juno comes; I know her by her gait.°   *bearing, carriage*
JUNO. How does my bounteous sister? Go with me[7]

---

1  Cupid, like his mother, represents sexual love. He is usually represented as blind.
2  According to Ovid's *Metamorphoses*, Venus and Cupid aided Pluto ("Dis"), god of the underworld, in his love for Proserpina, Ceres's daughter. Pluto kidnapped Proserpina and took her to the underworld. From then on, she had to spend part of the year there; the earth's surface experienced winter during the months Proserpina was confined underground.
3  Venus's home on Cyprus.
4  Refers both to consummation and to the marriage debt owed to Hymen, god of marriage.
5  Venus. The goddess of love was married to Vulcan, though she had an illicit affair with Mars, the god of war.
6  Traditionally regarded as lecherous creatures; associated with Venus.
7  Climb aboard the chariot.

To bless this twain,[1] that they may prosperous be
105   And honored in their issue.

*They sing.*

JUNO [AND CERES]
    Honor, riches, marriage-blessing,
    Long continuance and increasing,
    Hourly joys be still upon you!
    Juno sings her blessings on you.
110   Earth's increase, foison plenty,
    Barns and garners° never empty,                          *granaries*
    Vines with clustering bunches growing,
    Plants with goodly burthen bowing;
    Spring come to you at the farthest
115   In the very end of harvest![2]
    Scarcity and want shall shun you;
    Ceres' blessing so is on you.
FERDINAND. This is a most majestic vision, and
    Harmonious charmingly[3]—may I be bold
    To think these spirits?
120  PROSPERO.                    Spirits, which by mine art
    I have from their confines called to enact
    My present fancies.
FERDINAND.               Let me live here ever—
    So rare a wondered[4] father and a wise
    Makes this place paradise.
    PROSPERO.                   Sweet, now silence;
125   Juno and Ceres whisper seriously.
    There's something else to do: hush and be mute
    Or else our spell is marred.

---

1   The couple, Miranda and Ferdinand.
2   May there be no winter, but that spring follow autumn. A prayer for constant
abundance.
3   Ferdinand describes the music as both melodious and magically enchanting.
"Charm" carries the sense of "spell."
4   Performing marvelous wonders; awe-inducing.

JUNO *and* CERES *whisper and send* IRIS *on employment.*

IRIS. You nymphs called naiads[1] of the windering brooks,
    With your sedged crowns[2] and ever-harmless looks:
    Leave your crisp channels, and on this green land        130
    Answer your summons, Juno does command.
    Come, temperate nymphs, and help to celebrate
    A contract of true love—be not too late.

*Enter certain nymphs.*
    You sunburned sicklemen,° of August weary:[3]       *harvesters*
    Come hither from the furrow and be merry—        135
    Make holiday! Your rye-straw hats put on,
    And these fresh nymphs encounter every one
    In country footing.[4]

*Enter certain reapers, properly habited; they join with the nymphs in a graceful dance, towards the end whereof* PROSPERO *starts suddenly and speaks, after which, to a strange, hollow, and confused noise, they heavily vanish.*[5]

PROSPERO. [*Aside*] I had forgot that foul conspiracy
    Of the beast Caliban and his confederates        140
    Against my life; the minute of their plot
    Is almost come. [*To the spirits*] Well done: avoid.[6] No more.
FERDINAND. This is strange—your father's in some passion
    That works him strongly.
MIRANDA.               Never till this day
    Saw I him touched with anger so distempered.       145
PROSPERO. You do look, my son, in a moved sort,[7]
    As if you were dismayed. Be cheerful, sir.
    Our revels now are ended. These our actors,

---

1    Water nymphs.
2    Interwoven plant leaves.
3    Tired from harvesting.
4    Folk dancing.
5    Exit the stage sorrowfully or reluctantly.
6    Depart.
7    Worried, agitated condition.

As I foretold you, were all spirits and
150  Are melted into air—into thin air—
And, like the baseless fabric° of this vision,      insubstantial structure
The cloud-capped towers, the gorgeous palaces,
The solemn temples, the great globe itself,[1]
Yea, all which it inherit, shall dissolve,
155  And, like this insubstantial pageant faded
Leave not a rack[2] behind. We are such stuff
As dreams are made on,° and our little life      made of
Is rounded with a sleep.° Sir, I am vexed,   surrounded by; completed by
Bear with my weakness; my old brain is troubled.
160  Be not disturbed with my infirmity.
If you be pleased, retire into my cell
And there repose. A turn or two I'll walk
To still my beating mind.[3]
FERDINAND and MIRANDA. We wish your peace.
165  PROSPERO. [To ARIEL] Come with a thought.[4] [To FERDINAND and
MIRANDA] I thank thee. Exit [FERDINAND and MIRANDA].
Ariel: come.

Enter ARIEL.
ARIEL. Thy thoughts I cleave to; what's thy pleasure?
PROSPERO. Spirit,
We must prepare to meet with Caliban.
ARIEL. Ay, my commander. When I presented Ceres
170  I thought to have told thee of it, but I feared
Lest I might anger thee.
PROSPERO. Say again, where didst thou leave these varlets?

---

1  Prospero's reference to the earth registers a simultaneous evocation of the
Globe playhouse, whose theatrical magic is as ephemeral as the masque of Juno,
Ceres, and Iris.
2  Fog or cloud driven by the wind.
3  Prospero's speech belongs to an elegiac tradition dedicated to thinking about
the ephemerality of human life and of everything humans make. Shakespeare's
great contemporary, Edmund Spenser, ends his Faerie Queene by reflecting on our
"flowring pride, so fading and so fickle, / Short Time shall soon cut down with his
consuming sickle" (Book 8, lines 8–9).
4  Immediately, as fast as thought.

ARIEL. I told you, sir; they were red-hot[1] with drinking,
    So full of valor that they smote the air
    For breathing in their faces, beat the ground           175
    For kissing of their feet, yet always bending[2]
    Towards their project. Then I beat my tabor,
    At which like unbacked colts[3] they pricked their ears,
    Advanced their eyelids, lifted up their noses
    As° they smelt music—so I charmed their ears     *as if*  180
    That calf-like° they my lowing followed through    *compliant*
    Toothèd briars, sharp furze, pricking gorse[4] and thorns,
    Which entered their frail shins. At last I left them
    I'th' filthy-mantled° pool beyond your cell,     *scum-covered*
    There dancing up to th'chins that the foul lake     185
    O'erstunk their feet.
PROSPERO.          This was well done, my bird.
    Thy shape invisible retain thou still.
    The trumpery[5] in my house, go bring it hither
    For stale° to catch these thieves.     *decoy or trap*
ARIEL.              I go, I go.

                                  *Exit.*

PROSPERO. A devil—a born devil, on whose nature     190
    Nurture[6] can never stick; on whom my pains
    Humanely taken, all, all lost, quite lost!
    And as with age his body uglier grows,
    So his mind cankers.° I will plague them all     *rots, corrupts*
    Even to roaring. Come: hang them on this line.[7]     195

---

1    Red-faced from drinking and excited by bravado.
2    Turning, aiming.
3    Young, unbroken male horses.
4    Brambly bushes.
5    Fancy, yet cheaply made clothing.
6    In reference to Caliban; the traits acquired from birth (nature) override anything taught or learned in the course of one's life (nurture).
7    Either a clothesline or the branches of a stage-property lime or linden tree. Given the difficulties of hanging a line on the Elizabethan stage, the likelier answer seems to be a stage property tree, particularly given the later reference to "lime-grove" in the subsequent act (5.1.10, TLN 1958).

*Enter ARIEL, loaden with glistering apparel, etc. Enter CALIBAN,*
*STEPHANO, and TRINCULO, all wet.*

CALIBAN. Pray you, tread softly, that the blind mole[1] may not hear
a footfall; we now are near his cell.

STEPHANO. Monster, your fairy, which you say is a harmless fairy,
has done little better than played the jack[2] with us.

200 TRINCULO. Monster, I do smell all horse-piss, at which my nose is
in great indignation.

STEPHANO. So is mine. Do you hear, monster? If I should take a
displeasure against you, look you—

TRINCULO. Thou wert but a lost[3] monster.

205 CALIBAN. Good my Lord, give me thy favor still.
Be patient, for the prize I'll bring thee to
Shall hoodwink[4] this mischance; therefore speak softly—
All's hushed as midnight yet.

TRINCULO. Ay, but to lose our bottles in the pool!

210 STEPHANO. There is not only disgrace and dishonor in that, monster,
but an infinite loss.

TRINCULO. That's more to me than my wetting, yet this is your
harmless fairy, monster.

STEPHANO. I will fetch off[5] my bottle, though I be o'er ears for my
215 labor.

CALIBAN. Prithee, my King, be quiet. Seest thou here;
This is the mouth o'th' cell—no noise, and enter.
Do that good mischief which may make this island
Thine own for ever and I, thy Caliban,
220 For aye° thy foot-licker.                        *ever*

STEPHANO. Give me thy hand—I do begin to have bloody thoughts.

TRINCULO. O King Stephano![6] O peer! O worthy Stephano, look
what a wardrobe here is for thee!

---

1   Because moles could not see in their dark underground tunnels, they were
thought to have developed a heightened sensitivity to sound.
2   A knave or trickster.
3   Ruined.
4   A falconry term for placing a hood over the falcon's eyes, rendering it still and
relatively docile. Caliban suggests that the completion of the mission will gloss
over this misfortune.
5   Rescue, retrieve.
6   This is a reference to the old ballad "Take that old cloak about thee," which
satirizes low-born people seeking to dress in courtly clothing, just as Stephano
and Trinculo are seeking to do by taking the garments off the linden tree.

CALIBAN. Let it alone, thou fool; it is but trash.

TRINCULO. Oh ho, monster! We know what belongs to a frippery.[1]      225
O King Stephano!

STEPHANO. Put off that gown, Trinculo! By this hand, I'll have that
gown.

TRINCULO. Thy grace shall have it.

CALIBAN. The dropsy[2] drown this fool. What do you mean      230
To dote thus on such luggage?[3] Let's alone
And do the murder first—if he awake,
From toe to crown he'll fill our skins with pinches,[4]
Make us strange stuff.

STEPHANO. Be you quiet, monster. Mistress Line,[5] is not this my      235
jerkin?[6] Now is the jerkin under the line. Now, jerkin, you are
like to lose your hair and prove a bald jerkin.

TRINCULO. Do, do![7] We steal by line and level, an't like your grace.[8]

STEPHANO. I thank thee for that jest; here's a garment for't. Wit
shall not go unrewarded while I am king of this country. "Steal      240
by line and level" is an excellent pass of pate—there's another
garment for't.

TRINCULO. Monster, come put some lime[9] upon your fingers, and
away with the rest.

CALIBAN. I will have none on't—we shall lose our time      245
And all be turned to barnacles[10] or to apes
With foreheads villainous low.

---

1    Used-clothing shop.
2    A disease in which the body retains accumulated fluids.
3    Goods that are carried or "lugged"; in this case, the garments.
4    This can refer to the painful but not very harmful pinches inflicted by the
spirits of the island.
5    The stage-property tree that holds the clothes.
6    Sleeveless leather jacket, often trimmed with fur.
7    Words of encouragement or approval.
8    With clever precision, as your Grace sees fit. The expression is proverbial and
refers to carpentry terms (line and level).
9    Birdlime; a sticky substance that is painted on trees in order to trap birds.
10    Either shellfish or the barnacle goose, a traditionally stupid creature.
According to legend, geese metamorphosed from the crustaceans.

STEPHANO. Monster, lay to[1] your fingers: help to bear this away
where my hogshead[2] of wine is, or I'll turn you out of my king-
250   dom. Go to;[3] carry this.

---

1   Apply, put to work.
2   A cask of liquor.
3   Get moving.

4.1.253–59:          DOGS AND HOUNDS
                    (TLN 1929–40)

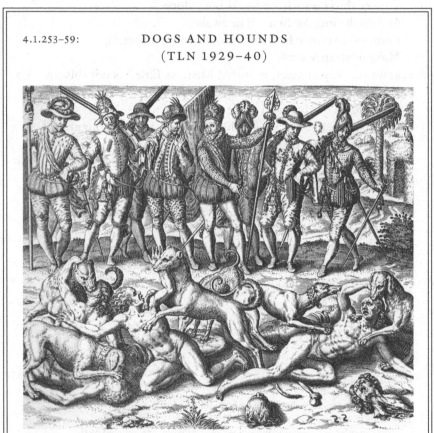

From Bartolomé de las Casas, *A relation of the first voyages and discoveries made by the Spaniards in America* (London: 1699).

The scene of Trinculo, Stephano, and Caliban being chased about the stage by actors in dog costumes can be played for laughs. In the 2010 film version, directed by Julie Taymor and starring Helen Mirren, the three

TRINCULO. And this.
STEPHANO. Ay, and this.

*A noise of hunters heard. Enter divers spirits in shape of dogs and hounds*
*hunting them about,* PROSPERO *and* ARIEL *setting them on.*

PROSPERO. Hey, Mountain, hey!

---

drunken men are chased by fiery CGI dogs in a scene both scary and
uproariously funny. But the text has a more serious dark side. Prospero
seems to call for the would-be assassins to suffer real terror and real pain.
"[G]rind their joints," he says; "With dry convulsions, shorten up their
sinews / With aged cramps" (4.1.225–57, TLN 1935–37). And there is an
even darker shadow over the scene. As Shakespeare would likely have
known, given his evident interest in writings about the Americas, the
Spanish conquistadors were notorious for their savage treatment of the
First Peoples. Bartolomé de las Casas (see Appendix D)—himself first
a member of the Spanish forces and later a convert both to the priesthood and to the defense of the native people—chronicled the barbarity
of his Spanish countrymen, including how they trained their hounds to
hunt those fleeing for their lives. Here, in a 1583 English translation, is
a glimpse of the horror of the conquest:

> ... all the people which coulde flee, hid themselues in the mountaynes,
> and mounted on the toppes of them, fled from the men so without
> all manhood, emptie of all pitie, behauing them as sauage beastes,
> the slaughterers and deadly enemies of mankinde: they taught their
> houndes, fierce dogs, to teare them in peeces at the first viewe, and in
> the space that one might say a Credo, assayled and deuoured an Indian
> as if it had been a swine.

Of course, the possible recollection of Spanish atrocities in the scene
doesn't mean we should see Prospero as one of the "deadly enemies of
mankind," but the picture of him setting "dogs and hounds" on three
men, one whose name—Caliban—reminds us of the "cannibals" of the
New World, does mean that we must keep our eyes open to the traces of
tyranny and violence that Prospero can never entirely shed.

ARIEL.                  Silver—there it goes—Silver!

PROSPERO. Fury, Fury! There, Tyrant,[1] there! Hark, hark!

255    Go charge my goblins that they grind their joints

     With dry convulsions, shorten up their sinews

     With aged cramps, and more pinch-spotted[2] make them

     Than pard° or cat o'mountain.               *leopard*

ARIEL.                  Hark, they roar!

PROSPERO. Let them be hunted soundly.° At this hour    *relentlessly*

260    Lies at my mercy all mine enemies.

     Shortly shall all my labors end, and thou

     Shalt have the air at freedom: for a little,

     Follow, and do me service.                  *Exeunt.*

## [5.1]

*Enter* PROSPERO, *in his magic robes, and* ARIEL.

PROSPERO. Now does my project gather to a head:[3]

     My charms crack[4] not, my spirits obey, and time

     Goes upright with his carriage.[5] [*To* ARIEL] How's the day?[6]

ARIEL. On the sixth hour—at which time, my Lord,

     You said our work should cease.

5 PROSPERO.                 I did say so

     When first I raised the tempest. Say, my spirit,

     How fares the King and's followers?

ARIEL.                  Confined together

     In the same fashion as you gave in charge,

     Just as you left them—all prisoners, sir,

10    In the lime-grove[7] which weather-fends[8] your cell;

     They cannot budge till your release.° The King,    *until you release them*

---

1   The names of the ghostly dogs; they are not traditional hound names.

2   Marked with bruises.

3   Approaches a climax. In alchemy, the expression refers to ingredients in a mixture reaching the boiling point.

4   Another alchemical reference: the failure of an experiment.

5   Time is personified as walking upright because his burden is lighter; Prospero's project is approaching a successful conclusion.

6   What time of day is it?

7   A grove of linden trees.

8   Protects from harsh weather.

His brother, and yours abide, all three distracted,
And the remainder mourning over them,
Brimful of sorrow and dismay—but chiefly
Him that you termed, sir, the good old lord Gonzalo:                    15
His tears runs down his beard like winter's drops
From eaves of reeds.[1] Your charm so strongly works 'em
That if you now beheld them, your affections°                    *emotions*
Would become tender.
PROSPERO.                    Dost thou think so, spirit?
ARIEL. Mine would, sir, were I human.
PROSPERO.                              And mine shall.                    20
Hast thou, which art but air, a touch, a feeling
Of their afflictions, and shall not myself,
One of their kind, that relish all as sharply
Passion as they,[2] be kindlier[3] moved than thou art?
Though with their high wrongs I am struck to th'quick,[4]                    25
Yet with my nobler reason 'gainst my fury
Do I take part. The rarer action is
In virtue than in vengeance; they being penitent,
The sole drift of my purpose doth extend
Not a frown further. Go, release them, Ariel:                    30
My charms I'll break, their senses I'll restore,
And they shall be themselves.
ARIEL.                              I'll fetch them, sir.
          *Exit [ARIEL while PROSPERO traces a magic circle on the stage].*

PROSPERO. Ye elves of hills, brooks, standing lakes, and groves,
And ye that on the sands with printless foot
Do chase the ebbing Neptune, and do fly° him                    *flee*   35
When he comes back; you demi-puppets[5] that
By moonshine do the green sour ringlets[6] make
Whereof the ewe not bites; and you whose pastime

---

1   Thatched roofs.
2   Feel passion as they feel passion.
3   Both "in a more human way" (Ariel is not a human being) and "with greater compassion."
4   Hit at the most sensitive and vital part.
5   Half-sized fairies or spirits.
6   Caused by the roots of toadstools, these rings were said to be formed by dancing fairies.

<pre>
       Is to make midnight-mushrooms that rejoice
40     To hear the solemn curfew,¹ by whose aid—
       Weak masters² though ye be—I have bedimmed
       The noontide sun, called forth the mutinous winds,
       And 'twixt the green sea and the azured vault°                sky
       Set roaring war; to the dread-rattling thunder
45     Have I given fire, and rifted° Jove's stout oak³             split
       With his own bolt! The strong-based promontory⁴
       Have I made shake, and by the spurs° plucked up             roots
       The pine and cedar. Graves at my command
       Have waked their sleepers, ope'd, and let 'em forth
50     By my so potent art.⁵ But this rough magic⁶
       I here abjure, and when I have required
       Some heavenly music,⁷ which even now I do,
       To work mine end upon their senses that
       This airy⁸ charm is for, I'll break my staff,
55     Bury it certain fathoms in the earth;
       And deeper than did ever plummet sound,
       I'll drown my book.
</pre>

*Solemn music. Here enters* ARIEL *before, then* ALONSO *with a frantic gesture, attended by* GONZALO. SEBASTIAN *and* ANTONIO *enter in like manner, attended by* ADRIAN *and* FRANCISCO. *They all enter the circle that* PROSPERO *has made, and there stand charmed.* PROSPERO, *observing, speaks.*

[*Aside to* GONZALO] A solemn air and the best comforter

---

1    The bell rung at nine o'clock, signaling curfew. Spirits were thought to roam the earth after this bell and to retire at sunrise.

2    Minister spirits; they maintain their own supernatural realms, but their powers are weaker than Prospero's.

3    Jove's sacred tree, an emblem of his power.

4    Solidly based large ridge of rock.

5    This speech paraphrases Medea's incantation in Book 7 of Ovid's *Metamorphoses*. See Appendix B, p. 169.

6    The artisanal, practical use of magic, as opposed to the refined study of magic, alchemy, and the purification of the soul.

7    Music was often supposed to have redemptive powers.

8    In the air, but also infers musicality, as in the previous mention of heavenly music.

To an unsettled fancy°—cure thy brains        *disturbed imagination*
(Now useless) boiled within thy skull. [*To courtiers*] There stand,    60
For you are spell-stopped.
[*Aside to* GONZALO]
Holy Gonzalo, honorable man,
Mine eyes, e'en sociable° to the show of thine,       *sympathetic*
Fall fellowly drops.[1] [*Aside*] The charm dissolves apace,
And as the morning steals upon the night,        65
Melting the darkness, so their rising senses
Begin to chase the ignorant fumes that mantle°     *cover, obstruct*
Their clearer reason. [*Aside to each character, in turn*] O good
     Gonzalo,
My true preserver, and a loyal sir
To him thou follow'st, I will pay thy graces        70
Home[2] both in word and deed. Most cruelly
Did thou, Alonso, use me and my daughter.
Thy brother was a furtherer in the act—
Thou art pinched for't now, Sebastian. Flesh and blood,
You, brother mine,[3] that entertained ambition,       75
Expelled remorse[4] and nature,[5] whom, with Sebastian
(Whose inward pinches therefore are most strong)
Would here have killed your King, I do forgive thee,
Unnatural though thou art. [*Aside*] Their understanding
Begins to swell, and the approaching tide        80
Will shortly fill the reasonable shore
That now lies foul and muddy.[6] Not one of them
That yet looks on me or would know me.[7] Ariel,
Fetch me the hat and rapier in my cell;

---

1   Cry empathetic tears.
2   Proverbial phrase meaning "to repay a debt entirely."
3   My brother (i.e., Antonio).
4   Pity, compassion.
5   Natural feeling, brotherly affection.
6   Like growing waves that approach and eventually wash over the shore, the lords' comprehension increases and will eventually clear their minds of all confusion.
7   The lords do not recognize Prospero because they have not yet fully recovered their wits.

85    I will discase[1] me, and myself present
      As I was sometime Milan.[2] Quickly, spirit—
      Thou shalt ere long be free.

*ARIEL fetches the items, returns, then sings as he helps to attire him.*

      ARIEL. Where the bee sucks, there suck I;
      In a cowslip's bell I lie—
90    There I couch when owls do cry.
      On the bat's back I do fly
      After° summer merrily.                    *chasing, pursuing*
      Merrily, merrily shall I live now
      Under the blossom that hangs on the bough.
95  PROSPERO. Why, that's my dainty Ariel! I shall miss thee
      But yet thou shalt have freedom. [*Ariel arranges his clothing.*] So,
        so, so.[3]
      To the King's ship, invisible as thou art:
      There shalt thou find the mariners asleep
      Under the hatches. The master and the boatswain
100  Being awake, enforce them to this place
      And presently, I prithee.
      ARIEL. I drink the air[4] before me and return
      Or ere your pulse twice beat!

                                      *Exit [ARIEL].*

      GONZALO. All torment, trouble, wonder, and amazement
105  Inhabits here! Some heavenly power guide us
      Out of this fearful country!
      PROSPERO.            [*To ALONSO*] Behold, Sir King,
      The wrongèd Duke of Milan, Prospero.
      For more assurance that a living prince
      Does now speak to thee, I embrace thy body,
      [*Embraces ALONSO.*]

---

1    Unclothe, take off the magic robes.
2    As I appeared when I was Duke of Milan.
3    Prospero expresses his approval of the adjustments Ariel makes to his ducal attire.
4    Orgel suggests that Ariel is adapting the Latin expression *viam vorare* (I devour the road) to "his own mode of travel."

And to thee and thy company I bid                                                110
A hearty welcome.
ALONSO.                    Whe'er thou be'st he or no,
Or some enchanted trifle° to abuse me                    *magical apparition*
(As late I have been[1]) I not know. Thy pulse
Beats as of flesh and blood, and since I saw thee,
Th'affliction of my mind amends,° with which             *heals, recovers*   115
I fear a madness held me. This must crave°                      *demand*
(And if this be at all°) a most strange story.       *is actually happening*
Thy dukedom I resign, and do entreat
Thou pardon me my wrongs. But how should Prospero
Be living, and be here?
PROSPERO.               [*To* GONZALO] First, noble friend,                120
Let me embrace thine age, whose honor cannot
Be measured or confined.
GONZALO.                   Whether this be
Or be not, I'll not swear.
PROSPERO.                   You do yet taste
Some subtleties[2] o' th'isle that will not let you
Believe things certain. Welcome, my friends all!                        125
[*Aside to* SEBASTIAN *and* ANTONIO] But you, my brace[3] of lords,
          were I so minded,
I here could pluck° his highness' frown upon you        *bring down*
And justify° you traitors. At this time                          *prove*
I will tell no tales.
SEBASTIAN.         The devil speaks in him.
PROSPERO. No!                                                             130
[*To* ANTONIO]
For you, most wicked sir—whom to call brother
Would even infect my mouth—I do forgive
Thy rankest fault[4] (all of them), and require
My dukedom of thee, which perforce° I know       *by necessity*
Thou must restore.
ALONSO.               If thou be'st Prospero,                            135

---

1   As these magical specters have lately abused or deceived me.
2   This refers to both magical hallucinations and elaborate sugary desserts served
at the end of banquets.
3   Pair, usually used to describe a pair of dogs or game animals.
4   Antonio's usurpation of the dukedom.

Give us particulars of thy preservation,
How thou hast met us here, whom three hours since
Were wracked upon this shore, where I have lost
(How sharp the point of this remembrance is!)
My dear son Ferdinand.

140 PROSPERO.               I am woe° for't, sir.         *sorry*

ALONSO. Irreparable is the loss, and patience
Says it is past her cure.°       *past the remedy of patience*

PROSPERO.          I rather think
You have not sought her help, of whose soft grace
For the like loss I have her sovereign aid,
And rest myself content.

145 ALONSO.            You the like loss?

PROSPERO. As great to me, as late; and supportable
To make the dear° loss have I means much weaker    *grievous*
Than you may call to comfort you;[1] for I
Have lost my daughter.

150 ALONSO. A daughter?
O heavens, that° they were living both in Naples,    *if only*
The King and Queen there! That they were, I wish
Myself were mudded in that oozy bed°      *the ocean floor*
Where my son lies. When did you lose your daughter?

155 PROSPERO. In this last tempest. [*Aside*] I perceive these lords
At this encounter do so much admire,
That they devour their reason, and scarce think
Their eyes do offices of truth, their words
Are natural breath.[2] [*To courtiers*] But howsoe'er you have

160 Been jostled from your senses, know for certain
That I am Prospero and that very Duke
Which was thrust forth of Milan, who most strangely[3]
Upon this shore, where you were wracked, was landed
To be the Lord on't.° No more yet of this,    *of it*

165 For 'tis a chronicle of day by day,°    *a story to be told over several days*

---

1   The general sense is "although we both have lost children, I have fewer means
to comfort myself for this grievous loss." Alonso has courtiers to console him;
Prospero has none.

2   The courtiers are so struck by amazement that they can't credit their own
thoughts or what their eyes see or the words they are speaking.

3   In an unusual way; miraculously.

Not a relation[1] for a breakfast, nor
Befitting this first meeting. [*To ALONSO*] Welcome, sir.
This cell's my court; here have I few attendants—
And subjects none abroad.[2] Pray you, look in.
My dukedom, since you have given me again,                    170
I will requite you with as good a thing,
At least bring forth a wonder to content ye
As much as me my dukedom.

*Here* PROSPERO *discovers*[3] FERDINAND *and* MIRANDA *playing at chess.*

MIRANDA. Sweet Lord, you play me false.°          *you are cheating*
FERDINAND.                              No, my dearest love,
I would not for the world.                                    175
MIRANDA. Yes, for a score of kingdoms you should wrangle,[4]
And I would call it fair play.
ALONSO.                        If this prove
A vision° of the island, one dear son          *a mirage*
Shall I twice lose.
SEBASTIAN.        A most high miracle!

[*FERDINAND sees ALONSO and the others.*]

FERDINAND. Though the seas threaten, they are merciful;      180
I have cursed them without cause.
ALONSO.                        Now all the blessings
Of a glad father compass thee about:
Arise, and say how thou cam'st here.
MIRANDA.                      O wonder!
How many goodly creatures are there here!
How beauteous mankind is! O brave new world      185
That has such people in't!
PROSPERO.              'Tis new to thee.
ALONSO. What is this maid with whom thou wast at play?
Your eld'st° acquaintance cannot be three hours.      *longest*

---

1  Story, report.
2  Anywhere else on the island.
3  Reveals.
4  Contend (perhaps dishonestly).

Is she the goddess that hath severed us
And brought us thus together?

190 FERDINAND.                    Sir, she is mortal,
But by immortal providence, she's mine.
I chose her when I could not ask my father
For his advice, nor thought I had one. She
Is daughter to this famous Duke of Milan,
195 Of whom so often I have heard renown,
But never saw before, of whom I have
Received a second life, and second father
This lady makes him to me.

---

5.1.174–77:                 PLAYING AT CHESS
                            (TLN 2141–47)

For an early-modern audience, the "discovery" of Ferdinand and
Miranda "at chess" might have brought to mind a long tradition of
courtly chess games between aristocratic young men and aristocratic
young women. In the lovely Italian painting on the facing page, we see
a perfect image of chess as such a pastime. The encounter between the
lovers in the play, however, while drawn with great delicacy, is far more
complicated than the painting.

When Prospero draws the curtain aside, our first sight is of two loving
young people at chess. But that changes with Miranda's first line, in which
she accuses Ferdinand of cheating. She doesn't sound angry—she calls
him "sweet lord" before she says, "you play me false"—but it still sounds
like she means it. He says that he would not cheat "for all the world." Her
last two lines might mean that she now believes he did not cheat; and that
even if, in some future game, he did cheat, she would forgive him so completely that she would call it fair play. Or her lines might simply reiterate
the accusation: you would cheat, and for a prize ("a score of kingdoms")
far smaller than the whole world, and I would still call it fair play.

As the scene suggests, chess was more than an innocent aristocratic
pastime. In his essay "False Play: Shakespeare and Chess," William Poole
tells us that it was also a game connected with "cheating, betting, beating,

ALONSO.               I am hers.[1]
But oh, how oddly will it sound that I
Must ask my child forgiveness.

PROSPERO.             There, sir, stop.         200
Let us not burden our remembrances with
A heaviness that's gone.

GONZALO.             I have inly wept,
Or should have spoke ere this: look down, you gods,
And on this couple drop a blessèd crown,
For it is you that have chalked forth the way[2]      205

---

1    I am a second father to her, just as Prospero is your second father.
2    Drew, as if with chalk, our pathway.

"Two Chess Players," attributed to Lorenzo Costa or Amico Aspertini, from Raimond van Marle, *Iconographie de l'art profane au Moyen-Age et à la Renaissance* (The Hague: Martinus Nijhoff, 1931), vol. 1, fig. 57.

fighting, class conflict, civil unrest, and seduction" (53). Indeed, chess is a way of playing at military strategy, political assassination, and total conquest, so this exchange between the young lovers bears on the history of struggle between their fathers and especially on the treachery practiced by Alonso to gain sovereignty over Milan. The scene suggests that Ferdinand might be more like his father than has first appeared. It also gives us new insight into Miranda: she seems able to be just as suspicious of others as her father is, but she is also someone wise enough to put her love above her distrust.

Which brought us hither.

ALONSO.                    I say amen, Gonzalo.[1]

GONZALO. Was Milan[2] thrust from Milan that his issue
    Should become kings of Naples? O rejoice
    Beyond a common joy, and set it down
210    With gold on lasting pillars! In one voyage
    Did Claribel her husband find at Tunis;
    And Ferdinand, her brother, found a wife
    Where he himself was lost; Prospero, his dukedom
    In a poor isle; and all of us, ourselves,
    When no man was his own.[3]

ALONSO.                         [To FERDINAND and MIRANDA] Give
215    me your hands:
    Let grief and sorrow still° embrace his heart       *forever*
    That doth not wish you joy.

GONZALO.                    Be it so, amen.


*Enter ARIEL, with the [Ship]master and Boatswain amazedly following.*
    O look, sir, look, sir, here is more of us!
    I prophesied if a gallows were on land,
220    This fellow could not drown.
    [To Boatswain]
    Now, blasphemy,[4]
    That swear'st grace o'erboard[5]—not an oath on shore?
    Hast thou no mouth by land?[6]
    What is the news?

225 BOATSWAIN. The best news is that we have safely found
    Our King and company; the next, our ship,
    Which but three glasses[7] since we gave out split,[8]

---

1   Even though Gonzalo summons gods, repeated words such as amen contain
the pagan spirit within a Christian frame of reference.
2   The Duke of Milan.
3   When we had neither self-awareness nor self-mastery.
4   One who blasphemes (a personification).
5   Gonzalo suggests that the Boatswain's strong language in the storm caused
God to abandon the ship to its fate.
6   No fighting words now that you are not on your boat.
7   Three hours. There is a discrepancy between the four hours that Prospero
thought his magic work would take (1.2.240, TLN 361) and the three hours speci-
fied by the Boatswain.
8   Proclaimed our ship sinking.

Is tight and yare and bravely rigged[1] as when
We first put out to sea.

ARIEL.                 [*Aside to* PROSPERO] Sir, all this service
Have I done since I went.

PROSPERO.            My tricksy° spirit!        *playful, sportive*   230

ALONSO. These are not natural events; they strengthen°    *grow*
From strange to stranger: say, how came you hither?

BOATSWAIN. If I did think, sir, I were well awake,
I'd strive to tell you: we were dead of sleep
And (how we know not) all clapped under[2] hatches,        235
Where, but even now—with strange and several noises
Of roaring, shrieking, howling, jingling chains,
And more diversity of sounds, all horrible!—
We were awaked, straightway at liberty,
Where we, in all our trim,[3] freshly beheld          240
Our royal, good, and gallant ship, our master
Cap'ring° to eye her. On a trice,[4] so please you,   *playfully skipping*
Even in a dream, were we divided from them[5]
And were brought moping° hither.           *bewildered*

ARIEL.                    Wast well done?

PROSPERO. Bravely, my diligence;° thou shalt be free.   *diligent one*  245

ALONSO. This is as strange a maze as e'er men trod,
And there is in this business more than nature
Was ever conduct of; some oracle
Must rectify our knowledge.

PROSPERO.              Sir, my liege,[6]
Do not infest your mind with beating on          250
The strangeness of this business. At picked leisure,
Which shall be shortly single, I'll resolve you,
Which to you shall seem probable, of every
These happened accidents.[7] Till when, be cheerful
And think of each thing well. [*To* ARIEL] Come hither, spirit:   255

---

1   Watertight, prepared for sea and finely equipped.
2   Confined beneath.
3   This could refer either to the mariners' garments or to the ship's rigging.
4   Immediately.
5   I.e., the other crewmen.
6   Referring to a superior or sovereign figure.
7   When, very soon, we are in an extended time of leisure, I will explain all of
these events in a way that will be capable of proof.

Set Caliban and his companions free;
Untie the spell. [*To* ALONSO] How fares my gracious sir?
There are yet missing of your company
Some few odd lads that you remember not.

*Enter* ARIEL, *driving in* CALIBAN, STEPHANO, *and* TRINCULO *in their stolen apparel.*

STEPHANO. [*To* TRINCULO *and* CALIBAN]

260    Every man shift for all the rest, and let
No man take care for himself,[1] for all is
But fortune. Coraggio,[2] bully-monster,[3] coraggio!

TRINCULO. [*Sees* PROSPERO *and the others.*] If these be true spies[4]
which I wear in my head, here's a goodly sight!

265    CALIBAN. O Setebos, these be brave spirits indeed!
How fine° my master is; I am afraid       *i.e., in his noble attire*
He will chastise me.

SEBASTIAN. Ha, ha!
What things are these, my Lord Antonio?
Will money buy 'em?

270    ANTONIO.             Very like—one of them
Is a plain fish and no doubt marketable.[5]

PROSPERO. Mark but the badges[6] of these men, my lords,
Then say if they be true. This misshapen knave—
His mother was a witch, and one so strong

275    That could control the moon, make flows and ebbs,
And deal in her command without her power.[7]
These three have robbed me, and this demi-devil

---

1    An inversion of the common phrase "every man for himself."
2    Italian for "courage."
3    "Bully" is a term of endearment or familiarity, generally hyphenated with another word.
4    Unmistaken eyes.
5    Antonio and Sebastian, like Stephano and Trinculo, perceive Caliban as a commodity. These lines also suggest Caliban's fishlike appearance, as Trinculo mentioned earlier (2.2.23–27, TLN 1064–69).
6    Emblems worn to identify the servants of noblemen.
7    Sycorax, like Ovid's Medea, was able to control the moon and the tides, which are caused by the moon. Sycorax was also able to exert her power beyond the realm of the moon's power.

(For he's a bastard one[1]) had plotted with them
To take my life. [*To ALONSO*] Two of these fellows you
Must know and own;° this thing of darkness[2] I          *acknowledge*          280
Acknowledge mine.

CALIBAN.                    I shall be pinched to death!

ALONSO. Is not this Stephano, my drunken butler?

SEBASTIAN. He is drunk now—where had he wine?

ALONSO. And Trinculo is reeling-ripe[3]—where should they
Find this grand liquor that hath gilded[4] 'em?          285
[*To TRINCULO*] How cam'st thou in this pickle?[5]

TRINCULO. I have been in such a pickle since I saw you last
That I fear me will never out of my bones.
I shall not fear flyblowing.

SEBASTIAN.                    Why, how now, Stephano?

STEPHANO. O touch me not; I am not Stephano, but a cramp.[6]          290

PROSPERO. You'd be king o'the isle, sirrah?[7]

STEPHANO. I should have been a sore one then.

ALONSO. This is a strange thing as e'er I looked on.

PROSPERO. He is as disproportioned in his manners
As in his shape. [*To CALIBAN*] Go, sirrah, to my cell:          295
Take with you your companions. As you look
To have my pardon, trim° it handsomely.          *decorate*

CALIBAN. Ay, that I will; and I'll be wise hereafter
And seek for grace.[8] [*Aside*] What a thrice-double ass
Was I to take this drunkard for a god          300
And worship this dull fool!

PROSPERO.                    Go to: away!

---

1    Prospero suggests that Caliban is the illegitimate offspring of his human
mother and a demonic father.
2    Prospero refers to what he views as Caliban's depravity. It also connects with
early modern ideas about the dark complexions of Africans and Native Americans.
3    So drunk as to be falling over.
4    With flushed or red faces.
5    The meaning is proverbial: "to be in a pickle" or sorry condition. The phrase
also alludes to liquor's function as a preservative.
6    He is in so much pain that he has become a cramp.
7    "Sirrah" is a mocking form of address, usually denoting someone deemed to
be inferior to the speaker.
8    Caliban means that he will seek a redemptive grace or that he will seek the
grace and favor of Prospero. The choice between a religious and a social meaning
depends on how the lines are spoken and to whom they are spoken, whether to
himself or to others on stage.

ALONSO. [*To* STEPHANO *and* TRINCULO] Hence, and bestow your
    luggage where you found it.
SEBASTIAN. Or stole it rather.

        [*Exeunt* CALIBAN, STEPHANO, *and* TRINCULO.]

    PROSPERO. Sir, I invite your highness and your train°     *entourage*
305    To my poor cell, where you shall take your rest
    For this one night, which part of it I'll waste[1]
    With such discourse as, I not doubt, shall make it
    Go quick away—the story of my life
    And the particular accidents gone by
310    Since I came to this isle. And in the morn
    I'll bring° you to your ship, and so to Naples,     *accompany*
    Where I have hope to see the nuptial
    Of these, our dear-belovèd, solemnized;
    And thence retire me to my Milan, where
    Every third thought shall be my grave.[2]
315  ALONSO.                          I long
    To hear the story of your life, which must
    Take the ear strangely.°     *amaze and delight the ears*
    PROSPERO.           I'll deliver all,
    And promise you calm seas, auspicious gales,
    And sail so expeditious that shall catch
320    Your royal fleet far off. [*Aside to* ARIEL] My Ariel, chick,[3]
    That is thy charge: then to the elements
    Be free, and fare thou well. [*To courtiers*] Please you, draw near.[4]
                                    *Exeunt omnes.*

---

1    Pass or occupy the time, with a gracious hint of self-deprecation.
2    A conventional meditation on death. It need not imply that Prospero is elderly
or near death.
3    A term of endearment. It recalls Prospero's earlier epithet for Ariel, "bird"
(4.1.186, TLN 1858). Both terms suggest Ariel's birdlike qualities.
4    Please come in (into my cell). ·

## EPILOGUE[1]

*spoken by* PROSPERO

Now my charms are all o'erthrown,
And what strength I have's mine own,
Which is most faint. Now, 'tis true
I must be here confined by you[2]
Or sent to Naples; let me not,                                        5
Since I have my dukedom got
And pardoned the deceiver, dwell
In this bare island[3] by your spell,
But release me from my bands°                    bonds of confinement
With the help of your good hands.°                    applause          10
Gentle breath of yours my sails
Must fill, or else my project fails,
Which was to please. Now I want°                              lack
Spirits to enforce, art to enchant;
And my ending is despair,                                            15
Unless I be relieved by prayer,
Which pierces so that it assaults
Mercy itself, and frees all faults.
    As you from crimes would pardoned be,
    Let your indulgence[4] set me free.                              20

                                                          *Exit.*

---

1    The speaker seems to be both the character of Prospero and the actor playing
him; it combines the actor's conventional request for applause and Prospero's peti-
tion for forgiveness.
2    Prospero's use of "confined" is important to the play's themes of power and
captivity. Prospero asks the audience to release him from the island and from his role
in the play.
3    Both the island and the stage in the playhouse.
4    Goodwill. This also suggests the Roman Catholic practice in which priests offer
remission for the punishment of sins.

# APPENDIX A: FROM ARISTOTLE, *POLITICS* (FOURTH CENTURY BCE)

[One of the fathers of the Western philosophical tradition, Aristotle (384–322 BCE) has shaped the way we have conceived of humanity over the last two millennia. His works cover the breadth of human existence, from biology, through science and the natural world, to ethics and governance. In the *Politics*, Aristotle discusses the city as a living (organic) community, whose well-functioning is as integral to human beings as is good health or family. The work deals with ideas about rule and authority as much as it deals with the notion of living a good life and performing noble actions.

Early in the *Politics* (I, iv), Aristotle introduces the idea that some people are born better suited to subjugation than they are to living autonomously. The natural slave, Aristotle explains, "is a living possession ... some men are by nature free, and others slaves, and that for these latter slavery is both expedient and right." Though he somewhat nuances the notion, arguing for a fair and respectful treatment of the slave whom he considers a living part of the master, the notion of "natural slaves" became an ideological cornerstone for many colonizing empires who argued that people of the New World were born to be ruled. Juan Ginés de Sepúlveda, who famously debated Bartolomé de las Casas on Spain's colonizing efforts in the New World, was one of the strongest advocates for Aristotle's "natural slave" theory.]

IV. Property is a part of the household, and the art of acquiring property is a part of the art of managing the household; for no man can live well, or indeed live at all, unless he be provided with necessaries. And as in the arts which have a definite sphere the workers must have their own proper instruments for the accomplishment of their work, so it is in the management of a household. Now instruments are of various sorts; some are living, others lifeless; in the rudder, the pilot of a ship has a lifeless, in the look-out man, a living instrument; for in the arts the servant is a kind of instrument. Thus, too, a possession is an instrument for maintaining life. And so, in the arrangement of the family, a slave is a living possession, and property a number of such instruments; and the servant is himself an instrument which takes precedence of all other instruments. For if every instrument could accomplish its own work, obeying or anticipating the will of others, like the statues of Daedalus,[1] or the tripods of Hephaestus,[2] which, says the poet[3] of their own accord entered the assembly of the Gods; if, in like manner, the shuttle would weave and the plectrum touch the lyre without a hand to guide them, chief workmen would not want servants, nor masters slaves. Here, however, another distinction must be drawn; the instruments commonly so called are instruments of production, whilst a possession is an instrument of action. The shuttle, for example, is not only of use; but something else is made by it, whereas of a garment or of a bed there is only the use. Further, as production and action are different in kind, and both require instruments, the instruments which they employ must likewise differ in kind. But life is action and not production, and therefore the slave is the minister of action. Again, a possession is spoken of as a part is spoken of; for the part is not only a part of something else, but wholly belongs to it; and this is also true of a possession. The master is only the master of the slave; he does not belong to him, whereas the slave is not only the slave of his master, but wholly belongs to him. Hence we see what is the nature and office of a slave; he who is by nature not his own but another's man, is by nature a slave; and he may be said to be another's man who, being a human being, is also a possession. And a possession may be defined as an instrument of action, separable from the possessor.

V. But is there any one thus intended by nature to be a slave, and for whom such a condition is expedient and right, or rather is not all slavery a violation of nature?

There is no difficulty in answering this question, on grounds both of reason and of fact. For that some should rule and others be ruled is a thing not only necessary, but expedient; from the hour of their birth, some are marked out for subjection, others for rule.

And there are many kinds both of rulers and subjects (and that rule is the better which is exercised over better subjects—for example, to

1   A craftsman in Greek mythology, mostly known for designing the labyrinth in which the Minotaur was imprisoned.
2   The Greek god of fire and metalworking, who acted as a blacksmith for other gods to forge their various weapons.
3   Referring to Homer.

rule over men is better than to rule over wild beasts; for the work is better which is executed by better workmen, and where one man rules and another is ruled, they may be said to have a work); for in all things which form a composite whole and which are made up of parts, whether continuous or discrete, a distinction between the ruling and the subject element comes to fight. Such a duality exists in living creatures, but not in them only; it originates in the constitution of the universe; even in things which have no life there is a ruling principle, as in a musical mode. But we are wandering from the subject. We will therefore restrict ourselves to the living creature, which, in the first place, consists of soul and body: and of these two, the one is by nature the ruler, and the other the subject. But then we must look for the intentions of nature in things which retain their nature, and not in things which are corrupted. And therefore we must study the man who is in the most perfect state both of body and soul, for in him we shall see the true relation of the two; although in bad or corrupted natures the body will often appear to rule over the soul, because they are in an evil and unnatural condition. At all events we may firstly observe in living creatures both a despotical and a constitutional rule; for the soul rules the body with a despotical rule, whereas the intellect rules the appetites with a constitutional and royal rule. And it is clear that the rule of the soul over the body, and of the mind and the rational element over the passionate, is natural and expedient; whereas the equality of the two or the rule of the inferior is always hurtful. The same holds good of animals in relation to men; for tame animals have a better nature than wild, and all tame animals are better off when they are ruled by man; for then they are preserved. Again, the male is by nature superior, and the female inferior; and the one rules, and the other is ruled; this principle, of necessity, extends to all mankind.

Where then there is such a difference as that between soul and body, or between men and animals (as in the case of those whose business is to use their body, and who can do nothing better), the lower sort are by nature slaves, and it is better for them as for all inferiors that they should be under the rule of a master. For he who can be, and therefore is, another's and he who participates in rational principle enough to apprehend, but not to have, such a principle, is a slave by nature. Whereas the lower animals cannot even apprehend a principle; they obey their instincts. And indeed the use made of slaves and of tame animals is not very different; for both with their bodies minister to the needs of life. Nature would like to distinguish between the bodies of freemen and slaves, making the one strong for servile labor, the other upright, and although useless for such services, useful for political life in the arts both of war and peace. But the opposite often happens—that some have the souls and others have the bodies of freemen. And doubtless if men differed from one another in the mere forms of their bodies as much as the statues of the Gods do from men, all would acknowledge that the inferior class should be slaves of the superior. And if this is true of the body, how much more just that a similar distinction should exist in the soul? but the beauty of the body is seen, whereas the beauty of the soul is not seen. It is clear, then, that some men are by nature free, and others slaves, and that for these latter slavery is both expedient and right.

VI. But that those who take the opposite view have in a certain way right on their side, may be easily seen. For the words slavery and slave are used in two senses. There is a slave or slavery by law as well as by nature. The law of which I speak is a sort of convention—the law by which whatever is taken in war is supposed to belong to the victors. But this right many jurists impeach, as they would an orator who brought forward an unconstitutional measure: they detest the notion that, because one man has the power of doing violence and is superior in brute strength, another shall be his slave and subject. Even among philosophers there is a difference of opinion. The origin of the dispute, and what makes the views invade each other's territory, is as follows: in some sense virtue, when furnished with means, has actually the greatest power of exercising force; and as superior power is only found where there is superior excellence of some kind, power seems to imply virtue, and the dispute to be simply one about justice (for it is due to one party identifying justice with goodwill while the other identifies it with the mere rule of the stronger). If these views are thus set out separately, the other views have no force or plausibility against the view that the superior in virtue ought to rule, or be master. Others, clinging, as they think, simply to a principle of justice (for law and custom are a sort of justice), assume that slavery in accordance with the custom of war is justified by law, but at the same moment they deny this. For what if the cause of the war be unjust? And again, no one would ever say he is a slave who is unworthy to be a slave. Were this the case, men of the highest rank would be slaves and the children of slaves if they or their parents chance to have been taken captive and sold. Wherefore Hellenes[1] do not like to call Hellenes slaves, but confine the term to barbarians. Yet, in using this language, they really mean the natural slave of whom we spoke at first; for it must be admitted that some are slaves everywhere, others nowhere. The same principle applies to nobility. Hellenes regard themselves as noble everywhere, and not only in their own country, but they deem the barbarians noble only when at home, thereby implying that there are two sorts of nobility and freedom, the one absolute, the other relative. The Helen of Theodectes[2] says:

Who would presume to call me servant who am on both sides sprung from the stem[3] of the Gods?

What does this mean but that they distinguish freedom and slavery, noble and humble birth, by the two principles of good and evil? They think that as men and animals beget men and animals, so from good men a good man springs. But this is what nature, though she may intend it, cannot always accomplish.

We see then that there is some foundation for this difference of opinion, and that all are not either slaves by nature or freemen by nature, and also that there is in some cases a marked distinction between the two classes, rendering it expedient and right for the one to be slaves and the others to be masters: the one practicing obedience, the others exercising the authority and lordship which nature intended them to have. The abuse of this authority is injurious to both; for the interests of part and whole, of body and soul, are the same, and the slave is a part of the master, a living but separated part of his bodily frame. Hence, where the relation of master and slave between them is natural they are friends and have a common interest, but where it rests merely on law and force the reverse is true.

---

1 Greeks.
2 Theodectes (c. 380–c. 340 BCE) was a Greek poet and rhetorician who wrote fifty tragedies, including *Helen*, which Aristotle quotes here.
3 Stem could be used either as a botanical metaphor (the stem is the main trunk of a plant out of which buds develop) or to infer a line of descent or ancestry (stock).

# APPENDIX B:
## FROM OVID, *METAMORPHOSES* (8 CE)

[The influence of Ovid (43 BCE–17 CE) on Shakespeare's drama is well documented: Ovid's seminal opus, the narrative poem *Metamorphoses*, echoes throughout Shakespeare's canon. The poem's massive span (over 11,000 lines divided into 15 books) provides a record of the history of the world up to the deification of Julius Caesar in 42 BCE. Salient themes of love, transformation, and power (among others) mingle throughout the poem as Ovid relates numerous stories, histories, and myths.

The poem first appeared in English in the fifteenth century. Both Chaucer and Gower reproduced sections of it in their works, but William Caxton provided the first complete translation of the poem (in prose) in 1480. Almost a century later in London (1567), Arthur Golding published a translation in rhyming couplets and iambic heptameter that proved highly influential. Golding's translation was the primary version of the poem that Shakespeare read and drew from.

Book 7 of Ovid's *Metamorphoses* focuses primarily on Medea, granddaughter of the Sun god Helios, known for her powers of sorcery. Prospero's "rough magic" speech (5.1.34–57, TLN 1984–2008) strongly echoes a speech Medea makes in Ovid's narrative about her abilities to control nature's elements. The speech also parallels the powers that the play attributes to the witch Sycorax, in particular the control over the moon and tides. We have modernized some of the spellings in this selection.]

> Three nights were yet as then to come. Soon as that she shone
> Most full of light, and did behold the earth with fulsome face,
> Medea with her hair not trussed so much as in a lace,
> But flaring on her shoulders twined, and barefoot, with her gown
> Unguarded, gat[1] her out of doors and wandered up and down
> Alone the dead time of the night: both man, and beast, and bird
> Were fast asleep: the serpents sly in trailing forward stirred
> So softly as ye would have thought they still asleep had been.
> The moisting air was whist:[2] no leaf ye could have moving seen.
> The stars alone fair and bright did in the welkin[3] shine

---

1   Got.
2   Silent.
3   Sky.

To which she lifting up her hands did thrice herself incline:
And thrice with water of the brook her hair besprinkled she:
And gasping thrice she opened her mouth: and bowing down her knee
Upon the bare hard ground, she said: "O trustee time of night
Most faithful unto purities, O golden stars whose light
Doth jointly with the moon succeed the beams that blaze by day
And thou three-headed Hecate who knows best the way
To compass this our great attempt and art our chiefest stay:
Ye charms & witchcrafts, & thou earth which both with herb & weed
Of mighty working furnishest the wizards at their need:
Ye airs and winds: ye eyes of hills, of brook, of woods alone,
Of standing Lakes, and of the night approached ye everychone.[1]
Through help of whom (the crooked banks much wondering at the thing)
I have compelled streams to run clean backward to their spring.
By charms I make the calm seas rough, & make ye rough seas plain,
And cover all the sky with clouds and chase them thence again.
By charms I raise and lay the winds, and burst the vipers jaw.
And from the bowels of the earth both stones and trees do draw.
Whole woods and forests I remove: I make the mountains shake,
And even the earth itself to groan and fearfully to quake.
I call up dead men from their graves: and thee O lightsome moon
I darken oft, though beaten brass abate thy peril soon.
Our sorcery dims the morning fair and darkens the sun at noon.
The flaming breath of fiery bulls ye quenched for my sake
And caused their unwieldy necks the bended yoke to take.
Among the earth bred brothers you a mortal war did set
And brought asleep the dragon fell whose eyes were never shut.
By means whereof deceiving him that had the golden fleece
In charge to keep, you sent it thence by Jason into Greece.
Now have I need of herbs that can by virtue of their juice
To flowering prime of lusty youth old withered age reduce.
I am assured ye will it grant. For not in vain have shone
These twinkling stars, nay yet in vain this chariot all alone
By draught of dragons hither comes." With that was from the sky
A chariot softly glanced down, and stayed hard[2] thereby.

---

1   Everyone.
2   Came to an abrupt stop.

## APPENDIX C: FROM JUAN GINÉS DE SEPÚLVEDA, *THE SECOND DEMOCRATE; OR, THE JUST CAUSES OF THE WAR AGAINST THE INDIANS* (1547)

[Juan Ginés de Sepúlveda (1494–1573) was a Spanish humanist scholar, translator of Aristotle into Latin, and author of numerous learned books on politics and religion. Today he is known only because of his role in a famous debate that took place in 1550 at the Colegio de San Gregorio in the city of Valladolid. Organized by King Charles V of Spain (r. 1516–58), the debate took up the question of morality of the Spanish conquest, colonization, and forced conversion to Christianity of the Indigenous peoples of the Americas. His opponent in the debate was Bartolomé de las Casas (see Appendix D), the justly renowned advocate in Spain for the humanity of the First Peoples. In the debate, as the selection below makes clear, Sepúlveda drew on Aristotle's idea that some human beings were "natural slaves," incapable of effective self-government and therefore in need of rule by fully rational, fully human beings like the Spanish colonizers. Sepúlveda also brought forward against the natives their practices of human sacrifice and cannibalism. Both sides claimed victory in the debate, though there was no officially declared winner. Most important, of course, was not who won the debate, but that, for the first time, Europeans found themselves considering the moral status of the colonization and forced conversion of Indigenous peoples.]

The man rules over the woman, the adult over the child, the father over his children. That is to say, the most powerful and most perfect rule over the weakest and most imperfect. This same relationship exists among men, there being some who by nature are masters and others who by nature are slaves. Those who surpass the rest in prudence and intelligence, although not in physical strength, are by nature the masters. On the other hand, those who are dim-witted and mentally lazy, although they may be physically strong enough to fulfill all the necessary tasks, are by nature slaves. It is just and useful that it be this way. We even see it sanctioned in divine law itself, for it is written in the Book of Proverbs: "He who is stupid will serve the wise man."[1] And

---

1 Proverbs 11:29.

so it is with the barbarous and inhumane peoples [the Indians] who have no civil life and peaceful customs. It will always be just and in conformity with natural law that such people submit to the rule of more cultured and humane princes and nations. Thanks to their virtues and the practical wisdom of their laws, the latter can destroy barbarism and educate these [inferior] people to a more humane and virtuous life. And if the latter reject such rule, it can be imposed upon them by force of arms. Such a war will be just according to natural law....

Now compare these natural qualities of judgment, talent, magnanimity, temperance, humanity, and religion [of the Spanish] with those of these pitiful men [the Indians], in whom you will scarcely find any vestiges of humanness. These people possess neither science nor even an alphabet, nor do they preserve any monuments of their history except for some obscure and vague reminiscences depicted in certain paintings, nor do they have written laws, but barbarous institutions and customs. In regard to their virtues, how much restraint or gentleness are you to expect of men who are devoted to all kinds of intemperate acts and abominable lewdness, including the eating of human flesh? And you must realize that prior to the arrival of the Christians, they did not live in that peaceful kingdom of Saturn [the Golden Age] that the poets imagine, but on the contrary they made war against one another continually and fiercely, with such fury that victory was of no meaning if they did not satiate their monstrous hunger with the flesh of their enemies.... These Indians are so cowardly and timid that they could scarcely resist the mere presence of our soldiers. Many times thousands upon thousands of them scattered, fleeing like women before a very few Spaniards, who amounted to fewer than a hundred....

In regard to those [the Aztecs] who inhabit New Spain and the province of Mexico, I have already said that they consider themselves the most civilized people [in the New World]. They boast of their political and social institutions, because they have rationally planned cities and nonhereditary kings who are elected by popular suffrage, and they carry on commerce among themselves in the manner of civilized people. But ... I dissent from such an opinion. On the contrary, in those same institutions there is proof of the coarseness, barbarism, and innate servility of these men. Natural necessity encourages the building of houses, some rational manner of life, and some sort of commerce. Such an argument merely proves that they are neither bears nor monkeys and that they are not totally irrational.

But on the other hand, they have established their commonwealth in such a manner that no one individually owns anything, neither a house nor a field that one may dispose of or leave to his heirs in his will, because everything is controlled by their lords, who are incorrectly called kings. They lived more at the mercy of their king's will than of their own. They are the slaves of his will and caprice, and they are not the masters of their fate. The fact that this condition is not the result of coercion but is voluntary and spontaneous is a certain sign of the servile and base spirit of these barbarians. They had distributed their fields and farms in such a way that one third belonged to the king, another third belonged to the religious cult, and only a third part was reserved for the benefit of everyone; but all of this they did in such a way that they themselves cultivated the royal and religious lands. They lived as servants of the king and at his mercy, paying extremely large tributes. When a father died, all his inheritance, if the king did not decide otherwise, passed in its entirety to the oldest son, with the result that many of the younger sons would either die of starvation or subject themselves to an even more rigorous servitude. They would turn to the petty kings for help and would ask them for a field on the condition that they not only pay feudal tribute but also promise themselves as slave labor when it was necessary. And if this kind of servitude and barbaric commonwealth had not been suitable to their temperament and nature, it would have been easy for them to take advantage of the death of a king, since the monarchy was not hereditary, in order to establish a state that was freer and more favorable to their interests. Their failure to do so confirms that they were born for servitude and not for the civil and liberal life....

Until now we have not mentioned their impious religion and their abominable sacrifices, in which they worship the Devil as God, to whom they thought of offering no better tribute than human hearts.... Interpreting their religion in an ignorant and barbarous manner, they sacrificed human victims by removing the hearts from the chests. They placed these hearts on their abominable altars. With this ritual they believed that they had appeased their gods. They also ate the flesh of the sacrificed men....

War against these barbarians can be justified not only on the basis of their paganism but even more so because of their abominable licentiousness, their prodigious sacrifice of human victims, the extreme harm that they inflicted on innocent persons, their horrible banquets of human flesh, and the impious cult of their idols. Since the evangelical law of the New Testament is more perfect and more gentle than the Mosaic law of the Old Testament (for the latter was a law of fear and the former is a law of grace, gentleness, and clemency), so also [since the birth of Christ] wars are now waged with more mercy and clemency. Their purpose is not so much to punish as to correct evils. What is more appropriate and beneficial for these barbarians than to become subject to the rule of those whose wisdom, virtue, and religion have converted them from barbarians into civilized men (insofar as they are capable of becoming so), from being torpid and licentious to becoming upright and moral, from being impious servants of the Devil to becoming believers in the true God? They have already begun to receive the Christian religion, thanks to the prudent diligence of the Emperor Charles, an excellent and religious prince. They have already been provided with teachers learned in both the sciences and letters and, what is more important, with teachers of religion and good customs.

# APPENDIX D: FROM BARTOLOMÉ DE LAS CASAS, *A SHORT ACCOUNT OF THE DESTRUCTION OF THE INDIES* (1552)

[Bartolomé de las Casas (1484–1566) was the most important and influential critic of the Spanish campaign of conquest, exploitation, and cultural genocide against the Indigenous peoples of Latin and South America.

De las Casas did not start out as an opponent of the Spanish conquest. In 1502, as an eighteen-year-old, he emigrated with his father to Hispaniola, an island in the Caribbean. The young man became a landowner and slave-owner. He took part with his fellow Spanish colonists in slave raids against the native populations and in the exploitation of the land and the people. He started to change his mind in 1510 when he was ordained as a priest and when he was confronted by a group of Dominican friars who denounced the cruelty of the Spanish. Over the next several years, he turned away from the inhumanity of colonialism and joined forces with what became an internal, Spanish opposition to the Spanish campaign of enslavement, exploitation, and murder. From 1514 onwards, he devoted his life to an attempt to civilize his countrymen's relationship with the Americas. He worked tirelessly, and with some success, to persuade the Spanish monarchy to implement governmental and juridical supervision of the conquistadors and colonists. Although he was dedicated throughout his life to the conversion of the natives to Christianity, he did help to convince the Pope to declare against the European program of forced conversion. The natives were rational beings, he said, who had to be converted to Christianity by rational and loving argument.

In 1550 in Valladolid in northern Spain, he faced off against Juan Ginés de Sepúlveda (see Appendix C) in a path-making debate concerning the morality of the Spanish treatment of the natives, with de Sepúlveda drawing on Aristotle to argue that the natives were "natural slaves" who could not function without their Spanish masters, and de las Casas arguing for the natives' humanity, rationality, and dignity—essential characteristics that they shared with the Spanish.

Among his many writings, *A Short Account of the Destruction of the Indies* (written in 1542, published in 1552) is a shocking account of the torture and murder of the Indigenous peoples. It was translated into many different languages. It helped promulgate the so-called "Black Legend," which characterized the Spanish as violent, greedy, and unchristian, and it contributed to the Christian reform of Spanish law and policy in the Americas. An extract from the *Short Account* is provided below, taken from one of the early modern English translations, where it appeared as part of the work *Popery truly Displayed in its Bloody Colours* by Thomas Dawson (1689).]

## OF THE ISLAND HISPANIOLA.

In this Isle, which, as we have said, the Spaniards first attempted, the bloody slaughter and destruction of men first began: for they violently forced away women and children to make them slaves, and ill-treated them, consuming and wasting their food, which they had purchased with great sweat, toil, and yet remained dissatisfied too, which every-one according to his strength and ability, and that was very inconsiderable or they provided no other food than what was absolutely necessary to support nature without superfluity, freely bestowed on them, and one individual *Spaniard* consumed more victuals in one day, than would serve to maintain three families a month, every one consisting of ten persons. Now being oppressed by such evil usage, and afflicted with such great torments and violent entertainment they began to understand that such men as those had not their mission from heaven; and therefore some of them concealed their provisions and others to their wives and children in lurking holes, but some, to avoid the obdurate and dreadful temper of such a nation, sought their refuge on the craggy tops of mountains; for the Spaniards did not only entertain them with cuffs, blows, and wicked cudgelling, but laid violent hands also on the governors of cities; and this arrived at length to that height of temerity and impudence, that a certain captain was so audacious as abuse the consort of the most puissant king of the whole Isle. From which time they began to consider by what ways and means they might expel the Spaniards out of their country, and immediately took up arms. But, good God, what arms, do you imagine? Namely such, both offensive and defensive, as resemble reeds wherewith boys sport with one another, more than manly arms and weapons.

Which the Spaniards no sooner perceived, but they, mounted on generous steeds, well weaponed with lances and swords, begin to exercise their bloody butcheries and stratagems, and overrunning their cities and towns, spared no age, or sex, nay not so much as women with child, but ripping up their bellies, tore them alive in pieces. They laid wagers among themselves, who should with a sword at one blow cut, or divide a man in two; or which of them should decollate or behead a man, with the greatest dexterity; nay farther, which should sheath his sword in the bowels of a man with the quickest dispatch and expedition.

They snatched young babes from the mothers' breasts, and then dashed out the brains of those innocents against the rocks; others they cast into rivers scoffing and jeering them, and called upon their bodies when falling with derision, the true testimony of their cruelty, to come to them, and inhumanely exposing others to their merciless swords, together with the mothers that gave them Life.

They erected certain gibbets, large, but low made, so that their feet almost reached the ground, every one of which was so ordered as to bear thirteen Persons in honour and reverence (as they said blasphemously) of our redeemer and his twelve apostles, under which they made a fire to burn them to ashes whilst hanging on them: but those they intended to preserve alive, they dismissed, their hands half cut, and still hanging by the skin, to carry their letters missive to those that fly from us and lie skulking on the mountains, as an approbation of their flight.

The lords and persons of noble extract were usually exposed to this kind of death; they ordered gridirons to be placed and supported with wooden forks, and putting a small fire under them, these miserable wretches by degrees and with loud shrieks and exquisite torments, at last expired.

I once saw four or five of their most powerful lords laid on these gridirons, and thereon roasted, and not far off, two or three more overspread with the same commodity, man's flesh; but the shrill clamours which were heard there being offensive to the captain, by hindering his repose, he commanded them to be strangled with a halter. The executioner (whose name and parents at *Seville* are not unknown to me) prohibited the doing of it; but stopped gags into their mouths to prevent the hearing of the noise (he himself making the fire) till that they died, when they had been roasted as long as he thought convenient. I was an eyewitness of these and an innumerable number of other cruelties: and because all men, who could lay hold of the opportunity, sought out lurking holes in the mountains, to avoid as dangerous rocks so brutish and barbarous a people, strangers to all goodness, and the extirpators and adversaries of men, they bred up such fierce hunting dogs as would devour an *Indian* like a hog, at first sight in less than a moment: now such kind of slaughters and cruelties as these were committed by the curs, and if at any time it happened, (which was rarely) that the *Indians* irritated upon a just account destroyed or took away the life of any *Spaniard*, they promulgated and proclaimed this law among them, that one hundred *Indians* should die for every individual *Spaniard* that should be slain....

### Of New Spain.

New *Spain* was discovered *Anno Domini.* 1517. And in the detection there was no first or second attempt, but all were exposed to slaughter. The year ensuing those Spaniards (who style themselves Christians) came thither to rob, kill and slay, though they pretend they undertook this voyage to people the country. From this year to the present, *viz.* 1542. the injustice, violence and tyranny of the Spaniards came to the highest degree of extremity: for they had shook hands with and bid adieu to all fear of God and the king, unmindful of themselves in this sad and deplorable condition, for the destructions, cruelties, butcheries, devastations, the demolishing of cities, depredations, *&c.* which they perpetrated in so many and such ample kingdoms, are such and so great, and strike the minds of men with so great horror, that all we have related before are inconsiderable comparatively to those which have been acted from the year 1518 to 1542, and to this very month of September that we now live to see the most heavy, grievous and detestable things are committed, that the rule we laid down before as a maxim might be indisputably verified, to wit, that from the beginning they ran headlong from bad to worse, and were overcome in their diabolical acts and wickedness only by themselves.

Thus from the first entrance of the Spaniards into New Spain, which happened on the 18th day of April in the said month of the year 1518, to 1530, the space of ten whole years, there was no end or period put to the destruction and slaughters committed by the merciless hands of the sanguinary and blood-thirsty Spaniard in the continent, or space of 450 Miles round about Mexico, and the adjacent or neighbouring parts, which might contain four or five spacious kingdoms, that neither for magnitude or fertility would give Spain herself the pre-eminence. This entire region was more populous than Toledo, Seville, Valladolid, Zaragoza, and Faenza;[1] and there is not at this day in all of them so many people, nor when they flourished in their greatest height and splendour was there such a number, as inhabited that region, which embraced in its circumference, four hundred and eighty miles. Within these twelve years the Spaniards have destroyed in the said continent, by spears, fire and sword, computing men, women, youth, and children above four millions of people in these their acquests or conquests (for under that word they mask their cruel actions) or rather those of the Turk himself,[2] which are reported of them, tending to the ruin of the Catholic cause, together with their invasions and unjust wars, contrary to and condemned by divine as well as human laws; nor are they reckoned in this number who perished by their more than Egyptian bondage and usual oppressions.

There is no tongue, art, or human knowledge can recite the horrid impieties, which these capital enemies to government and all mankind have been guilty of at several times and in several nations; nor can the circumstantial aggravations of some of their wicked acts be unfolded or displayed by any manner of industry, time or writing, but yet I will say somewhat of every individual particular thing, which this protestation and oath, that I conceive I am not able to comprehend one of a thousand.

### *Of* New Spain *in particular.*

Among other slaughters this also they perpetrated in the most spacious city of *Cholula*, which consisted of thirty thousand families; all the chief rulers of that region and neighbouring places, but first the priests with their high priest going to meet the Spaniards in pomp and state, and to the end they might give them a more reverential and honourable reception appointed them to be in the middle of the solemnity, that so being entertained in the apartments of the most powerful and principal noblemen, they might be lodged in the city. The Spaniards presently consult about their slaughter or castigation (as they term it)

---

1   Cities in Spain.
2   The Ottoman Empire.

that they might fill every corner of this region by their cruelties and wicked deeds with terror and consternation; for in all the countries that they came they took this course, that immediately at their first arrival they committed some notorious butcheries, which made those Innocent sheep tremble for fear. To this purpose therefore they sent to the governors and nobles of the cities, and all places subject unto them, together with their supreme lord, that they should appear before them, and no sooner did they attend in expectation of some capitulation or discourse with the Spanish commander, but they were presently seized upon and detained prisoners before anyone could advertise or give them notice of their captivity. They demanded of them six thousand Indians to drudge for them in the carriage of their bag and baggage; and as soon as they came the Spaniards clapped them into the yards belonging to their houses and there enclosed them all. It was a thing worthy of pity and compassion to behold this wretched people in what a condition they were when they prepared themselves to receive the burdens laid on them by the Spaniards. They came to them naked, their privities only veiled, their shoulders loaded with food; only covered with a net, they laid themselves quietly on the ground, and shrinking in their bodies like poor wretches, exposed themselves to their swords: thus being all gathered together in their yards, some of the Spaniards armed held the doors to drive them away if attempting to approach, and others with lances and swords butcher these innocents so that not one of them escaped, but two or three days after some of them, who hid themselves among the dead bodies, being all over besprinkled with blood and gore, presented themselves to the Spaniards, imploring their mercy and the prolongation of their lives with tears in their eyes and all imaginable submission, yet they, not in the least moved with pity or compassion, tore them in pieces: but all the chief governors who were above 100 in number, were kept bound, whom the captain commanded to be affixed to posts and burnt; yet the king of the whole country escaped, and betook himself with a train of 30 or 40 gentlemen, to a temple (called in their tongue *Quu*) which he made use of as a castle or place of defence, and there defended himself a great part of the day, but the Spaniards who suffer none to escape out of their clutches, especially soldiers, setting fire to the temple, burnt all those that were there enclosed, who break out into these dying words and exclamations. O profligate men, what injury have we done you to occasion our death! Go, go to Mexico, where our supreme Lord *Montencuma* will revenge our cause upon your persons. And it's reported, while the Spaniards were engaged in this tragedy destroying six or seven thousand men, that their commander with great rejoicing sang this following air;

*Mira Nero de* Tarpeia, Roma *como se ardia,*
*Gritos de ninos y viejo, y el de nadase dolia.*

*From the* Tarpeian *still Nero espies*
Rome *all in flames with unrelenting eyes,*
*And hears of young and old the dreadful cries.*[1]

They also committed a very great butchery in the city *Tepeara*, which was larger and better stored with houses than the former; and here they massacred an incredible number with the point of the sword.

---

1    "Mira Nero de Tarpeia" is derived from a Spanish romance of the same name. This is an example of a process called "confractation," by which sixteenth-century Brazilian dramatists would include musical numbers in their works derived from Iberian romances. See Neto.

# APPENDIX E: FROM MICHEL DE MONTAIGNE, "OF THE CANNIBALS" (1578–80)

[Michel de Montaigne (1533–92) remains one of the most influential writers of the sixteenth century and a pioneer of the essay form. First published in Paris in the 1580s, his book of essays covers a myriad of aspects of the human condition, from good manners and conversation, to feelings, vices, and more existential queries. Montaigne's essays were a lifelong project which he continuously added to and revised. His work was widely popular and circulated across early modern Europe by the time Shakespeare began writing. He most likely read Montaigne in John Florio's English translation (1603); we have modernized some of Florio's spellings in this selection.

"Of the Cannibals," which describes the customs and practices of the Tupinambá people in Brazil and relativizes their so-called barbarism in contrast with the rampant cruelty displayed in sixteenth-century Europe, is an important source for *The Tempest*. The essay offers an empathetic account of the Natives' way of life, with Montaigne's trademark wit most evident in his tongue-in-cheek criticism of colonialism and ethnocentric philosophy. While the essay offers interesting parallels with Caliban and with the play's exploration of servitude and imperialism, Montaigne's influence is most notable in Gonzalo's commonwealth speech (2.1.39–59, TLN 824–846), which draws closely from the essay's envisioning of a utopia.]

At what time King Pyrrhus came into Italy, after he had survived the marshalling of the army, which the Romans sent against him: "I know not," said he, "what barbarous men these are" (for so were the Grecians wont to call all strange nations) "but the disposition of this army, which I see, is nothing barbarous." So said the Grecians of that which Flaminius[1] sent into their country: And Philip[2] viewing from a tower the order and distribution of the Roman camp, in his kingdom under Publius Sulpicius Galba.[3] See how a man ought to take heed,

---

1 Titus Quinctius Flamininus (c. 228–174 BCE) was a Roman general who defeated King Philip V of Macedon (r. 221–179 BCE) and conquered Greece in 198 BCE.
2 Philip V of Macedon.
3 Roman officer and politician (fl. late third to early second century BCE).

lest he overweeningly follow vulgar opinions, which should be measured by the rule of reason, and not by the common report.

I have had long time dwelling with me a man, who for the space of 10 or 12 years had dwelt in that other world which in our age was lately discovered in those parts where Villegaignon[1] first landed, and surnamed Antartike France.[2] This discovery of so infinite and vast a country, seemed worth great consideration. I know not whether I can warrant myself, that some other be not discovered hereafter, sithence so many worthy men, and better learned than we are, have so many ages been deceived in this. I fear me our eyes be greater than our bellies, and that we have more curiosity than capacity. We embrace all, but we fasten nothing but wind.

Plato brings in Solon to report that he had learned of the priests of the city of Saïs in Egypt, that whilom, and before the general Deluge, there was a great land called Atlantis, situated at the mouth of the strait of Gibraltar, which contained more firm land than Africa and Asia together. And that the kings of that country did not only possess that land, but had so far entered into the main land, that of the breadth of Africa, they held as far as Egypt; and of Europe's length, as far as Tuscany: and that they undertook to invade Asia, and to subdue all the nations that compass the Mediterranean Sea, to the gulf of Mare-Maggiore [the Black Sea], and to that end they traversed all Spain, France and Italie, so far as Greece, where the Athenians made head against them; but that a while after, both the Athenians themselves, and that great land, were swallowed up by the Deluge. It is very likely this extreme ruin of waters wrought strange alterations in the habitations of the earth; as some hold that the sea hath divided Sicily from Italy,

> *Hæc loca vi quandam, et vasta convulsa ruina*
> *Dissiluisse ferunt, cum protinus utraque tellus*
> *Vna foret. —*

---

1    Nicolas Durand de Villegaignon (1510–71) was a French naval officer who tried to establish a French colony in Brazil but was defeated and eventually driven out by the Portuguese in 1558.
2    Antarctic France was to be the name of the colony that Villegaignon tried building in present-day Rio de Janeiro on behalf of Henry II.

Then say, sometimes this land by that forsaken,
And that by this, we are split, and ruin-shaken,
Whereas till then both lands as one were taken.
        Virgil Aeneid. iii 414, 416.

Cyprus from Syria, the land of Negroponto from the main land of Boeotia, and in other places joined lands that were sundried by the sea, filling with mud and sand the channels between them.

> —— *sterilisque diu palus aptaque remis*
> *Vicinas urbes alit, et grave sentit aratrum.*

The fenne long barren, to be row'd in, now
Both feeds the neighbor towns, and feels the plow.
        Horatius Art of Poetry Poet. 65.

But there is no great appearance the said land should be the new world we have lately discovered; for it well-nigh touched Spain, and it were an incredible effect of inundation to have removed the same more than twelve hundred leagues, as we see it is. Besides, our modern navigations have now almost discovered that it is not an land, but rather firm land, and a continent, with the East Indies on one side, and the countries lying under the two poles on the other; from which if it be divided, it is with so narrow a strait and interval, that it no way deserved to be named an land: For, it seemed there are certain motions in these vast bodies, some natural, and other some febricitant, as well as in ours. When I consider the impression my river of Dordogne[1] worked in my time, toward the right shore of her descent, and how much it hath gained in 20 years, and how many foundations of divers houses it hath overwhelmed and violently carried away; I confess it to be an extraordinary agitation: for, should it always keep one course, or had it ever kept the same, the figure of the world had ere this been overthrown: but they are subject to changes and alterations. Sometimes they overflow and spread themselves on one side, sometimes on another; and other times they contain themselves in their natural beds or channels: I speak not of sudden inundations, whereof we now treat the causes. In Medoc

---

1    A river in the south of France.

along the seacoast, my brother the Lord of Arsacke, may see a town of his buried under the sands, which the sea cast up before it: The tops of some buildings are yet to be discerned. His rents and domaines have been changed into barren pastures. The inhabitants thereabouts affirm, that some years since, the sea encroached so much upon them, that they have lost four leagues[1] of firm land: These sands are her fore-runners. And we see great hillocks of gravel moving, which march half a league before it, and usurp on the firm land.

The other testimony of antiquity, to which some will refer this discovery, is in Aristotle (if at least that little book of unheard-of wonders be his) where he reported that certain Carthaginians having sailed athwart the Atlantic Sea, without the strait of Gibraltar, after long time, they at last discovered a great fertile land, all replenished with goodly woods, and watered with great and deep rivers, far distant from all land, and that both they and others, allured by the goodness and fertility of the same, went thither with their wives, children, and household, and there began to inhabit and settle themselves. The lords of Carthage seeing their country by little and little to be dispeopled, made a law and express inhibition, that upon pain of death no more men should go thither, and banished all that were gone thither to dwell, fearing (as they said) that in success of time, they would so multiply as they might one day supplant them, and overthrow their own estate. This narration of Aristotle hath no reference unto our new-found countries.

This servant I had, was a simple and rough-hewn fellow: a condition fit to yield a true testimony. For, subtle people may indeed mark more curiously, and observe things more exactly, but they amplify and glose[2] them: and the better to persuade, and make their interpretations of more validity, they cannot choose but somewhat alter the story. They never represent things truly, but fashion and make them according to the visage they saw them in; and to purchase credit to their judgment, and draw you on to believe them, they commonly adorn, enlarge, yea, and hyperbolize the matter. Wherein is required either a most sincere reporter, or a man so simple, that he may have no invention to build upon, and to give a true likelihood unto false devices, and be not wedded to his own will. Such a one was my man; who besides his own report,

---

1    A unit of distance (from the French *lieue*) existing in several variants, from about 3.25 to about 4.68 km.

2    Give them a deceptively attractive appearance.

hath many times showed me divers mariners and merchants, whom he had known in that voyage. So am I pleased with his information, that I never enquire what cosmographers[1] say of it.

We had need of topographers to make us particular narrations of the places they have been in. For some of them, if they have the advantage of us, that they have seen Palestine, will challenge a privilege, to tell us news of all the world besides. I would have every man write what he knows, and no more: not only in that, but in all other subjects. For one may have particular knowledge of the nature of one river, and experience of the quality of one fountain, that in other things knows no more than another man: who nevertheless to publish this little scantling,[2] will undertake to write of all the physics. From which vice proceed divers great inconveniences.

Now to return to my purpose I find (as far as I have been informed) there is nothing in that nation that is either barbarous or savage, unless men call that barbarism which is not common to them. As indeed, we have no other aim of truth and reason, than the example and idea of the opinions and customs of the country we live in. There is ever perfect religion, perfect policy, perfect and complete use of all things. They are even savage, as we call those fruits wild which nature of herself and of her ordinary progress hath produced: whereas indeed, they are those which ourselves have altered by our artificial devices, and diverted from their common order, we should rather term savage. In those are the true and most profitable virtues, and natural properties most lively and vigorous, which in these we have bastardized, adapting them to the pleasure of our corrupted taste. And if notwithstanding, in divers fruits of those countries that were never tilled, we shall find that in respect of ours they are most excellent, and as delicate unto our taste; there is no reason, art should gain the point of honor of our great and puissant mother Nature. We have so much by our inventions surcharged the beauties and riches of her works, that we have altogether over chocked[3] her: yet wherever her purity shined, she makes our vain and frivolous enterprises wonderfully ashamed.

---

1    Those who study cosmography, the science that maps the general features of the cosmos or universe.
2    A small sample or amount of something.
3    Smothered.

*Et veniunt haderæ sponte sua melius,*
*Surgit et in solis formsior arbutus antris.*
*Et volucres nulla dulcius arte canunt.*—

Ivies spring better of their owne accord,
Unhaunted spots much fairer trees afford.
Birds by no art much sweeter notes record.
Propert. i El. ii. 10.

All our endeavor or wit cannot so much as reach to represent the
nest of the least birdlet, its contexture, beauty, profit and use, no nor
the web of a seely[1] spider. All things (said Plato) are produced either by
nature, by fortune, or by art. The greatest and fairest by one or other
of the two first, the least and imperfect by the last.

Those nations seem therefore so barbarous unto me, because
they have received very little fashion from human wit, and are yet near
their original naturalitie. The laws of nature do yet command them
which are but little bastardized by ours, and that with such purity, as
I am sometimes grieved the knowledge of it came no sooner to light,
at what time there were men that better than we could have judged
of it. I am sorry Lycurgus[2] and Plato had it not: for me seemed that
what in those nations we see by experience, doth not only exceed all
the pictures wherewith licentious Poesy hath proudly embellished the
golden age, and all her quaint inventions to faine[3] a happy condition
of man, but also the conception and desire of philosophy. They could
not imagine a genuitie[4] so pure and simple as we see it by experience;
nor ever believe our society might be maintained with so little art and
human combination. It is a nation, would I answer Plato, that hath
no kind of traffic, no knowledge of letters, no intelligence of numbers,
no name of magistrate, nor of politic superiority; no use of service, of
riches or of poverty; no contracts, no successions, no partitions, no
occupation but idle; no respect of kindred, but common, no apparel but
natural, no manuring of lands, no use of wine, corn, or mettle. The very

---

1   Puny.
2   Legendary Greek figure (c. 820 BCE) reputed to have brought military and community reforms to Sparta.
3   Archaic spelling of feign.
4   Naturalness.

words that import lying, falsehood, treason, dissimulations, covetous-
ness, envy, detraction, and pardon, were never heard of amongst them.
How dissonant would he find his imaginary commonwealth from this
perfection?

*Hos natura modos primum dedit.*

Nature at first uprise,
these manners did devise.[1]

Furthermore, they live in a country of so exceeding pleasant and
temperate situation, that as my testimonies have told me, it is very rare
to see a sick body amongst them; and they have further assured me, they
never saw any man there either shaking with the palsy, toothless, with
eyes dropping, or crooked and stooping through age. They are seated
along the sea-coast, encompassed toward the land with huge and steep
mountains, having between both, a hundred leagues or thereabout of
open and champaine[2] ground. They have great abundance of fish and
flesh, that have no resemblance at all with ours, and eat them without
any sauces or skill of cookery, but plain boiled or broiled. The first man
that brought a horse thither, although he had in many other voyages
conversed with them, bred so great a horror in the land, that before they
could take notice of him, they slew him with arrows. Their buildings
are very long, and able to contain two or three hundred souls, covered
with barks of great trees, fastened in the ground at one end, interlaced
and joined close together by the tops, after the manner of some of our
granges;[3] the covering whereof hangs down to the ground, and steadied
them as a flank. They have a kind of wood so hard, that riveting and
cleaving the same, they make blades, swords, and gridirons to broil
their meat with. Their beds are of a kind of cotton cloth, fastened to
the house roof, as our ship-cabins: every one hath his several couch for
the women lie from their husbands.

---

1    Montaigne does not provide the reference in his essay: the quotation is from
Virgil's *Georgics* (II, 20).
2    Unforested or flat.
3    Barns.

They rise with the sun, and feed for all day, as soon as they are up: and make no more meals after that. They drink not at meal, as Suidas[1] reported, of some other people of the east, which drank after meals but drink many times a day, and are much given to pledge carouses. Their drink is made of a certain root, and of the color of our claret wines, which lasted but two or three days; they drink it warm. It hath somewhat a sharp taste, wholesome for the stomach, nothing heady, but laxative for such as are not used unto it, yet very pleasing to such as are accustomed unto it. Instead of bread, they use a certain white composition, like unto Corianders confected.[2] I have eaten some, the taste whereof is somewhat sweet and wallowish.[3] They spend the whole day in dancing. Their young men go a hunting after wild beasts with bows and arrows. Their women busy themselves there whilst with warming of their drink, which is their chiefest office. Some of their old men, in the morning before they go to eating, preach in common to all the household, walking from one end of the house to the other, repeating one self-same sentence many times, till he have ended his turn (for their buildings are a hundred paces in length) he commends but two things unto his auditory. First valor against their enemies, then lovingness unto their wives. They never miss (for their restraint) to put men in mind of this duty, that it is their wives which keep their drink lukewarm and well-seasoned. The form of their beds, cords, swords blades, and wooden bracelets, wherewith they cover their hand wrists, when they fight, and great canes open at one end, by the sound of which they keep time and cadence in their dancing, are in many places to be seen, and namely in mine own house. They are shaven all over, much more close and cleaner than wee are, with no other razors than of wood or stone. They believe their souls to be eternal, and those that have deserved well of their gods to be placed in that part of heaven where the sun rises, and the cursed toward the west in opposition.

They have certain prophets and priests which commonly abide in the mountains, and very seldom show themselves unto the people; but when they come down there is a great feast prepared, and a solemn

---

1 The Suidas (or Suda), named after its purported author, is a large tenth-century Byzantine encyclopedia of the ancient Mediterranean world, spanning nearly 30,000 entries.
2 Like preserved coriander.
3 Flat or insipid.

assembly of main townships together (each grange as I have described made a village, and they are about a French league one from another). The prophet speaks to the people in public, exhorting them to embrace virtue, and follow their duty. All their moral discipline contained but these two articles; first an undismayed resolution to war then an inviolable affection to their wives. He doth also prognosticate of things to come, and what success they shall hope for in their enterprises he neither swayed or dissuade them from war but if he chance to miss of his divination, and that it succeed otherwise than he foretold them, if he be taken, he is hewn in a thousand pieces, and condemned for a false prophet. And therefore he that hath once misreckoned himself is never seen again. Divination is the gift of God; the abusing whereof should be a punishable imposture. When the divines amongst the Scythians had foretold an untruth, they were couched along upon hurdles full of heath or brushwood, drawn by oxen, and so manacled hand and foot, burned to death. Those which manage matters subject to the conduct of man's sufficiency are excusable, although they show the utmost of their skill. But those that gull and cony-catch[1] us with the assurance of an extraordinary faculty, and which is beyond our knowledge, ought to be double punished; first because they perform not the effect of their promise, then for the rashness of their imposture and unadvised of their fraud.

They war against the nations that lie beyond their mountains, to which they go naked, having no other weapons than bows or wooden swords, sharp at one end as our broaches[2] are. It is an admirable thing to see the constant resolution of their combats, which never end but by effusion of blood and murder: for they know not what fear or routs[3] are. Every victor brings home the head of the enemy he hath slain as a trophy of his victory, and fastened the same at the entrance of his dwelling place. After they have long time used and entreated their prisoners well, and with all commodities they can devise, he that is the master of them; summoning a great assembly of his acquaintance; tied a cord to one of the prisoners arms, by the end whereof he holds him fast, with some distance from him, for fear he might offend him, and gives the

---

1 Deceive or cheat.
2 This could refer to a variety of pointed or tapered tools (such as spikes for roasting meat) or cutting tools.
3 A state of wild confusion or disorderly retreat.

other arm, bound in like manner, to the dearest friend he hath, and both in the presence of all the assembly kill him with swords: which done, they roast and then eat him in common, and send some slices of him to such of their friends as are absent. It is not, as some imagine, to nourish themselves with it (as anciently the Scythians want to do), but to represent an extreme and inexpiable revenge. Which we prove thus; some of them perceiving the Portugals, who had confederated themselves with their adversaries, to use another kind of death when they took them prisoners; which was, to bury them up to the middle, and against the upper part of the body to shoot arrows, and then being almost dead, to hang them up; they supposed, that the people of the other world (as they who had sowed the knowledge of many vices amongst their neighbors, and were much more cunning in all kinds of evils and mischief than they) undertook not this manner of revenge without cause, and that consequently it was more smart and cruel than theirs, and thereupon began to leave their old fashion to follow this.

I am not sorry we note the barbarous horror of such an action, but grieved, that prying so narrowly into their faults we are so blinded in ours. I think there is more barbarism in eating men alive, than to feed upon them being dead; to mangle by tortures and torments a body full of lively sense, to roast him in pieces, and to make dogs and swine to gnaw and tear him in mammocks[1] (as we have not only read, but seen very lately, yea and in our own memory, not amongst ancient enemies, but our neighbors and fellow-citizens; and which is worse, under pretence of piety and religion[2]) than to roast and eat him after he is dead. Chrysippus and Zeno, arch-pillars of the Stoicke sect,[3] have supposed that it was no hurt at all in time of need, and to what end so ever, to make use of our carrion bodies, and to feed upon them, as did our forefathers, who being besieged by Cæsar in the city of Alexia, resolved to sustain the famine of the siege, with the bodies of old men, women, and other persons unserviceable and unfit to fight.

---

1   Tear into scraps or small pieces.
2   Montaigne seems to be referencing the Inquisition here.
3   Stoicism was a school of Greek philosophy build around a logical understanding of personal ethics and in relation to the natural world. Zeno of Citium (c. 334–c. 262 BCE) is held to be the founder of the Stoic school of philosophy. Chrysippus of Soli (c. 279–c. 206 BCE) later expanded upon Zeno's doctrines and became known as the second founder of the Stoic movement.

*Vascones (fama est) alimentis talibus usi*
*Produxere ammas.—*

Gascoynes (as fame reports)
Liv'd with meats of such sortes.
                    Juven. Sat. xv. 93.

And physicians fear not, in all kinds of compositions available to our health, to make use of it, be it for outward or inward applications. But there was never any opinion found so unnatural and immodest, that would excuse treason, treachery, disloyalty, tyranny, cruelty, and such like, which are our ordinary faults.

We may then well call them barbarous, in regard to reasons rules, but not in respect of us that exceed them in all kinds of barbarism. Their wares are noble and generous and have as much excuse and beauty as this humane infirmity may admit: they aim at naught so much, and have no other foundation amongst them, but the mere jealousy of virtue. They contend not for the gaining of new lands; for to this day they yet enjoy that natural ubertie [*sic*] and fruitfulness, which without laboring toil, doth in such plenteous abundance furnish them with all necessary things, that they need not enlarge their limits. They are yet in that happy estate as they desire no more than what their natural necessities direct them: whatsoever is beyond it, is to them superfluous. Those that are much about one age, do generally enter ... call one another brethren, and such as are younger they call children, and the aged are esteemed as fathers to all the rest. These leave this full possession of goods in common, and without division to their heirs, without other claim or title but that which nature doth plainly impart unto all creatures, even as she brings them into the world.

If their neighbors chance to come over the mountains to assail or invade them, and that they get the victory over them, the victors' conquest is glory, and the advantage to be and remain superior in valor and virtue: else have they nothing to do with the goods and spoils of the vanquished, and so return into their country, where they neither want any necessary thing, nor lack this great portion, to know how to enjoy their condition happily, and are contented with what nature afforded them. So do these when their turn comes. They require no other ransom of their prisoners, but an acknowledgement and confession that they are vanquished. And in a whole age, a man shall not find one that doth not rather embrace death, than either by word or countenance remissibly to yield one jot of an invincible courage. There is none seen that would not rather be slain and devoured, than sue for life, or show any fear. They use their prisoners with all liberty, that they may so much the more hold their lives dear and precious, and commonly entertain them with threats of future death, with the torments they shall endure, with the preparations intended for that purpose, with mangling and slicing of their members, and with the feast that shall be kept at their charge. All which is done, to wrest some remiss, and exact some faint yielding speech of submission from them, or to possess them with a desire to escape or run away; that so they may have the advantage to have daunted and made them afraid, and to have forced their constancy. For certainly true victory consisted in that only point.

> —————— *Victoria nulla est*
> *Quam quæ confessos animo quoque subjugat hostes.*

> No conquest such, as to suppresse
> Foes hearts, the conquest to confesse.
> — Claud. vi. Cons. Hon. Pan. 245.

[...]

But to return to our history, these prisoners, howsoever they are dealt withal, are so far from yielding, that contrariwise during two or three months that they are kept, they ever carry a cheerful countenance, and urge their keepers to hasten their trial, they outrageously dote and injure them. They upbraid them with their cowardliness, and with the number of battles they have lost again theirs. I have a song made by a prisoner, wherein is this clause, let them boldly come altogether, and flock in multitudes, to feed on him; for with him they shall feed upon their fathers and grandfathers, that heretofore have served his body for food and nourishment: "these muscles," said he, "this flesh, and these veins, are your own; fond men as you are, know you not that the substance of your forefathers' limbs is yet tied unto ours? Taste them well for in them shall you find the relish of your own flesh": an invention, that hath no show of barbarism. Those that paint them dying, and that represent this action, when they are put to execution, delineate the prisoners spitting in their executioners' faces, and making mows at them. Verily, so long as breath is in their body they never cease to brave and defy them, both in speech and countenance. Surely in respect of us these are very savage men: for either they must be so in good sooth or we must be so indeed; there is a wondrous difference between their form and ours.

Their men have many wives, and by how much more they are reputed valiant so much the greater is their number. The manner and beauty of their marriages is wondrous strange and remarkable: for, the same jealousy our wives have to keep us from the love and affection of other women, the same have theirs to procure it. Being more careful for their husbands' honor and content than of any thing else, they endeavor and apply all their industry to have as many rivals as possibly they can, forasmuch as it is a testimony of their husbands' virtue. Our women would count it a wonder, but it is not so: it is virtue properly matrimonial, but of the highest kind. And in the Bible, Leah, Rachel, Sarah, and Jacob's wives brought their fairest maiden servants into their husband's beds. And Livia seconded the lustful appetites of Augustus to her great prejudice. And Stratonica, the wife of King Deiotarus did not only bring the most beauteous chambermaid that served her to her husband's bed, but very carefully brought up the children he begot on her, and by all possible means aided and furthered them to succeed in their father's royalty. And least a man should think that all this is done by a simple and servile or awful duty unto their custom, and by the impression of their ancient custom's authority, without discourse or judgment, and because they are so blockish and dull-spirited, that they can take no other resolution, it is not amiss we allege some evidence of their sufficiency. Besides what I have said of one of their warlike songs, I have another amorous canzonet,[1] which begins in this sense: "Adder stay, stay good adder, that my sister may by the pattern of thy parti-colored coat draw the fashion and work of a rich lace, for me to give unto my love; so may thy beauty, thy nimbleness or disposition be ever preferred before all other serpents." The first couplet is the burthen[2] of the song. I am so conversant with poesy that I may judge this invention hath no

---

1    A light song resembling a madrigal.
2    Refrain or chorus.

barbarism at all in it, but is altogether anacreontic.[1] Their language is a kind of pleasant speech, and hath a pleasing sound, and some affinity with the Greek terminations.

Three of that nation, ignorant how dear the knowledge of our corruptions will one day cost their repose, security, and happiness, and how their ruin shall proceed from this commerce, which I imagine is already well advanced (miserable as they are to have suffered themselves to be so cozened by a desire of new-fangled novelties, and to have quit the calmness of their climate to come and see ours), were at Rouen in the time of our late King Charles the ninth,[2] who talked with them a great while. They were shown our fashions, our pomp, and the form of a fair city; afterward some demanded their advice, and would needs know of them what things of note and admirable they had observed amongst us: they answered three things, the last of which I have forgotten, and am very sorry for it, the other two I yet remember. They said, "First they found it very strange that so many tall men with long beards, strong and well armed, as it were about the king's person (it is very likely they meant the Switzers of his guard) would submit themselves to obey a beardless child, and that we did not rather choose one amongst them to command the rest." Secondly (they have a manner of phrase whereby they call men but a moiety[3] one of another.) "They had perceived there were men amongst us full gorged with all sorts of commodities, and others which, hunger starved and bare with need and poverty, begged at their gates: and found it strange these moieties so needy could endure such an injustice, and that they took not the others by the throat, or set fire on their houses." I talked a good while with one of them, but I had so bad an interpreter, who did so ill apprehend my meaning, and who through his foolishnesses was so troubled to conceive my imaginations, that I could draw no great matter from him. Touching that point, wherein I demanded of him what good he received by the superiority he had amongst his countrymen (for he was a captain and our mariners called him king), he told me it was to march foremost in any charge of war: further, I asked him how many men did follow him, he showed me a distance of place, to signify they were as many as might be contained in so much round, which I guessed to be about four or five thousand

---

1   Resembling the style of the Greek lyric poet Anacreon (c. 582–c. 485 BCE).
2   Charles IX ruled France from 1560 until his death in 1574.
3   From the French *moitié*: they behold men as halves of one another.

men: moreover, demanded if when wars were ended, all his authority expired; he answered, that he had only this left him, which was, that when he went on progress, and visited the villages depending of him, the inhabitants prepared paths and highways athwart the hedges of their woods, for him to pass through at ease. All this is not very ill; but what of that? They wear no kind of breeches nor hosen.

# APPENDIX F: FROM WILLIAM STRACHEY, *A TRUE REPORTORY OF THE WRACKE* (1610)

[The writings of William Strachey (1572–1621) offer one of the first accounts of England's colonial efforts in North America. He is best known for his eyewitness account of the shipwreck of the colonial vessel *Sea Venture* in 1609, when he and other survivors ended up stranded on the island of Bermuda for the better part of a year after being blown off course by a hurricane. They eventually managed to construct two small ships and reach their intended destination in Virginia.

In 1610, Strachey wrote a detailed account of this ordeal in a letter addressed to an anonymous female reader (referred to in the text only as "Excellent Lady"). The letter was eventually published in 1625 by Samuel Purchas as part of his collection of travel stories, *Purchas his Pilgrimes*.

Strachey's letter, which is believed to have been widely circulated in manuscript prior to publication, is generally believed to be the key source for Shakespeare's play.]

> *A true repertory of the wrake, and redemption of Sir* Thomas Gates *Knight; upon, and from the Islands of the* Bermudas: *his coming to* Virginia, *and the state of that Colony then, and after, under the government of the Lord* La Warre, *July 15, 1610. Written by* William Strachey, *Esquire.*

> *A most dreadful Tempest (the manifold deaths whereof are here to the life described) their wrack on* Bermuda; *and the description of those Islands*

Excellent Lady, know that upon Friday late in the evening, we broke ground out of the Sound of Plymouth,[1] our whole fleet then consisting of seven good ships, and two pinnaces,[2] all which from the said second of June, unto the twenty-three of July, kept in friendly consort together, not a whole watch at any time, losing the sight each of other. Our course when we came about the height of between 26 and 27 degrees, we declined to the Northward ..., and found the wind to this course indeed as friendly, as in the judgment of all seamen, it is upon

---

1   Plymouth Sound (or The Sound) is a bay on the English Channel at Plymouth, in the south of England.
2   Light sailing ships.

a more direct line, and by Sir George Somers our admiral had been likewise in former time sailed, being a gentleman of approved assuredness, and ready knowledge in seafaring actions, having often carried commands, and chief charge in many ships royal of her Majesty's, and in sundry voyages made many defeats and attempts in the time of the Spaniards quarrelling with us, upon the Islands and Indies, etc. We had followed this course so long, as now we were within seven or eight days at the most, by Captain Newport's reckoning, of making Cape Henry upon the coast of Virginia: When on St. James his day, July 24, being Monday (preparing for no less all the black night before) the clouds gathering thick upon us, and the winds singing, and whistling most unusually, which made us to cast off our pinnace, towing the same until then astern, a dreadful storm and hideous began to blow from out the northeast, which swelling, and roaring as it were by fits, some hours with more violence than others, at length did beat all light from heaven; which like an hell of darkness turned black upon us, so much the more fuller of horror, as in such cases horror and fear use to overrun the troubled, and overmastered senses of all, which (taken up with amazement) the ears lay so sensible to the terrible cries, and murmurs of the winds, and distraction of our company, as who was most armed, and best prepared, was not a little shaken. For surely (noble Lady) as death comes not so sudden nor apparent, so he comes not so elvish and painful (to men especially even then in health and perfect habitudes of body) as at sea; who comes at no time so welcome, but our frailty (so weak is the hold of hope in miserable demonstrations of danger) it makes guilty of many contrary changes, and conflicts: for indeed death is accompanied at no time, nor place with circumstances every way so incapable of particularities of goodness and inward comforts, as at sea. For it is most true, there arises commonly no such unmerciful tempest, compound of so many contrary and diverse nations, but that it worked upon the whole frame of the body, and most loathsomely affected all the powers thereof: and the manner of the sickness it lays upon the body, being so insufferable, gives not the mind any free and quiet time, to use her judgment and empire.... For four and twenty hours the storm in a restless tumult, had blown so exceedingly, as we could not apprehend in our imaginations any possibility of greater violence, yet did we still find it, not only more terrible, but more constant, fury added to fury, and one storm urging a second more outrageous then the former; whether it so wrought upon our fears, or indeed met with new forces: Sometimes strikes in our ship amongst women, and passengers, not used to such hurly and discomforts, made us look one upon the other with troubled hearts, and panting bosoms: our clamours drowned in the winds, and the winds in thunder. Prayers might well be in the heart and lips, but drowned in the outcries of the officers: nothing heard that could give comfort, nothing seen that might encourage hope. It is impossible for me, had I the voice of Stentor,[1] and expression of as many tongues, as his throat of voices, to express the outcries and miseries, not languishing, but wasting his spirits, and art constant to his own principles, but not prevailing. Our sails wound up lay without their use, and if at any time we bore but a hillock,[2] or half fore course,[3] to guide her before the sea, six and sometimes eight men were not enough to hold the whip staff in the steerage, and the tiller below in the gunner room, by which may be imagined the strength of the storm: In which, the sea swelled above the clouds, and gave battle unto heaven. It could not be said to rain, the waters like whole rivers did flood in the air. And this I did still observe, that whereas upon the land, when a storm hath powered itself forth once in drifts of rain, the wind as beaten down, and vanquished therewith, not long after endured: here the glut of water (as if throttling the wind erewhile) was no sooner a little emptied and qualified, but instantly the winds (as having gotten their mouths now free, and at liberty) spoke more loud, and grew more tumultuous, and malignant: What shall I say? Winds and seas were as mad, as fury and rage could make them; for mine own part, I had been in some storms before, as well upon the coast of Barbary[4] and Algeria, in the Levant,[5] and once more distressful in the Adriatic Gulf, in a bottom of Candy[6].... Yet all

---

1 A Greek herald in the Trojan War noted for his loud voice.
2 Small hill.
3 Course, in nautical terms, refers to a ship's lowermost sails on a mast. The fore course (or foresail) would be set on the foremast. "Half fore course" means the ship has hoisted the sails at half length.
4 The Barbary Coast (or Barbary) was an early modern geographical location encompassing the northern coast of Africa (what would today be Algeria, Morocco, Libya, and Tunisia).
5 A geographical location referring to a large area of Western Asia (most notably Syria).
6 A derivative of the original Arabic name for the island of Crete (*Candia* in Latin, *Candy* in English).

that I had ever suffered gathered together, might not hold comparison with this: there was not a moment in which the sudden splitting, or instant oversetting of the ship was not expected. Howbeit this was not all; it pleased God to bring a greater affliction yet upon us; for in the beginning of the storm we had received likewise a mighty leak. And the ship in every joint almost, having spewed out her Ocam,[1] before we were aware (a casualty more desperate than any other that a voyage by sea draws with it) was grown five foot suddenly deep with water above her ballast, and we almost drowned within, whilst we sat looking when to perish from above. This imparting no less terror than danger, ran through the whole ship with much fright and amazement, startled and turned the blood, and took down the braves of the most hardy mariner of them all, insomuch as he that before happily felt not the sorrow of others, now began to sorrow for himself, when he saw such a pond of water so suddenly broken in, and which he knew could not (without present avoiding) but instantly sink him. So as joining (only for his own sake, not yet worth the saving) in the public safety; there might be seen master, master's mate, boatswain, quarter master, coopers, carpenters, and who not, with candles in their hands, creeping along the ribs viewing the sides, searching every corner, and listening in every place, if they could hear the water run. Many a weeping leak was this way found and hastily stopped, and at length one in the gunner room made up with I know not how many pieces of beef: but all was to no purpose, the leak (if it were but one) which drunk in our greatest seas, and took in our destruction fastest, could not then be found, nor ever was, by any labor, council, or search. The waters still increasing, and the pumps going, which at length choked with bringing up whole and continual biscuit[2] (and indeed all we had, ten thousand weight) it was conceived, as most likely, that the leak might be sprung in the bread room, whereupon the carpenter went down, and ripped up all the room, but could not find it so.

I am not able to give unto your ladyship every man's thought in this perplexity, to which we were now brought; but to me, this leakage

---

1    Oakum, the fiber from ropes used in the caulking of wooden ships.
2    Hardtack was a kind of biscuit or cracker designed specifically for sea voyages. It would be baked to be extremely hard and virtually inedible in its original form but would soften over time with prolonged exposure to humidity. It proved an extremely useful food item for lengthy sea voyages.

appeared as a wound given to men that were before dead. The Lord knew, I had as little hope, as desire of life in the storm, and in this, it went beyond my will; because beyond my reason, why we should labor to preserve life; yet we did, either because so dear are a few lingering hours of life in all mankind, or that our Christian knowledge taught us, how much we owed to the rites of nature, as bound, not to be false to ourselves, or to neglect the means of our own preservation; the most despairing things amongst men, being matters of no wonder nor moment with him, who is the rich fountain and admirable essence of all mercy.

Our governor, upon the Tuesday morning (at what time, by such who had been below in the hold, the leak was first discovered) had caused the whole company, about 140, besides women, to be equally divided into three parts, and opening the ship in three places (under the forecastle, in the waste, and hard by the Bitacke[1]) appointed each man where to attend; and thereunto every man came duly upon his watch, took the bucket or pump for one hour and rested another. Then men might be seen to labor, I may well say, for life, and the better sort, even our governor, and admiral themselves, not refusing their turn, and to spell each the other, to give example to other. The common sort stripped naked, as men in galleys, the easier both to hold out, and to shrink from under the salt water, which continually leapt in among them, kept their eyes waking, and their thoughts and hands working, with tired bodies, and wasted spirits, three days and four nights destitute of outward comfort, and desperate of any deliverance, testifying how mutually willing they were, yet by labor to keep each other from drowning, albeit each one drowned whilst he labored. Once so huge a sea broke upon the poop and quarter,[2] upon us, as it covered our ship from stern to stem,[3] like a garment or a vast cloud. It filled her brim full for awhile within, from the hatches up to the spare deck.[4] This force or confluence of water was so violent, as it rushed and carried the helmsman from the helm,

1 The forecastle is the upper deck of a sailing ship, while the waste (or waist) is the central deck of a ship (between the forecastle and the quarter deck). Bitacke likely refers to beakhead (or beak), the protruding part at the very front of a ship.
2 The poop deck is a deck that forms the roof of a cabin built in the rear of a ship. The quarterdeck is the part of the upper deck raised behind the mainmast, including the poop deck, usually reserved for ship's officers, guests, and passengers.
3 The bow or prow of a ship.
4 An upper deck of light construction above the main deck.

and wrested the whip staff out of his hand, which so flew from side to side, that when he would have ceased the same again, it so tossed him from starboard to larboard, as it was god's mercy it had not split him: it so beat him from his hold, and so bruised him, as a fresh man hazarding in by chance fell fair with it, and by main strength bearing somewhat up, made good his place, and with much clamor encouraged and called upon others; who gave her now up, rent in pieces and absolutely lost. Our governor was at this time below at the Capstone, both by his speech and authority heartening every man unto his labor. It struck him from the place where he sat, and grovelled him, and all us about him on our faces, beating together with our breaths all thoughts from our bosoms, else, than that we were now sinking. For my part, I thought her already in the bottom of the Sea; and I have heard him say, wading out of the flood thereof, all his ambition was but to climb up above hatches to die in *Aperto coelo*,[1] and in the company of his old friends. It so stunned the ship in her full pace, that she stirred no more, than if she had been caught in a net, or than, as if the fabulous Remora[2] had stuck to her forecastle. Yet without bearing one inch of sail, even then she was making her way nine or ten leagues in a watch. One thing, it is not without his wonder (whether it were the fear of death in so great a storm, or that it pleased God to be gracious unto us) there was not a passenger, gentleman, or other, after he began to stir and labor, but was able to relieve his fellow, and make good his course; and it is most true, such as in all their lifetimes had never done hour's work before (their minds now helping their bodies) were able twice 48 hours together to toil with the best.

During all this time, the heavens looked so black upon us, that it was not possible the elevation of the pole[3] might be observed: nor a star by night, not sunbeam by day was to be seen. Only upon the Thursday night, Sir George Somers being upon the watch, had an apparition of a little round light, like a faint star, trembling, and streaming along with

---

1  Latin expression meaning "in open heaven"; i.e., he climbed up so he could die in open air.
2  A remora, more commonly known as a suckerfish, is a fish from the ray family known to attach itself to other marine animals and ships. They were believed to be able to stop ships from sailing.
3  In astronomy, the elevation of the pole is a way to determine latitude: "the altitude of the pole above the horizon of any place is equal to the latitude of that place" (Taylor 103).

a sparkling blaze, half the height upon the main mast, and shooting sometimes from shroud to shroud, attempting to settle as it were upon any of the four shrouds; and for three or four hours together, or rather more, half the night it kept with us, running sometimes along the main yard to the very end, and then returning.[1] At which, Sir George Somers called divers about him, and showed them the same, who observed it with much wonder, and carefulness: but upon a sudden, towards the morning watch, they lost the sight of it, and knew not what way it made. The superstitious seamen make many constructions of this sea-fire, which nevertheless is usual in storms: The same (it may be) which the Grecians were wont in the Mediterranean to call Castor and Pollux, of which, if one only appeared without the other, they took it for an evil sign of great tempest. The Italians, and such, who lie open to the Adriatic and Tyrrene Sea,[2] call it (a sacred body) *Corpo sancto*: the Spaniards call it Saint Elmo, and have an authentic and miraculous legend for it. Be it what it will, we laid other foundations of safety or ruin than in the rising or falling of it, could it have served us now miraculously to have taken our height[3] by, it might have struck amazement, and a reverence in our devotions, according to the due of a miracle. But it did not light us any whit the more to our known way, who ran now (as do hoodwinked[4] men) at all adventures, sometimes North, and Northeast, then North and by West, and in an instant again varying two or three points, and sometimes half the compass. East and by South we steered away as much as we could to bear upright, which was no small carefulness nor pain to do, albeit we much unrigged our ship, threw overboard much luggage, many a trunk and chest (in which I suffered no mean loss) and staved many a butt of beer, hogsheads of oil, cider, wine, and vinegar, and heaved away all our ordnance on the starboard side, and had now purposed to have cut down the main mast, the more to lighten her, for we were much spent, and our men so weary, as their strengths together failed them, with their hearts, having

1    Strachey here describes a phenomenon known as "St. Elmo's Fire" (named after the patron Saint of sailors, Erasmus of Formia), by which luminous plasma appears following electrical reactions in the atmosphere such as those happening during thunderstorms. It is generally thought to be a good omen by sailors who witness it.
2    The Tyrrhenian Sea is part of the Mediterranean Sea, off the west coast of Italy.
3    To have found our way.
4    Blindfolded.

travailed now from Tuesday till Friday morning, day and night, without either sleep or food; for the leakage taking up all the hold, we could neither come by beer nor fresh water; fire we could keep none in the cook room to dress any meat, and carefulness, grief, and our turn at the pump or bucket, were sufficient to hold sleep from our eyes. And surely madam, it is most true, there was not any hour (a matter of admiration) all these days, in which we freed not twelve hundred barricos[1] of water, the least whereof contained six gallons, and some eight, besides three deep pumps continually going, two beneath at the capstone,[2] and the other above in the half deck, and at each pump 4,000 strokes at the least in a watch; so as I may well say, every four hours, we quitted 100 tons of water: and from Tuesday noon till Friday noon, we bailed and pumped 2,000 tons, and yet do what we could, when our ship held least in her, after Tuesday night second watch she bore ten foot deep, at which stay our extreme working kept her one eight glasses,[3] forbearance whereof had instantly sunk us, and it being now Friday, the fourth morning, it wanted little, but that there had been a general determination, to have shut up hatches, and commending our sinful souls to God, committed the ship to the mercy of the sea: surely, that night we must have done it, and that night had we then perished: but see the goodness and sweet introduction of better hope, by our merciful God given unto us. Sir George Somers, when no man dreamed of such happiness, had discovered, and cried land. Indeed the morning now three quarters spent, had won a little clearness from the days before, and it being better surveyed, the very trees were seen to move with the wind upon the shore side: whereupon our governor commanded the helmsman to bear up, the boatswain sounding at the first, found it 13 fathom, & when we stood a little in seven fathom; and presently heaving his lead the third time, had ground at four fathom, and by this, we had got her within a mile under the Southeast point of the land, where we had somewhat smooth water. But having no hope to save her by coming to an anchor in the same, we were enforced to run her ashore, as near the land as we could, which brought us within three quarters of a mile of shore, and by the mercy of God unto us, making out our boats, we had ere night

---

1  A barrico is a small cask.
2  The capstan is a mechanized axle that multiplies the seamen's pulling force when hauling ropes on a ship.
3  Kept the ship whole for eight hours.

brought all our men, women, and children, about the number of one hundred and fifty, safe into the Island.

We found it to be the dangerous and dreaded Island, or rather Islands of the Bermuda ... because they be so terrible to all that ever touched on them; and such tempests, thunders, and other fearful objects are seen and heard about them that they be called commonly the Devil's Islands ... Yet it pleased our merciful God to make even this hideous and hated place both the place of our safety and means of our deliverance....

## APPENDIX G: FROM JOHN DRYDEN AND WILLIAM DAVENANT, *THE TEMPEST*; *OR, THE ENCHANTED ISLAND* (1670)

[A new version of Shakespeare's *Tempest*, by John Dryden (1631–1700) and William Davenant (1606–68), appeared in 1667. *The Tempest; or, The Enchanted Island* added characters and expanded the music and spectacle of the original play. In 1677, Thomas Shadwell (c. 1642–92) added even more music and dance. The Dryden-Davenant-Shadwell version, with all its operatic embellishments, displaced Shakespeare's play from the stage for the next 150 years.

In *The Enchanted Island*, Miranda is given a sister named Dorinda. There is also on the island the handsome son of the late, deposed Duke of Mantua. His name is Hippolito. Prospero keeps him and the young women apart since Hippolito's horoscope predicted that he would die if he ever saw a woman. It remains unexplained how the young people failed to notice each other on the little boat that brought them and Prospero to the island years before. The shipwreck brings Ferdinand to the island and, as in the original, he and Miranda fall in love at first sight. However, the presence of the other young people, Dorinda and Hippolito, occasions a series of misunderstandings, a duel between Ferdinand and Hippolito, and the unintended death of Hippolito. That brings matters to what surely would have been an unhappy ending. Indeed, the ever-angry Prospero reveals to his old enemy Alonso that his son Ferdinand is alive, but only to make Alonso's grief sharper when Prospero tells him that his son is to die for the murder of Hippolito. The happy ending is saved by the initiative of Ariel, who magically restores the life of the apparently dead man.

Caliban is given a sister, Sycorax, whom he seeks to wed to "Trincalo" (Shakespeare's Trinculo is given a slightly new name and appears as the Boatswain rather than as a jester). Trincalo, Caliban, and Sycorax are joined in the comic subplot by Stephano (in this version, he is the Master of the Ship) and two other sailors. The four mariners, the monster servant, and his sister take part in a contest for rule of the island, where "Duke Stephano" and his two sailor Viceroys are challenged by Trincalo, who claims the throne on the basis of his engagement to Sycorax and alliance with Caliban. The competition for rule triggers a comic civil war. At the end of Dryden and Davenant's deeply conservative rewriting of Shakespeare's play, all the lower-rank characters are put back in their subjugated places and all the upper-rank characters are secure in their places at the top of the social hierarchy.

In the Preface, Dryden—full of praise for his recently deceased co-author—suggests how Davenant's changes to *The Tempest* actually improved it. But in the verse Prologue to the play, Dryden pulls back from the idea (one that became dominant in the eighteenth century) that Shakespeare's plays needed to be cleansed of possible playhouse corruption and civilized for modern readers and spectators by way of judicious adaptation. Shakespeare's play, Dryden concludes, is the best that drama can be. "Shakespeare's magic," he says, "could not copied be, / Within that circle none durst walk but he."

We have modernized some of the spellings in the selection here.]

## PREFACE TO THE ENCHANTED ISLAND

The writing of prefaces to plays was probably invented by some very ambitious poet, who never thought he had done enough, perhaps by some ape of the French eloquence, which uses to make a business of a letter of gallantry, an examen[1] of a farce; and in short, a great pomp and ostentation of words on every trifle. This is certainly the talent of that nation, and ought not to be invaded by any other. They do that out of gaiety, which would be an imposition upon us.

We may satisfy ourselves with surmounting them in the scene, and safely leave them those trappings of writing and flourishes of the pen, with which they adorn the borders of their plays, and which are indeed no more than good landskips[2] to a very indifferent picture. I must proceed no farther in this argument, lest I run myself beyond my excuse for writing this. Give me leave therefore to tell you, Reader, that I do it not to set a value on anything I have written in this play, but out of gratitude to the memory of Sir William Davenant, who did me the honor to join me with him in the alteration of it.

It was originally Shakespeare's, a poet for whom he had particularly a high veneration, and whom he first taught me to admire. The play

---

1    Examination.
2    Landscapes.

itself had formerly been acted with success in the Blackfriars.[1] And our excellent Fletcher[2] had so great a value for it, that he thought fit to make use of the same design, not much varied, a second time. Those who have seen his *Sea Voyage*[3] may easily discern that it was a copy of Shakespeare's *Tempest*: the storm, the desert island, and the woman who had never seen a man, are all sufficient testimonies of it. But Fletcher was not the only poet who made use of Shakespeare's plot. Sir John Suckling,[4] a professed admirer of our author, has followed his footsteps in his *Goblins*—his Regmella being an open imitation of Shakespeare's Miranda; and his spirits, though counterfeit, yet are copied from Ariel.[5] But Sir William Davenant, as he was a man of quick and piercing imagination, soon found that somewhat might be added to the design of Shakespeare, of which neither Fletcher nor Suckling had ever thought; and therefore to put the last hand to it, he designed the counterpart to Shakespeare's plot, namely that of a man who had never seen a woman; that by this means those two characters of innocence and love might the more illustrate and commend each other. This excellent contrivance he was pleased to communicate to me, and to desire my assistance in it. I confess that from the very first moment it so pleased me, that I never wrote anything with more delight. I must likewise do him that justice to acknowledge that my writing received daily his amendments, and that is the reason why it is not so faulty as the rest which I have done without the help or correction of so judicious a friend. The comical parts of the sailors were also his invention, and for the most part his writing, as you will easily discover by the style. In the time I wrote with him, I had the opportunity to observe somewhat more nearly of him than I had formerly done, when I had only a bare acquaintance with him. I found him then of so quick a fancy, that nothing was proposed to him, on which he could not suddenly produce a thought extremely pleasant and surprising.... And as his fancy was quick, so likewise were

---

1    One of the more popular theaters in early modern London, known for innovations in drama and staging.

2    Jacobean playwright John Fletcher (1579–1625).

3    *The Sea Voyage* (1622) is a play by Fletcher and Philip Massinger (1583–1640).

4    English poet and dramaturge (1609–41) working in the Cavalier tradition (works known for careless gaiety and wit).

5    The reference here is to one of Suckling's comedies, *The Goblins* (1638), which offers multiple echoes to *The Tempest*. The play's heroine, Regmella (or Reginella) is recognized as a close copy of Miranda.

the products of it remote and new. He borrowed not of any other; and his imaginations were such as could not easily enter into any other man. His corrections were sober and judicious, and he corrected his own writings much more severely than those of another man, bestowing twice the time and labor in polishing, which he used in invention.[1] It had perhaps been easy enough for me to have arrogated[2] more to myself than was my due in the writing of this play, and to have passed by his name with silence in the publication of it, with the same ingratitude which others have used to him, whose writings he hath not only corrected, as he has done this, but has had a greater inspection over them, and sometimes added whole scenes together, which may as easily be distinguished from the rest as true gold from counterfeit by the weight. But besides the unworthiness of the action which deterred me from it (there being nothing so base as to rob the dead of his reputation) I am satisfied I could never have received so much honor in being thought the author of any poem how excellent soever, as I shall from the joining my imperfections with the merit and name of Shakespeare and Sir William Davenant.

December 1, 1669.

JOHN DRYDEN.

### PROLOGUE TO THE TEMPEST, OR THE *ENCHANTED ISLAND*.

As when a tree's cut down, the secret root
Lives underground, and thence new branches shoot,
So from old Shakespeare's honored dust, this day,
Springs up and buds a new reviving play.
Shakespeare, who (taught by none) did first impart
To Fletcher wit, to laboring Jonson[3] art.
He, monarch-like, gave those his subjects law,
And is that Nature which they paint and draw.

---

1   He spent twice as much time revising his text than he spent composing it.
2   Claimed without justification.
3   English playwright Ben Jonson (1572–1637).

Fletcher reached that which on his heights did grow,
Whilst Jonson crept and gathered all below.
This did his love, and this his mirth digest:
One imitates him most, the other best.
If they have since out-writ all other men,
'Tis with the drops which fell from Shakespeare's pen.
The storm which vanished on the Neighb'ring shore,
Was taught by Shakespeare's *Tempest* first to roar.
That innocence and beauty which did smile
In Fletcher, grew on this enchanted isle.
But Shakespeare's magic could not copied be,
Within that circle none durst walk but he.
I must confess 'twas bold, nor would you now,
That liberty to vulgar wits allow,
Which works by magic supernatural things;
But Shakespeare's power is sacred as a king's.
Those legends from old priesthood were received,
And he then writ, as people then believed.
But if for Shakespeare we your grace implore,
We for our theatre shall want it more:
Who by our dearth of youths are forced to employ
One of our women to present a boy.
And that's a transformation you will say
Exceeding all the magic in the play.
Let none expect in the last Act to find,
Her sex transformed from man to womankind.
What e'er she was before the play began,
All you shall see of her is perfect man.
Or if your fancy will be farther led,
To find her woman, it must be abed.

## [FROM ACT II]

[This section of the play takes us into the subplot of a brewing civil war. Mustacho and Ventoso are two sailors who have been made Viceroys under the self-declared Duke Stephano in the play's comic version of lower-rank government. Trincalo, declared a rebel by Stephano, seeks to take over the rule of the island. He finds an ally in the servant-monster Caliban and looks forward to meeting Caliban's sister, Sycorax.]

[Page 22]

MUSTACHO. Art thou mad *Trincalo?* Wilt thou disturb a settled government?

TRINCALO. I say this island shall be under *Trincalo*, or it shall be a commonwealth; and so my bottle is my buckler, and so I draw my sword. [*Draws.*]

VENTOSO. Ah *Trincalo*, I thought thou hadst had more grace,
And thy two lawful viceroys.

MUSTACHO. Wilt not thou take advice of two that stand
For old counsellors here, where thou art a mere stranger
To the laws of the country?

TRINCALO. I'll have no laws.

VENTOSO. Then civil war begins.

[*Ventoso and Mustacho draw.*]

STEPHANO. Hold, hold! I'll have no blood shed;
My subjects are but few. Let him make a rebellion
By himself. And a rebel, I Duke *Stephano* declare him:
Viceroys, come away.

TRINCALO. And Duke *Trincalo* declares that he will make open war
wherever he meets thee or thy viceroys.

> [*Exeunt. Stephano, Mustacho and Ventoso.*
> *Enter Caliban with wood upon his back.*]

TRINCALO. Hah! Who have we here?

CALIBAN. All the infections that the sun sucks up from fogs, fens, flats, on *Prospero* fall; and make him by inch-meal a Disease! His spirits hear me, and yet I needs must curse, but they'll not pinch, fright me with urchin shows, pitch me i'th' mire, nor lead me in the dark out of my way, unless he bid 'em. But for every trifle he sets them on me. Sometimes like baboons they mow[1] and chatter at me, and often bite me; like hedge-hogs then they mount their prickles at me, tumbling before me in my barefoot way. Sometimes I am all wound about with adders, who with their cloven tongues hiss me to madness. Hah! Yonder stands one of his spirits sent to torment me.

TRINCALO. What have we here, a man or a fish?
  This is some monster of the isle. Were I in *England*,
  As once I was, and had him painted;
  Not a holiday fool there but would give me
  Sixpence for the sight of him. Well, if I could make
  Him tame, he were a present for an emperor.
  Come hither pretty monster, I'll do thee no harm.
  Come hither!

CALIBAN. Torment me not!
  I'll bring thee wood home faster.

TRINCALO. He talks none of the wisest, but I'll give him
  A dram o'th' bottle. That will clear his understanding.
  Come on your ways Master Monster, open your mouth.
  How now, you perverse moon-calf! What,
  I think you cannot tell who is your friend!
  Open your chops, I say.

[*Pours wine down his throat.*]

CALIBAN. This is a brave god, and bears coelestial[2] liquor.
  I'll kneel to him.

TRINCALO. He is a very hopeful monster. Monster, what say'st thou, art thou content to turn civil and sober, as I am? For then thou shalt be my subject.

CALIBAN. I'll swear upon that bottle to be true, for the liquor is not earthly. Did'st thou not drop from Heaven?

TRINCALO. Only out of the moon. I was the man in her when time was. By this light, a very shallow monster.

---

1  Grimace.
2  Celestial (from the Latin *caelestis*).

CALIBAN. I'll shew thee every fertile inch i'th' isle, and kiss thy foot. I
    prithee be my god, and let me drink. [*Drinks again.*]
TRINCALO. Well drawn, Monster, in good faith.
CALIBAN. I'll shew thee the best springs, I'll pluck thee berries,
    I'll fish for thee, and get thee wood enough.
    A curse upon the tyrant whom I serve! I'll bear him
    No more sticks, but follow thee.
TRINCALO. The poor monster is loving in his drink.
CALIBAN. I prithee let me bring thee where crabs grow,
    And I with my long nails, will dig thee pig-nuts,
    Shew thee a jay's nest, and instruct thee how to snare
    The marmoset; I'll bring thee to clustered filberts;
    Wilt thou go with me?
TRINCALO. This monster comes of a good natured race.
    Is there no more of thy kin in this island?
CALIBAN. Divine, here is but one besides myself—
    My lovely sister, beautiful and bright as the full moon.
TRINCALO. Where is she?
CALIBAN. I left her clamb'ring up a hollow oak,
    And plucking thence the dropping honeycombs.
    Say my king, shall I call her to thee?
TRINCALO. She shall swear upon the bottle too.
    If she proves handsome, she is mine: here Monster,
    Drink again for thy good news; thou shalt speak
    A good word for me. [*Gives him the Bottle.*]
CALIBAN. Farewell, old master, farewell, farewell.
    *Sings.* No more dams I'll make for fish,
    Nor fetch in firing at requiring,
    Nor scrape trencher, nor wash dish,
    Ban, Ban, Cackaliban
    Has a new master, get a new man.
    Heigh-day, Freedom, freedom!
TRINCALO. Here's two subjects got already, the monster,
    And his sister: well, Duke Stephano, I say, and say again,
    Wars will ensue, and so I drink. [*Drinks.*]
    From this worshipful monster, and mistress,
    Monster his sister,
    I'll lay claim to this island by alliance.

Monster, I say thy sister shall be my spouse:
Come away Brother Monster, I'll lead thee to my butt[1]
And drink her health.

[*Exeunt.*]

[FROM ACT IV]

[Here Ferdinand and the unworldly and romantically (and sexually) overwrought Hippolito begin their quarrel about the two young women, Miranda and Dorinda. Hippolito wants both women for himself. Ferdinand is ready to fight for what he sees as his sexual rights, but first Hippolito must learn something about fighting and about weaponry. Ferdinand, who knows where he can find a second sword, lends his opponent his own sword so that the complete novice Hippolito can practice for their upcoming duel.]

[*Enter Ferdinand.*]

FERDINAND. O! well encountered, you are the happy man!
   Y' have got the hearts of both the beauteous women.
HIPPOLITO. How! Sir? Pray, are you sure on't?
FERDINAND. One of 'em charged me to love you for her sake.
HIPPOLITO. Then I must have her.
FERDINAND. No, not till I am dead.
HIPPOLITO. How dead? What's that? But whatsoe'er it be
   I long to have her.
FERDINAND. Time and my grief may make me die.
HIPPOLITO. But for a friend you should make haste. I ne'er asked
   Anything of you before.
FERDINAND. I see your ignorance,
   And therefore will instruct you in my meaning.
   The woman, whom I love, saw you and loved you.
   Now, Sir, if you love her, you'll cause my death.
HIPPOLITO. Be sure I'll do't then.
FERDINAND. But I am your friend;
   And I request you that you would not love her.
HIPPOLITO. When friends request unreasonable things,

---

1   A cask or wooden barrel typically used for wine or ale.

Sure they're to be denied. You say she's fair,
And I must love all who are fair; for, to tell
You a secret, Sir, which I have lately found
Within myself: they all are made for me.

FERDINAND. That's but a fond conceit. You are made for one,
And one for you.

HIPPOLITO. You cannot tell me, Sir,
  I know I'm made for twenty hundred women.
  (I mean if there so many be i'th' world)
  So that if once I see her I shall love her.

FERDINAND. Then do not see her.

HIPPOLITO. Yes, Sir, I must see her.
  For I would fain have my heart beat again,
  Just as it did when I first saw her sister.

FERDINAND. I find I must not let you see her then.

HIPPOLITO. How will you hinder me?

FERDINAND. By force of arms.

HIPPOLITO. By force of arms?
  My arms perhaps may be as strong as yours.

FERDINAND. He's still so ignorant that I pity him, and fain
  Would avoid force. Pray, do not see her, she was
  Mine first; you have no right to her.

HIPPOLITO. I have not yet considered what is right, but, Sir,
  I know my inclinations are to love all women.
  And I have been taught that to dissemble what I
  Think is base. In honor then of truth, I must
  Declare that I do love, and I will see your woman.

FERDINAND. Would you be willing I should see and love your
  Woman, and endeavor to seduce her from that
  Affection which she vowed to you?

HIPPOLITO. I would not you should do it, but if she should
  Love you best, I cannot hinder her.
  But, Sir, for fear she should, I will provide against
  The worst, and try to get your woman.

FERDINAND. But I pretend no claim at all to yours;
  Besides you are more beautiful than I,
  And fitter to allure unpracticed hearts.
  Therefore I once more beg you will not see her.

HIPPOLITO. I'm glad you let me know I have such beauty.
   If that will get me women, they shall have it
   As far as e'er 'twill go; I'll never want 'em.
FERDINAND. Then since you have refused this act of friendship,
   Provide yourself a sword, for we must fight.
HIPPOLITO. A sword—what's that?
FERDINAND. Why such a thing as this.
HIPPOLITO. What should I do with it?
FERDINAND. You must stand thus, and push against me,
   While I push at you, till one of us fall dead.
HIPPOLITO. This is brave sport,
   But we have no swords growing in our world.
FERDINAND. What shall we do then to decide our quarrel?
HIPPOLITO. We'll take the sword by turns and fight with it.
FERDINAND. Strange ignorance! You must defend your life,
   And so must I; but since you have no sword
   Take this; for in a corner of my cave [*Gives him his sword.*]
   I found a rusty one; perhaps 'twas his who keeps
   Me pris'ner here. That I will fit;
   When next we meet, prepare yourself to fight.
HIPPOLITO. Make haste then, this shall ne'er be yours again.
   I mean to fight with all the men I meet, and
   When they are dead, their women shall be mine.
FERDINAND. I see you are unskillful; I desire not to take
   Your life, but if you please we'll fight on
   These conditions: he who first draws blood,
   Or who can take the other's weapon from him,
   Shall be acknowledged as the conqueror,
   And both the women shall be his.
HIPPOLITO.                          Agreed,
   And ev'ry day I'll fight for two more with you.
FERDINAND. But win these first.
HIPPOLITO. I'll warrant you I'll push you.

                                   [*Exeunt severally.*]

# WORKS CITED AND SELECT BIBLIOGRAPHY

## EDITIONS OF SHAKESPEARE

Bevington, David, editor. *The Complete Works of Shakespeare*. Updated 4th ed., Longman, 1997.

Blakemore, Evans G., editor. *The Riverside Shakespeare*. 2nd ed., Houghton Mifflin, 1997.

Johnson, Samuel, and George Steevens, editors. *Plays*. 15 vols., London, 1793.

Kermode, Frank, editor. *The Tempest*. Arden Shakespeare, Harvard UP, 1954.

Lindley, David, editor. *The Tempest*. New Cambridge Shakespeare, Cambridge UP, 2002.

Mowat, Barbara A., and Paul Werstine, editors. *The Tempest*. Folger Shakespeare Library, Simon & Schuster, 1994.

Orgel, Stephen, editor. *The Tempest*. Oxford Shakespeare, Oxford UP, 1987.

Rowe, Nicholas, editor. *The Works of Mr. William Shakespeare*. 6 vols., London, 1709.

Theobald, Lewis, editor. *The Works of Shakespeare*. 7 vols., London, 1733.

Vaughan, Virginia Mason, and Alden T. Vaughan, editors. *The Tempest*. Arden Shakespeare, Thomson, 1999.

## OTHER WORKS

Aristotle. *Aristotle's Poetics*. Translated by S.H. Butcher, introduction by Francis Fergusson, Hill and Wang, 1961.

Bakhtin, Mikhail. *Speech Genres and Other Essays*. Translated by Vern W. McGee, U of Texas P, 1986.

Bate, Jonathan. *Shakespeare and Ovid*. Clarendon, 1993.

Berger, Harry, Jr. "Miraculous Harp: A Reading of Shakespeare's *Tempest*." *Shakespeare Studies*, vol. 5, 1969, pp. 255–57.

Brower, Reuben Arthur. "'The Mirror of Analogy': *The Tempest*." *The Fields of Light: An Experiment in Critical Reading*, Oxford UP, 1951.

Carroll, Lewis. *Complete Works*. Introduction by Alexander Woollcott, Modern Library, n.d.

Césaire, Aimé. *A Tempest.* Translated by Richard Miller, Ubu Repertory Theater Publications, 1992.

Chambers, E.K. *William Shakespeare: A Study of Facts and Problems.* 2 vols., Clarendon, 1930.

de las Casas, Bartolomé. *Popery truly Displayed in its Bloody Colours.* London[, 1689].

Dekker, Thomas. *The Honest Whore, Part 2. The Dramatic Works of Thomas Dekker,* vol. 2, edited by Fredson Bowers, Cambridge UP, 1953–61.

Dryden, John. *The Works of John Dryden.* Vol. 10, U of California P, 1970.

Falconer, A.F. *Shakespeare and the Sea.* Constable, 1964.

Fanon, Frantz. *Black Skin, White Masks.* Translated by Charles Lam Markmann, Grove P, 1967.

Fletcher, John. *The Faithful Shepherdess. The Dramatic Works in the Beaumont and Fletcher Canon.* Edited by Fredson Bowers, 10 vols., Cambridge UP, 1966.

*Forbidden Planet.* Directed by Fred M. Wilcox, written by Cyril Hume, Metro Goldwyn-Meyer, 1956. Screenplay available at http://www.script-o-rama.com/movie_scripts/f/forbidden-planet-script-transcript-leslie.html. Accessed 21 July 2020.

Frey, Charles. "The Tempest and the New World." *Shakespeare Quarterly,* vol. 30, no. 1, Winter 1979, pp. 29–41.

Frye, Northrop. *The Secular Scripture: A Study of the Structure of Romance.* Harvard UP, 1976.

*The Geneva Bible: A Facsimile of the 1560 Edition.* Edited by Lloyd E. Berry, U of Wisconsin P, 1969.

Greg, W.W. *The Shakespeare First Folio: Its Bibliographical and Textual History.* Clarendon, 1955.

Hinman, Charlton. *The Printing and Proof-Reading of the First Folio of Shakespeare,* 2 vols. Clarendon, 1963.

Howard-Hill, Trevor. *Ralph Crane and Some Shakespeare First Folio Comedies.* UP of Virginia, 1972.

Jonson, Ben. *Bartholomew Fair.* Edited by Suzanne Gossett, The Revels Plays, Manchester UP, 2000.

———. *Every Man Out of His Humour.* Edited by Helen Ostovich, The Revels Plays, Manchester UP, 2001.

Lee, Sidney. *A Life of William Shakespeare.* Smith, Elder, & Co., 1898.

Lewton-Brain, Anna. "Dynamic Conversions: Grief and Joy in
George Herbert's Musical Verse." *Conversion Machines: Apparatus,
Artifact, Body*, edited by Bronwen Wilson and Paul Yachnin,
Edinburgh UP, forthcoming.

Mannoni, O. *Prospero and Caliban: The Psychology of Colonialism*.
Translated by Pamela Powesland, Methuen, 1956.

Montaigne, Michel de. *The Essays of Montaigne*. Translated by John
Florio, introduction by J.I.M. Stewart, Modern Library, 1933.

Neto, Luiz Costa-Lima. *Music, Theater, and Society in the Comedies
of Luiz Carlos Martin Penna (1833–1846)*. Translated by Stephen
Thomson Moore, Lexington Books, 2017.

Ovid. *Metamorphoses*. Translated by Arthur Golding, imprinted by
Robert Walde-graue, 1587.

Poole, William. "False Play: Shakespeare and Chess." *Shakespeare
Quarterly*, vol. 55, 2004, pp. 50–70.

Schalkwyk, David. *Shakespeare, Love and Service*. Cambridge UP,
2008.

Sepúlveda, Juan Ginés de. "Just War in the Indies." c. 1547. *Early
Modern Spain: A Documentary History*, by Jon Cowans, U of
Pennsylvania P, 2003.

——. *The Second Democrate; or, The Just Causes of the War against the
Indians*. 1550. Edited and translated by Angel Losada, 2nd ed.,
reprint of 1951 edition, Instituto Francisco de Vitoria, 1984.

Smith, Emma. *The Making of Shakespeare's First Folio*. Bodleian
Library, Oxford UP, 2015.

Spenser, Edmund. *The Faerie Queene*. Edited by A.C. Hamilton,
Longman, 1977.

Strachey, William. *A True Reportory of the Wracke and Redemption of
Sir Thomas Gates. Purchas his Pilgrim*, by Samuel Purchas, London,
1625.

Taylor, Janet. *An Epitome of Navigation, and Nautical Astronomy, with
the Improved Lunar Tables*. Taylor, 1842.

Vaughan, Alden T. "William Strachey's 'True Reportory' and
Shakespeare: A Closer Look at the Evidence." *Shakespeare
Quarterly*, vol. 59, 2008, pp. 245–73.

Vaughan, Alden T., and Virginia Mason Vaughan. *Shakespeare's
Caliban: A Cultural History*. Cambridge UP, 1991.

Virgil. *The Aeneid*. Translated by H. Rushton Fairclough, 2 vols.,
    Harvard UP, 1916.
Wells, Stanley. "Shakespeare and Romance." *Later Shakespeare*,
    edited by John Russell Brown and Bernard Harris, Edward
    Arnold, 1966.
Wiltenburg, Robert. "The *Aeneid* in *The Tempest*." *Shakespeare Survey*,
    vol. 39, 1987, pp. 159–68.
Yachnin, Paul, and Myrna Wyatt Selkirk. "Metatheatre and
    Character: *The Winter's Tale*." *Shakespeare and Character: Theory,
    History, Performance, and Theatrical Persons*, edited by Yachnin and
    Jessica Slights, Palgrave, 2009, pp. 139–57.
Zabus, Chantal. *Tempests After Shakespeare*. Palgrave, 2002.

## FROM THE PUBLISHER

A name never says it all, but the word "Broadview" expresses a good deal of the philosophy behind our company. We are open to a broad range of academic approaches and political viewpoints. We pay attention to the broad impact book publishing and book printing has in the wider world; for some years now we have used 100% recycled paper for most titles. Our publishing program is internationally oriented and broad-ranging. Our individual titles often appeal to a broad readership too; many are of interest as much to general readers as to academics and students.

Founded in 1985, Broadview remains a fully independent company owned by its shareholders—not an imprint or subsidiary of a larger multinational.

For the most accurate information on our books (including information on pricing, editions, and formats) please visit our website at www.broadviewpress.com. Our print books and ebooks are also available for sale on our site.

BROADVIEW PRESS
WWW.BROADVIEWPRESS.COM

This book is made of paper from well-managed FSC® - certified
forests, recycled materials, and other controlled sources.